Exploring the Role of Analytical Scale in Archaeological Interpretation

Edited by

James R. Mathieu
Rachel E. Scott

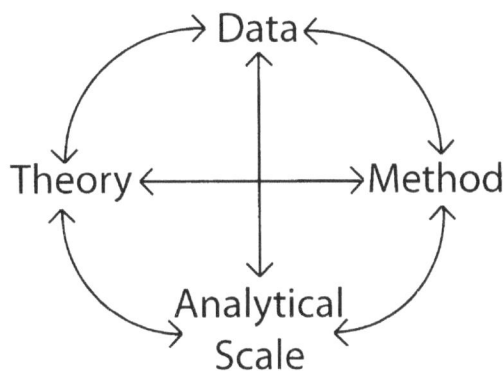

Data

Theory ← → Method

Analytical
Scale

BAR International Series 1261
2004

Published in 2016 by
BAR Publishing, Oxford

BAR International Series 1261

Exploring the Role of Analytical Scale in Archaeological Interpretation

ISBN 978 1 84171 619 0

BAR Publishing is the trading name of British Archaeological Reports (Oxford) Ltd.
British Archaeological Reports was first incorporated in 1974 to publish the BAR
Series, International and British. In 1992 Hadrian Books Ltd became part of the BAR
group. This volume was originally published by Archaeopress in conjunction with
British Archaeological Reports (Oxford) Ltd / Hadrian Books Ltd, the Series principal
publisher, in 2004. This present volume is published by BAR Publishing, 2016.

Printed in England

BAR
PUBLISHING

BAR titles are available from:

     BAR Publishing
     122 Banbury Rd, Oxford, OX2 7BP, UK
EMAIL   info@barpublishing.com
PHONE +44 (0)1865 310431
FAX   +44 (0)1865 316916
     www.barpublishing.com

Table of Contents

List of Contributors . . . . *iv*

Preface . . . . *v*

Introduction: Exploring the Role of Analytical Scale in Archaeological Interpretation
    – *James R. Mathieu and Rachel E. Scott* 1

Scale Factors in Early European Farming
    – *Peter Bogucki* 11

Analytical Scale, Populations, and the Mesolithic-Neolithic Transition in the Far North-west
    of Europe
    – *Timothy Darvill* 19

Scale and its Discontents
    – *D. Blair Gibson* 27

The Four Scales of Technical Analysis; or, How to Make Archaeometry More Useful
    – *Elizabeth Hamilton* 45

Faces in a Crowd or a Crowd of Faces? Archaeological Evidence for Individual and Group
    Identity in Early Anglo-Saxon East Anglia
    – *Genevieve Fisher* 49

The City and Complexity: Change and Continuity in Late Antique Volterra
    – *Rae Ostman* 59

Distinguishing the Local from the Regional: Irish Perspectives on Urbanization in Early
    Medieval Europe
    – *John Soderberg* 67

Patterns in Time and the Tempo of Change: A North Atlantic Perspective on the Evolution
    of Complex Societies
    – *Kevin P. Smith* 83

Discussion
    – *Peter S. Wells* 101

Discussion
    – *Dean R. Snow* 103

List of Contributors

Peter Bogucki
School of Engineering and Applied Science
ACE-23 Engineering Quadrangle
Princeton University
Princeton, NJ 08544, USA
Email: bogucki@princeton.edu

Timothy Darvill
School of Conservation Sciences
Bournemouth University
Fern Barrow, Poole
Dorset BH12 5BB
United Kingdom
Email: tdarvill@bournemouth.ac.uk

Genevieve Fisher
Peabody Museum of Archaeology and Ethnology
Harvard University
Cambridge, MA 02238, USA
Email: gfisher@husc.harvard.edu

D. Blair Gibson
Division of Behavioral and Social Sciences
El Camino College
16007 Crenshaw Blvd
Torrance, CA 90506, USA
Email: Bgibson100@cs.com

Elizabeth Hamilton
University of Pennsylvania Museum
3260 South Street
Philadelphia, PA 19104-6398, USA
Email: hamilt@unagi.cis.upenn.edu

James R. Mathieu
University of Pennsylvania Museum
3260 South Street
Philadelphia, PA 19104-6398, USA
Email: jmathieu@sas.upenn.edu

Rae Ostman
Department of Anthropology
New York University
25 Waverly Place
New York, NY 10003, USA
Email: rmo0948@is2.nyu.edu

Rachel E. Scott
Department of Anthropology
University of Pennsylvania Museum
3260 South Street
Philadelphia, PA 19104-6398, USA
Email: rescott@sas.upenn.edu

Kevin P. Smith
Haffenreffer Museum of Anthropology
Brown University
300 Tower Street
Bristol, RI 02809, USA
Email: kevin_p_smith@brown.edu

Dean R. Snow
Pennsylvania State University
409 Carpenter Building
University Park, PA 16802
Email: drs17@psu.edu

John Soderberg
Department of Anthropology
395 Hubert H. Humphrey Center
University of Minnesota
301 19th Avenue South
Minneapolis, MN 55455, USA
Email: sode0018@tc.umn.edu

Peter S. Wells
Department of Anthropology
395 Hubert H. Humphrey Center
University of Minnesota
301 19th Avenue South
Minneapolis, MN 55455, USA
Email: wells001@umn.edu

Preface

This volume grew out of a symposium session entitled *Continuity and Change: The Role of Analytical Scale in European Archaeology* that was co-organized by James R. Mathieu and Rachel E. Scott for the Society for American Archaeology Annual Meetings in Philadelphia, Pennsylvania in April 2000. Of the original fifteen presentations at that session, revised versions of eleven are included here.

The basic premise behind this volume is that the scale at which we pursue our research, the analytical scale, effects our interpretations of the archaeological record. The purpose of this volume is to encourage an explicit discussion of this relationship in order to develop a clearer understanding of its impact on research. This is done by highlighting some aspects of the role played by analytical scale in the analysis and interpretation of the archaeology of Europe.

It must be noted from the start that this volume is only an initial step in the explicit consideration of the role of analytical scale in archaeological interpretation. As such, it does not attempt to provide a definitive assessment, but rather to encourage thought on the topic by presenting some of the different ways that scholars have attempted to conceive of analytical scale and its impact.

Note that beyond the volume editors' attempts to encourage the authors to discuss the nature of, and the role played by, the chosen scale(s) of analysis, no overarching conception of analytical scale has been imposed and a substantial degree of variation exists within the volume. This is felt to be advantageous, particularly at this early stage of consideration, and it is hoped that this variation will lead to further exploration of the underlying nature of analytical scale and its effects on archaeological interpretation.

During the time it has taken to put together this volume, we have received the support and encouragement of a number of people. Here we would like to thank especially the authors of the various papers and David Davison of BAR for their patience during this process, the Kolb Foundation of the University of Pennsylvania Museum of Archaeology and Anthropology for financial support during graduate school, and Dr. Bernard Wailes for the mentoring he provided and for his unflagging support throughout the years.

Finally, we would like to dedicate this volume to our parents for all they have done for us.

James R. Mathieu
Rachel E. Scott
Philadelphia, PA
April 2004

Introduction: Exploring the Role of Analytical Scale in Archaeological Interpretation

James R. Mathieu and Rachel E. Scott

Introduction

At present there seems to be a distinct lack of conceptual literature within the discipline of archaeology on the topic of analytical scale and its influence on archaeological interpretation (see Stein and Linse 1993 for a rare exception bridging the disciplines of geology and archaeology). This volume is intended as a preliminary exploration of the role played by analytical scale in archaeological interpretation. In this introduction, we will present our general ideas concerning the concept of analytical scale and will provide a brief synopsis of the papers in the volume.

The Concept of Analytical Scale

Archaeological research is undertaken at a variety of analytical scales—from small-scale studies focused on artifacts within individual buildings used by specific people over short periods of time, to large-scale studies concerned with evolutionary processes occurring over millennia, across continents, and involving large groups of people.[1] By *analytical scale*, we are referring to the scale(s) of analysis used by a research project in terms of its spatial, temporal, and formal dimensions (cf. Spaulding 1960).[2]

The concept of analytical scale includes at least two complementary components. The first is the *scalar extent* or overall scope of the study. In other words, the maximum spatial, temporal, and formal limits of a research project form one aspect of its analytical scale (**Figure 1**).

For example, the scalar extent of the primary author's geographical study focused on medieval English royal castles (Mathieu 2001) ranges spatially over England, Wales, and parts of Scotland (**Figure 2**), while its temporal focus concentrates on the 600 or so years after AD 1066.[3] The formal extent of such a study ideally consists of the entire body of English royal castles that existed in these places during this period.

In general, the scalar extent of a study is probably best conceived of as the contiguous spatial area, the continuous temporal period, and/or the complete assemblage of material under investigation. However, in practical terms, this is probably never fully attainable. Archaeologists are often required to assume that the evidence under study is either complete in its spatial and temporal distribution or that it is representative as an accurate sample of the material that previously existed in the past. This may not always be a good assumption depending on the true scalar extent of the research undertaken.

In those cases where archaeological interpretations are made on the basis of research focused clearly on non-contiguous spaces, non-continuous time periods, and/or incomplete assemblages, an appreciation of the limited scalar extent of the study can highlight the potential limitations of the interpretations generated.

For example, a hypothetical study that compares the human remains from three different cemeteries representing three different time periods or regions can produce useful normative (generalized) interpretations about changes in past human health over time or across regions. However, there is the danger that unrepresented cemeteries from intervening periods or regions could alter or even contradict these generalized findings. In such instances, an explicit recognition that the true scalar extent of the study consists of the largest contiguous, continuous, and complete unit analyzed would help contextualize and qualify the interpretations made. In other words, noting that the scalar extent of this hypothetical study consisted of single cemeteries, we can emphasize that the interpretations derived from comparing these three cemeteries may not be fully representative of other intervening areas, time periods, and cemeteries.

The second component of analytical scale is the *scalar resolution* of the study. This refers to the smallest, consistently discernible unit achieved, studied, and/or used for analysis within the spatial, temporal, and formal dimensions (cf. Stein 1993:2) (**Figure 1**).

For example, in the study of medieval English royal castles mentioned above the spatial resolution consists of the accurate location of geographical features to the nearest kilometer (**Figure 2**), while the temporal resolution can discern yearly changes thanks to an abundance of historical records (**Figure 3**). The formal resolution of this study could conceivably identify individually diagnostic architectural elements, from window decorations and fireplace fittings, to specialized structural building types (e.g. shell-keeps, gatehouses, or circular towers), or the overall organization of the castle's plan (e.g. motte and bailey, ringwork, quadrangular, or concentric). For the purposes of this research, however, the formal resolution simply distin-

---

[1] We follow the typical archaeological usage of "small-scale" for relatively small things and "large-scale" for relatively large things. This differs from other fields such as photography and mapping where "small-scale" refers to low resolution images (and often large phenomena) while "large-scale" refers to high resolution images (and often relatively small phenomena).

[2] We generally agree with those researchers who prefer multi-scalar approaches (e.g. Blanton et al. 1993; Crumley and Marquardt 1987; de Montmollin 1988; Marquardt 1992:108; and see Last 1995 for a similar assessment of the Annales School of Bloch, Febvre, and Braudel) as the best way to identify patterning and to determine the *effective scale* of particular phenomena—i.e. "the scale at which pattern is recognized and meaning inferred" (Crumley 1995:2; Crumley 1979:166; Marquardt and Crumley 1987:2; Marquardt 1992:107; cf. Toumey 1981:469). However, we also realize that the realities of current research often require scholars to pursue studies focused solely on one analytical scale at a time.

[3] The Norman Conquest (1066) is generally accepted as the date for the introduction of castles to England. Their final use by the Crown (particularly for military purposes) occurred during the English Civil War (1642-1649).

guishes which castles were capable of functioning in administrative, defensive, and/or residential capacities at any given point in time (**Figure 2b**), thereby allowing one to track the administrative, military, and residential organization of royal castles over time.

Needless to say, the scalar extent and resolution of particular research projects can vary widely. In general, studies can be classified as small-scale or large-scale based on the size of their scalar extent – particularly their spatial extent. It is important to note, however, that large-scale studies with a high degree of scalar resolution are also amenable to smaller-scale analyses. For example, although Mathieu (2001) focused on the geographical patterning of royal castles at the national level, the one kilometer spatial resolution of the data could have allowed smaller-scale regional and local analyses. Similarly, while the research was aimed at understanding long-term changes in medieval England's political complexity over time, the one year temporal resolution of the data allowed much finer analyses and resulted in the identification of significant events in the overall process of state development.

The Dimensions of Analysis

As alluded to above, all archaeological studies incorporate *at least* three dimensions of analysis (cf. Spaulding 1960), though this often remains implicit.[4] The first two dimensions, *space* and *time*, are the ones most commonly discussed by and familiar to archaeologists when addressing issues of analytical scale (e.g. Clarke 1977; Crumley and Green 1987:22; Crumley and Marquardt 1987; de Montmollin 1988; Last 1995).

The third dimension, *form*, refers to the archaeological material, component, or complex that is actually under investigation (e.g. lithics, ceramics, metal, faunal, floral, and other remains, burials, architecture, site plans, and settlement patterns). For clarity in the following discussion, this dimension will be referred to as *material form*. This dimension can range in scale from microscopic attributes of artifacts, to assemblages of material (or compound artifacts such as buildings), and even to entire archaeological complexes (or 'cultures').

Interestingly, the common archaeological terms used to discuss the larger-scale phenomena within the dimension of material form are also often used to refer to constellations of things that extend across space and/or time—e.g. distributions, settlement patterns, horizons, and traditions. These terms have become so ubiquitous and loaded in archaeological circles that it is often difficult to conceive of some particular material forms without implicit reference to their spatial and/or temporal dimensions. For example, some material forms, like settlement patterns, imply relatively large spatial and/or temporal scales.

Two points arise from this implicit correspondence. First, the linking of scales among these different dimensions of analysis suggests that there may be some standard correlations in scale that exist between different dimensions. For example, intui-

tively it might seem that studies of large material forms would go hand-in-hand with studies of large spaces and long time periods.

However, this is often not the case in archaeological research. Consider those excavations which try to understand developments over a 1000 year period by excavating deep, but spatially limited trenches on a well-stratified site. Here, a large temporal scale is used with a very small spatial scale. Furthermore, if only certain artifacts are analyzed in this sounding, then a relatively small scale of material form would also be employed.

Alternatively, many large-scale surface survey projects that explore thousands of square kilometers of land are most interested in finding the archaeological remains from one particular time period (albeit one that may have lasted a couple hundred years). In this case, a large spatial scale is used with a relatively small temporal scale.

The first point to be made is that even if some of these dimensions seem to correspond roughly in terms of their relevant scales, there is no 1:1 or necessary correlation between these scales. The second point to make about the relationship between these different dimensions of analysis is that some researchers argue explicitly for a correspondence between certain material forms (often described in spatial terms) and the inferred past social units they are thought to indicate. For example, both de Montmollin (1988:64, table 1) and Neitzel (2000:27, fig. 2.1) infer a direct relationship between 'spatial units' (material form?) and 'social units' (**Figure 4**).[5]

An interesting ramification of this scheme is that, in effect, they are identifying a fourth dimension of analysis—the actual social units we as archaeologists infer from archaeological remains—what we refer to as *social form*. This dimension ranges in scale from individuals, to groups, communities, societies, and even larger agglomerations such as civilizations and/or world systems.[6]

However, though this correlation may be heuristically useful in identifying some past social groupings in certain settings, we would caution that again there does not have to be a 1:1 correlation between any of these dimensions of 'spatial scale' (material form) and social form. In other words, a house does not necessarily correlate to a household (Ashmore and Wilk 1988) and a site does not necessarily equate to a community (Yaeger and Canuto 2000:9). This is clearly illustrated by Hare (2000) who tries unsuccessfully to find a good correspondence between the material forms he identified in the archaeological record (e.g. houses, patio groups, villages, towns, and cities) and the social forms recorded in ethnohistoric census documents.

Furthermore, this perceived 1:1 correlation between material form and social form obscures the fact that an archaeologist

---

[4] Note that some of the other papers in this volume discuss aspects of analytical scale which might also be considered further dimensions.

[5] However, de Montmollin (1990:164-165) notes that these correlations become more difficult to sustain with bridging arguments as the scale of the phenomena increases.

[6] Identifying individuals is often limited to historically-documented contexts or burials. In prehistoric contexts, archaeologists usually focus on inferring interpretations concerning small groups (e.g. domestic groups), communities (e.g. villages or sometimes towns), and societies (e.g. chiefdoms and states).

studying a single structure and its development over time can make significant inferences about a variety of social units. For example, excavating a late 17th century colonial house in New England could provide not only information pertinent to understanding the specific household group that lived in the house, but also information relevant to the local colonial community, the wider colonial and British society, and even the extent and influence of the world system then in operation.

Overall, this breaking down of the perceived 1:1 correlation between different dimensions of analytical scale suggests that each dimension can be independently scaled to provide a plethora of analytical scale combinations, each with the potential to provide a different perspective on the past.

Why Is Analytical Scale Important?

The papers in this volume (see below for a summary of each) suggest that the analytical scale of a project has the potential to determine, channel, or at least influence the interpretations resulting from archaeological research (Toumey 1981:469). Building on this realization, we suggest that the role of analytical scale in archaeological interpretation needs to be better understood.

To achieve this, a logical first step would involve developing a better appreciation of how archaeologists decide which analytical scales to employ in their research. Unfortunately, this decision is often simply the result of following accepted traditional disciplinary behavior (Stein 1993:1-3; Stein and Linse 1993:v), without any conscious thought given to the issue. When pressed to consider the matter, most archaeologists would probably say that the analytical scale of their research is determined by the *research questions* they are investigating (e.g. de Montmollin 1988:63). But this begs the question, what determines the research questions deemed worthy of research?

Further probing might elicit an acknowledgement that one's *theoretical perspective* (de Montmollin 1988:63, 65), or preferred *research methods,* or the availability of certain *types of data* played a significant role in the decision (cf. Stein 1993:1). This implies that much of today's research is pursued simply because certain types of analyses are considered traditional, popular, and/or practical. For example, researchers typically use approaches with which they are more familiar and which may be relatively easier, more cost efficient, and/or enjoyable than others. These are all valid reasons, but they all imply that the analytical scale of a study is simply a dependent variable determined by one (or more) of the elements indicated in **Figure 5a**.

In contrast, we argue that analytical scale is, in fact, its own independent variable—and one that can vary and influence interpretations as much as these other factors (**Figure 5b**). This suggestion is based initially on the realization that many archaeological methods can be used at a variety of analytical scales. For example, GIS (geographic information systems), though typically associated with relatively large-scale, regional analysis, can actually be used for spatial studies at any scale from microscopic to global. In other words, there is no 1:1 correlation between theory, method, data, and analytical scale—

they are all independent variables.

Given this, the next logical step is to determine the influence certain analytical scales may have on archaeological interpretation. This could be approached by trying to identify which analytical scales tend to produce which sorts of interpretations. In other words, which analytical scales produce which different perspectives on the past? For example, just consider for a moment the likely influence of a research strategy using a coarse temporal scale and environmental data in order to explain the development of state-level societies. Is it likely that it would be more apt to show change as resulting from climatic and environmental variables as opposed to individual agency?

What about a study which had access to detailed historical narratives concerning the motivations and actions of powerful elites? Would it be more likely to place the locus of change and causality in the hands of individual agents because it had a much finer temporal resolution and documentary remains to analyze?

This comparison of differing analytical scales and their resulting implications about the past suggests that our failure to consider the influence of analytical scale and its role in archaeological interpretation may be causing us to pursue only certain perspectives on the past. How are we to obtain a full understanding of what may have transpired if we are not even aware of the influence our analytical scales have had? How can we correct for this biased perspective?

One way would be to try to identify those analytical scales which have been typically employed by archaeologists in certain circumstances, and those which have not. Then, by making a concerted effort to pursue atypical research by "playing with our analytical scales", we might be better able to understand the limitations of our traditional interpretations, complement them with new interpretations, and in the process appreciate the role that our different analytical scales played in leading us to each.

The Papers in this Volume

The papers presented in this volume are arranged in approximate chronological order from the Mesolithic-Neolithic transition through to the late Middle Ages. They span Europe east to west from Poland to Iceland and north to south from Iceland to Italy. Though as editors we encouraged the authors to consider explicitly the role of analytical scale in archaeological interpretation, we did not insist upon any one particular understanding of the concept of analytical scale and/or its significance in archaeology. In fact, many of the authors offer perspectives and definitions of analytical scale that differ from ours. In general, we find these different perspectives intriguing, particularly in how they overlap (or diverge) and how they may potentially complement each other. Given the exploratory nature of this discussion, we consider this a strength of the volume and welcome future contributions which further develop and explore the role played by analytical scale in archaeological interpretation.

Peter Bogucki illustrates the impact of differing analytical scales on the perception of early farming communities in central

Europe. Throughout his paper, he offers a number of "morals" for us to learn in order to avoid interpretive pitfalls. Beginning with a historical perspective, he describes how the size of excavation units has influenced the interpretation of early farm dwellings, their perceived duration of occupation, and in turn the speed at which farming spread across central Europe. Turning to his own fieldwork in north-central Poland, his understanding of the density of Neolithic settlement systems changed dramatically after he shifted from a single-site to a multi-site research strategy. Similarly, whether one views the Mesolithic-Neolithic transition as a relatively continuous development or attributes the introduction of agriculture to a dramatic in-migration of farming colonizers relies much upon the spatial and temporal scales at which the analysis is undertaken, as well as the choice of material culture studied. Where smaller-scale analyses and those focused on stone tool assemblages suggest the former, larger-scale analyses focused on sub-continental patterning and studies of house forms, settlement patterns, and other artifact types suggest the latter. Finally, by considering the proposed correlation of the recently hypothesized Black Sea flood with the spread of farming into Europe, he concludes that if the flood occurred as suggested, it happened at such smaller spatial and temporal scales it could not have affected the spread of agriculture significantly.

Timothy Darvill notes that despite the long archaeological interest in the Mesolithic-Neolithic transition, few sites in the British Isles actually document this transition. Moreover, none of the current theoretical perspectives successfully incorporate people because they all fail to link the scale of social action and human behavior with the material found in the archaeological record. To solve these difficulties, he argues that we need to match our problem scale—the social and spatial scale of our target populations from individuals to societies—with our analytical scale—the scale at which we carry out our research. Most studies of the Mesolithic-Neolithic transition have operated at a wide problem scale, designed to assess population continuity versus population change. Their analytical scale has involved either the excavation of a small number of sites or the analysis of large regional distributions. Darvill suggests that a better approach would be to focus on an intermediate spatial scale, one that recognizes that human activity occurs along a horizontal plane and that would allow the recovery of horizontal stratigraphies in areas where long vertical sequences do not exist. Arguing that postprocessual approaches to landscape are particularly appropriate because they provide an underlying theory based on the social use of space, he uses a series of nested analytical scales to examine the area around Billown on the Isle of Man. By uncovering recurrent patterns in the use of projectiles, pits, and quartz pebbles and noting the introduction of new social practices, he suggests continued community presence and social action over a wide geographic area from the Mesolithic into the Neolithic.

Though he defines analytical scale as the "geographical extent of the focus of research, as in 'regional scale', or the size or ranking of the social entity under consideration, as in site or single-polity", **D. Blair Gibson** chooses to focus his paper on a discussion of social evolution and the role, if any, played by "scale"—"the spatial dimensions of a polity or the size of its population". Framing his discussion in terms of a critique of the political economy school (which he prefers to call neo-Boasian), Gibson provides a neo-evolutionist perspective on the usefulness of scale as a meaningful measure of complexity. Adopting a substantivist position, Gibson argues that scale is not a useful measure of complexity since the size of both territory and population depends on the productive potential of a region and on the particular subsistence economy. Arguing that social organization is a better measure of complexity, he draws on his fieldwork in the Burren region of Ireland to suggest that the Late Neolithic/Early Bronze Age period was characterized by simple chiefdoms. Evidence for this consists of systems of field walls which unite individual households into larger neighborhoods, massive wedge tombs whose construction required labor on a larger corporate scale, and a variety of other tomb types which imply the practice of ancestor veneration. He concludes by noting that "scale is clearly a dependent variable, and so is of questionable analytical value, at least by itself".

Archaeometry, the detailed laboratory analysis of materials, is often limited to determining the material composition of artifacts and their means of production. However, **Elizabeth Hamilton** argues that archaeometry can also answer questions of broader archaeological significance. Though one could focus on the technical scales of analysis from microscopic to macroscopic, she chooses to consider four different "levels of culture" which can be studied using archaeometry. These include the individual producer and the choices he/she made, the production group which possesses the required knowledge and techniques, the wider culture which assigns status, value, and meaning to the production process and the resulting artifacts, and finally, the greater interaction area where technology and its associated meanings circulate and change. Using her analysis of artifacts from the Titelberg in Luxembourg, she notes how archaeometry helped identify the first use of brass in transalpine Europe, as well as changes in labor organization, the creation of new meanings associated with this alloy, and the probability of contact between Belgic Gaul and Asia Minor. Turning to Dunmisk, an early medieval glass-making site in Northern Ireland, she illustrates how archaeometry can inform us about different levels of culture by posing a series of questions that could be addressed beyond the conclusions presented by the site's excavators.

Genevieve Fisher presents a multi-scalar analysis of female dress ornaments from six early Anglo-Saxon cemeteries in East Anglia, England. By examining the distribution of brooches at kingdom-wide, community-level, and individual scales, she examines changing identities during the period of early Anglo-Saxon kingdom formation. For example, the increasing popularity of certain dress accessories within East Anglia as a whole attests to the emergence of a regional costume for women and the creation of an insular Anglian identity. In contrast, comparing the different types of brooches found at particular East Anglian sites indicates that different communities preferred particular brooches although they had a shared costume. Furthermore, comparisons of individual burial assemblages show many idiosyncratic brooch combinations that suggest a high degree of variation within communities. Fisher argues that this contrast between general community conformity in preferred brooch types and individual variation in particular brooch combinations suggests conflicting interests between the individual or kin-group and the wider community during this period. More generally, her research demonstrates how perceived patterns in material culture and their corresponding interpretations vary according to the analytical scale at which they are observed.

Inspired by a consideration of the role of analytical scale in archaeological interpretation, **Rae Ostman** develops a new perspective for examining the relationship between cities and decreasing social complexity in the past. Large-scale, comparative studies, with the generalizing goal of creating cross-cultural models, emphasize the disjunction and discontinuity caused by the collapse of complex societies. In contrast, more detailed analyses of particular cases highlight the evidence for social and cultural continuity, portraying decreasing complexity as a process of transition and transformation rather than decline and collapse. In order to understand the simpler societies that emerged, she argues that it is necessary to examine the process on an even smaller scale—the individual city, where local and state interests intersect. She applies this perspective to the city of Volterra, Italy in order to understand the development of late Antique society out of the dissolution of the Roman Empire. Noting that recent research at Volterra challenges general models of collapse by documenting a basic stability in the surrounding rural settlement pattern and agricultural economy in contrast to striking changes in the city itself, she proposes a detailed analysis of Volterra's ceramics. This is designed to illuminate how pottery production and consumption changed as Volterra became part of the broader imperial economy, and also how these changes later contributed to the creation of late Antique society.

Like Ostman, **John Soderberg** discusses the relationship between urbanism, social complexity, and analytical scale. He begins by noting that current models for the development of urban centers in early medieval Europe use a regional scale of analysis. Employing a theory of elite competition and coercion, these models see elites establishing trade emporia to acquire the foreign prestige goods needed to expand their power. As long-distance trade fostered the growth of early market exchange, these emporia became increasingly urban in character. Once introduced, these regional social dynamics spread to the local level, replacing earlier socioeconomic strategies of cooperation and commonality. Thus, in such regional approaches, a distinct local scale of analysis does not exist. However, citing research on early monastic sites in Ireland, Soderberg argues that this regional orientation is insufficient. In particular, the preliminary analysis of animal bones from Clonmacnoise suggests a slaughter pattern characteristic of the provisioning found at urban centers in Britain and at later Viking Dublin. To explain how such monastic urban sites arose during a period lacking a highly developed social hierarchy or extensive long-distance trade, he contends that the social behaviors associated with a local scale of analysis must be reintegrated into the process of urbanization and conceptions of social complexity. This would also allow variations in the process of urbanization to be seen as resulting from differences in the mediation between local and regional social dynamics, rather than simply viewing them as mere epiphenomena.

Kevin P. Smith explores the role of analytical scale in archaeological interpretation by questioning the validity of archaeo-

logical models for the development of complex societies. Given that people operate at much finer temporal and social scales than those monitored by archaeological methods, he asks to what extent are the changes we detect in the archaeological record actually those we hope to understand? He addresses this issue by focusing on the transformation of medieval Iceland from a network of decentralized simple chiefdoms into a unified proto-state. This process and the motivations behind it were uniquely described in writing by the participants involved. These historical texts document a series of events which occurred too rapidly—over a span of less than three generations, or half the duration of a common archaeological phase—and on too small a social scale to be observed by most archaeological methods. Moreover, the texts suggest that the actors were motivated by factors quite different from those typically given significance in archaeological models. In particular, the subtle changes in the scale and organization of households, the shifts in the proportions of cattle or sheep herded, and the fluctuations in the environment and the regional resource base—all typical archaeological data—occurred over periods of time too long to have been perceived as important by most actors in the past. As a result, Smith concludes that archaeology might provide more information about the context of sociopolitical change than it does its causes. However, changes in this context may help to explain why similar actions undertaken at different points in time produced markedly different results.

The finally two articles in the volume are discussion papers written by **Peter S. Wells** and **Dean R. Snow**. These highlight some of the key issues discussed in the volume.

Biographical Sketches

James R. Mathieu received his B.A. (1992), M.A. (1992), and Ph.D. (2001) in Anthropology from the University of Pennsylvania and his M.A. (1995) in Medieval Archaeology from the University of York, England. His field experience includes surveys and excavations in North Carolina, Maine, Virginia, Syria, France, England, Wales, Belize, Tunisia, and Guatemala. His research interests include the development of complex societies, experimental archaeology, the archaeology of Europe and the circum Mediterranean area, the use of GIS and other spatial analyses, and castle studies.

Rachel E. Scott received her B.A. (1994) in Anthropology from the University of Chicago and an H.Dip. (1995) in Celtic Archaeology from Unversity College Dublin, Ireland. She is currently a Ph.D. candidate in Anthropology at the University of Pennsylvania. She has participated in fieldwork in Ireland, Iceland, France, and Spain. Her research interests include bioarchaeology, human skeletal analysis, the cultural and biological body, and the archaeology of Europe (particularly Ireland).

References Cited

Ashmore, W. and R.R. Wilk 1988 'Household and community in the Mesoamerican past' in R.R. Wilk and W. Ashmore (eds) *Household and Community in the Mesoamerican Past* University of New Mexico Press (Albuquerque, NM):1-27.
Blanton, R.E., S.A. Kowalewski, G.M. Feinman, and L.M. Finsten 1993 *Ancient Mesoamerica: A Comparison of Change*

in Three Regions 2nd ed. Cambridge University Press (Cambridge).

Clarke, D. 1977 'Spatial information in archaeology' in D. Clarke (ed) *Spatial Archaeology* Academic Press (New York):1-32.

Crumley, C. 1979 'Three locational models: an epistemological assessment for anthropology and archaeology' in M.B. Schiffer (ed) *Advances in Archaeological Method and Theory* Vol. 2 Academic Press (New York):141-173.

Crumley, C.L. 1995 'Heterarchy and the analysis of complex societies' in R.M. Ehrenreich, C.L. Crumley, and J.E. Levy (eds) *Heterarchy and the Analysis of Complex Societies* Archaeological Papers of the American Anthropological Association No. 6 (Arlington, VA):1-5.

Crumley, C.L. and P.R. Green 1987 'Environmental setting' in C.L. Crumley and W.H. Marquardt (eds) *Regional Dynamics: Burgundian Landscapes in Historical Perspective* Academic Press (London):19-39.

Crumley, C.L. and W.H. Marquardt 1987 (eds) *Regional Dynamics: Burgundian Landscapes in Historical Perspective* Academic Press (New York).

de Montmollin, O. 1988 'Settlement scale and theory in Maya archaeology' in N.J. Saunders and O. de Montmollin (eds) *Recent Studies in Pre-Columbian Archaeology* British Archaeological Reports, International Series 421(i) (Oxford):63-104.

de Montmollin, O. 1990 'Scales of settlement study for complex societies: analytical issues from the Classic Maya area' *Journal of Field Archaeology* 15:151-168.

Hare, T.S. 2000 'Between the household and the empire: structural relationships within and among Aztec communities and polities' in M.-A. Canuto and J. Yaeger (eds) *Archaeology of Communities:A New World Perspective* Routledge (New York):78-101.

Last, J. 1995 'The nature of history' in I. Hodder, M. Shanks, A. Alexandri, V. Buchli, J. Carman, J. Last, and G. Lucas (eds) *Interpreting Archaeology: Finding Meaning in the Past* Routledge (New York):141-157.

Marquardt, W.H. 1992 'Dialectical archaeology' in M.B. Schiffer (ed) Archaeological Method and Theory, Vol. 4, University of Arizona Press (Tucson, AZ):101-140.

Marquardt, W.H. and C.L. Crumley 1987 'Theoretical issues in the analysis of spatial patterning' in C.L. Crumley and W.H. Marquardt (eds) *Regional Dynamics: Burgundian Landscapes in Historical Perspective* Academic Press (London):1-18.

Mathieu, J.R. 2001 *Assessing Political Complexity in Medieval England: An Analysis of Royal Buildings and Strategies* Unpublished Ph.D. dissertation, University of Pennsylvania (Philadelphia).

Neitzel, J.E. 2000 'What's a regional system? Issues of scale and interaction in the prehistoric Southwest' in M. Hegmon (ed) *The Archaeology of Regional Interaction* Univ. of Colorado Press (Boulder):25-40.

Spaulding, A. 1960 'The dimensions of archaeology' in G.E. Dole and R.L. Carneiro (eds) *Essays in the Science of Culture* Cromwell (New York):437-456.

Stein, J.K. 1993 'Scale in archaeology, geosciences, and geoarchaeology' in J.K. Stein and A.R. Linse (eds) *Effects of Scale on Archeological and Geoscientific Perspectives* Geological Society of America, Special Paper No. 283 (Boulder, CO):1-10.

Stein, J.K. and A.R. Linse (eds) 1993 *Effects of Scale on Archeological and Geoscientific Perspectives* Geological Society of America, Special Paper No. 283 (Boulder, CO).

Toumey, C.P. 1981 'Pattern and scale in archaeological regions' in P.D. Francis, F.J. Kense, and P.G. Duke (eds) *Networks of the Past: Regional Interaction in Archaeology* Proceedings of the 12th Annual Chacmool Conference (Calgary, Alberta):467-476.

Yaeger, J. and M.A. Canuto 2000 'Introducing an archaeology of communities' in M.-A. Canuto and J. Yaeger (eds) *Archaeology of Communities:A New World Perspective* Routledge (New York):1-15.

Spatial Extent and Spatial Resolution

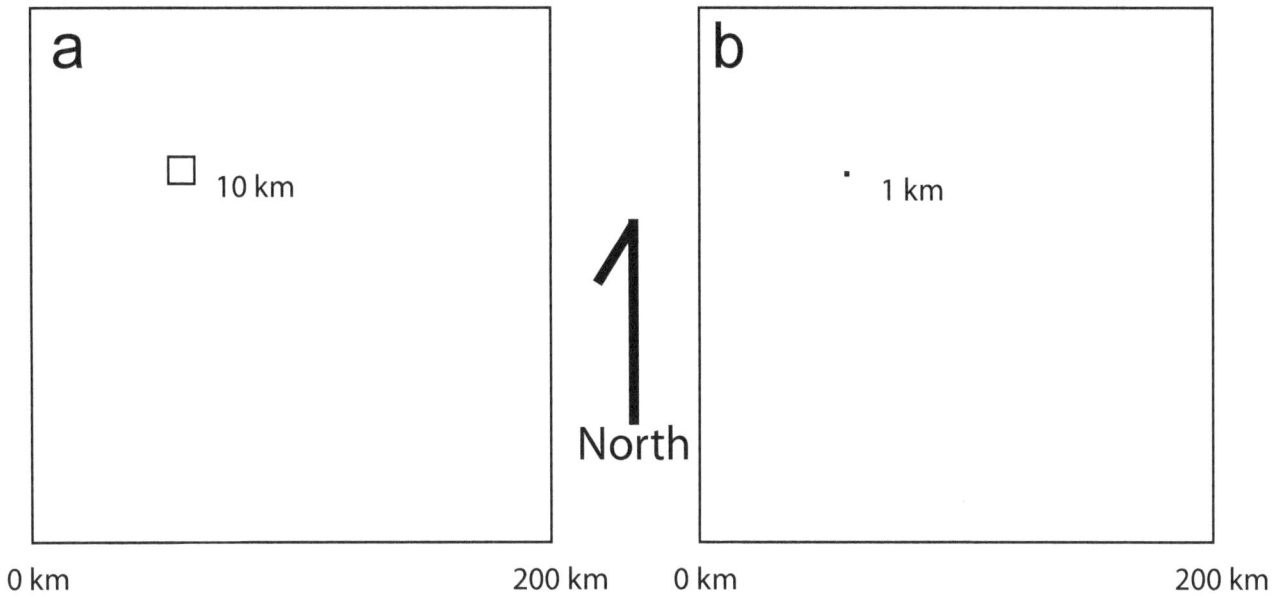

a

□ 10 km

↑
North

b

. 1 km

0 km · · · · · · · · · · · · · · · · · · · 200 km · 0 km · · · · · · · · · · · · · · · · · · · 200 km

Figure 1a-b: The concepts of spatial extent and spatial resolution. 1a, the spatial extent is 400 square km, while the resolution consists of 10 km survey blocks; 1b, the spatial extent has not changed, but the resolution is now to the nearest kilometer. During excavation, spatial resolution may improve to the nearest centimeter or so, though this usually requires that the spatial extent of the excavation unit also be reduced drastically to a matter of square meters.

Temporal Extent and Temporal Resolution

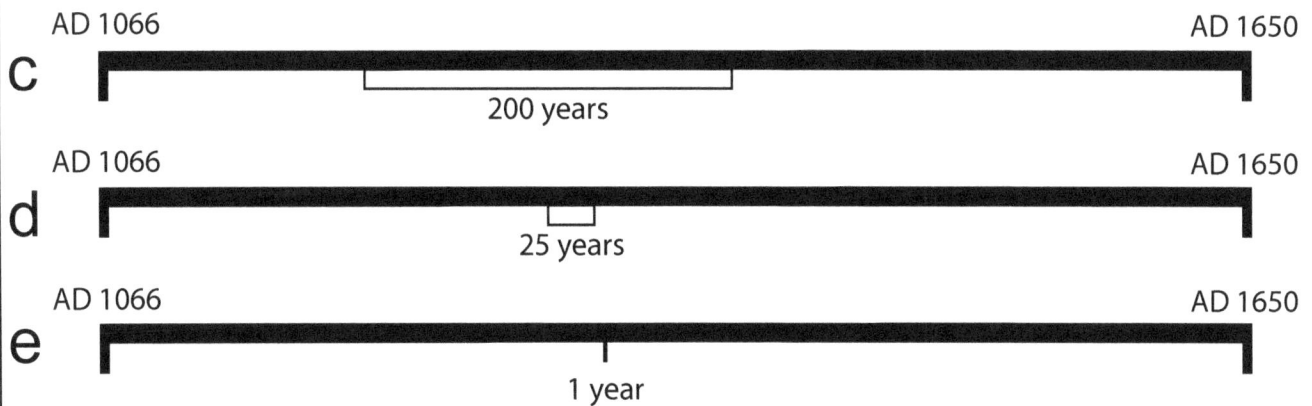

c   AD 1066 ————————————————— AD 1650
200 years

d   AD 1066 ————————————————— AD 1650
25 years

e   AD 1066 ————————————————— AD 1650
1 year

Figure 1c-e: The concepts of temporal extent and temporal resolution. 1c, the temporal extent is 585 years, while the resolution consists of 200 year long periods--typical of some prehistoric archaeology; 1d, the temporal extent has not changed, but the resolution is now improved to 25 year blocks; 1e, the temporal extent again is the same, but the resolution discerns individual years--through the use of historical records.

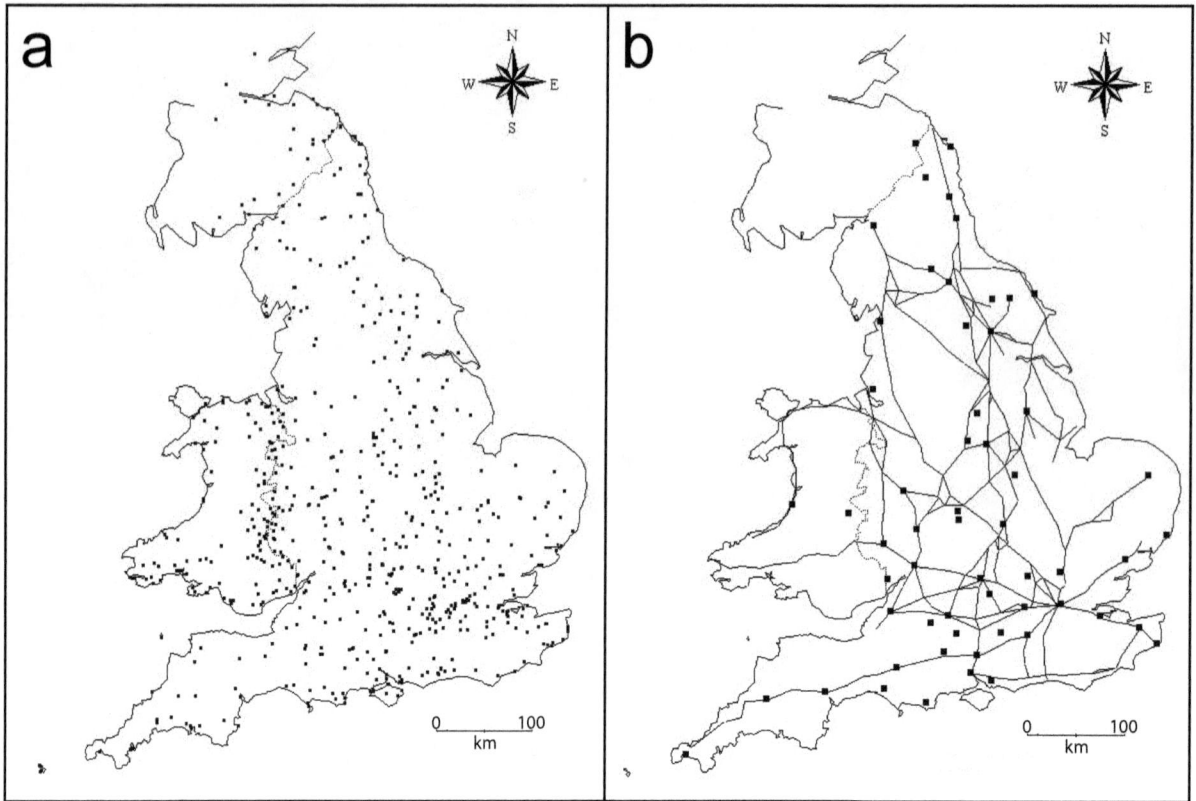

Figure 2: The spatial and formal extent of Mathieu's (2001) research consisted of (a) all the royal buildings in England, Wales, and Scotland between AD 1066-1650. However, with a spatial resolution to the nearest kilometer and a temporal resolution to a given year, very specific distribution maps could be produced. For example, (b) shows the location of all royal castles in AD 1219 in relation to the major road network.

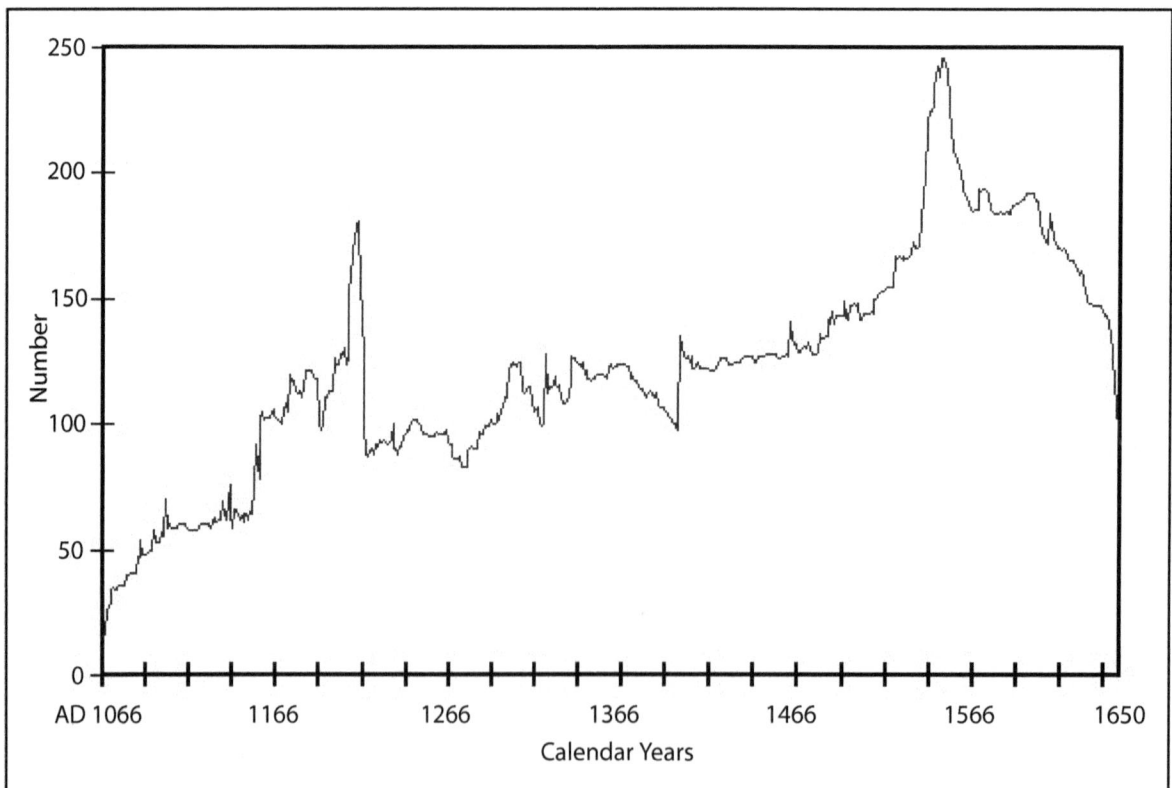

Figure 3: The temporal extent of Mathieu's (2001) reserch covered the period AD 1066-1650. But detailed historical information resulted in a temporal resolution that allowed yearly fluctuations in the number of buildings owned by the English Crown to be monitored. This made it easy to select specific significant years for the mapping of spatial patterns and the indentification of change and its causes.

Neitzel's (2000) Correlates		de Montmollin's (1988) Correlates	
"Spatial Unit"	*"Social Unit"*	*"Domestic Settlement"*	*"Society"*
Structure	Household/family	Dwelling structure	Nuclear household
		House group	Nuclear-extended household
		Cluster	Corporate group
Site	Settlement	Site	Community
Local area	Local system	Sub-basin	District
		Basin	Kingdom-polity
Region	Regional system	Region	Polity network
Macroregion	Macroregional system		
Macro-macroregion?	World system		

Figure 4: Attempts to correlate "spatial units" or material form to "social units" or social form.

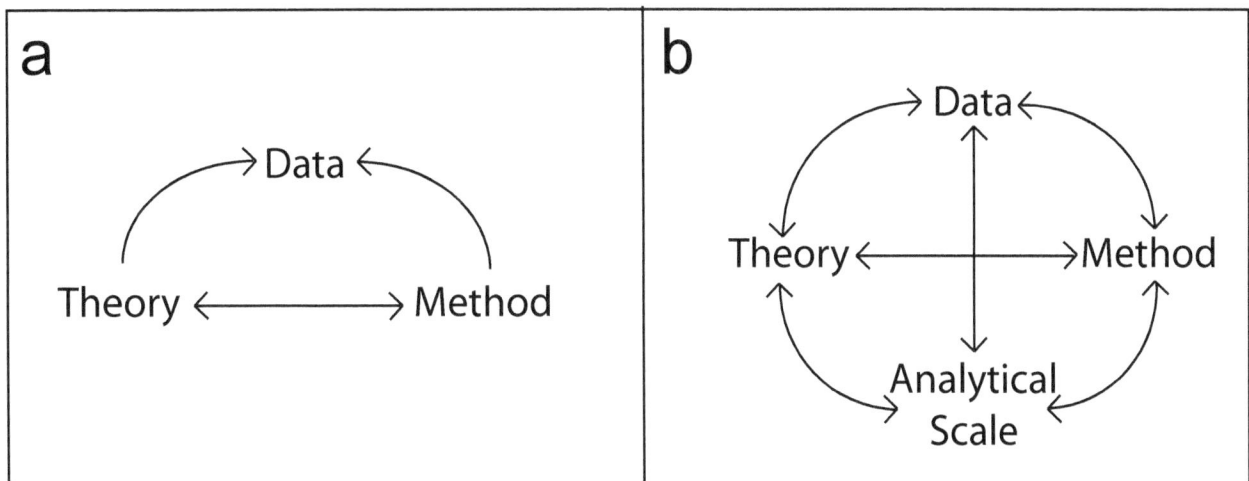

Figure 5: Alternative ways to conceive of the independent influence of the major elements involved in interpretive research strategies.

Scale Factors and Early European Farming

Peter Bogucki

Abstract

The study of the process of the establishment of farming communities throughout central Europe between 7500 and 5000 years ago is particularly sensitive to the choice of analytical units and scales. This process may appear strikingly different depending on the geographical and temporal scales chosen to define the scope of the investigation. Moreover, analysis of single artifact classes may contradict the picture obtained when many cultural subsystems are studied together. The issue has particular relevance for the discussion of whether the establishment of farming communities occurred through the adoption of agriculture by indigenous foragers or through the rapid dispersal of agricultural peoples.

The study of early farmers in central Europe has been particularly affected by the choice of units of temporal and spatial scale by archaeologists over the last 150 years.[1] In this paper, I would like to consider several cases from Neolithic continental Europe in which the choice of spatial and temporal scales of field research and analysis has had an impact on archaeological interpretation (**Figure 1**). These include:

- pithouses vs. longhouses as the primary dwellings of early farmers;
- Neolithic settlement systems that I have studied in Poland;
- Neolithic colonization vs. indigenous agriculture in south-central Europe;
- the hypothesized Black Sea flood and agricultural dispersals across Europe.

The goal of this exercise is to sharpen awareness that choice of analytical scale is as important an aspect of archaeological research as the choice of excavation strategy or interpretive approach and that the articulation among different temporal and spatial scales must be taken into consideration.

Pithouses vs. Longhouses

A classic early example of the impact of the choice of analytical scale is the pithouse vs. longhouse discussion of the first half of the twentieth century. Limited areas of excavation on early Neolithic sites in Germany, Poland, and neighboring countries had exposed large pits associated with postholes. This led to the conclusion that the early farmers of this region lived in large semi-subterranean structures with uneven floors characterized by many nooks and hollows. Moreover, the realization that living conditions in such hovels would degrade rapidly was, I believe, a major contributing factor to the early formulation of the model of *Brandwirtschaft*, or shifting slash-and-burn agriculture, as the prime mover behind the dispersal of agriculture in central Europe. Thus settlements were interpreted as short-term occupations, abandoned as soon as soil fertility declined.

As excavated areas became larger, such as the Köln-Lindenthal excavations of the early 1930s, archaeologists were reluctant to abandon this model. Werner Buttler (1936; Buttler and Haberey 1936) steadfastly believed that the large post structures (**Figure 2**) that he discovered at Köln-Lindenthal were barns, while the human inhabitants of the settlement remained in their muddy pithouses (**Figure 3**). A few years later, however, Konrad Jażdżewski (1938), excavating at Brześć Kujawski in Poland, listened to a voice of reason from one of his laborers. Jażdżewski had also found long timber structures and large irregular pits. One of the workers remarked that if he had to live in one of these muddy pits, he would break his leg slipping around in it. Jażdżewski concluded that the timber structures really were the houses.

Despite the outbreak of World War II, this debate continued in central Europe, and Oscar Paret published a compelling discussion in *Germania* in 1942 that effectively demolished the pithouse hypothesis. While the rest of European prehistory generally stood still between 1939 and 1946, there was a complete revolution in the understanding of Neolithic habitation structures. By 1949, V. Gordon Childe was able to write:

> Ten years ago the prehistoric soil of Europe was literally riddled with "pit dwellings" in which our ancestors slept and cooked, huddled together like soldiers in a bell tent. I suppose it was wraithes from Tacitus and Xiphilinus combining in the minds of 16th century antiquaries with more exact travelers' tales of the earth lodges of the Red Indians that caused this overcrowding of the pits. For the holes in the ground are there right enough: it is only in the last ten years that Bersu and Paret have evicted their human occupants to make room for the pigs and weevils these would properly accommodate. Thanks to them we realize that neither Stone Age Danubians nor Iron Age Britons were housed in subterranean silos or semi-subterranean sties . . . . Today it is plain that such farm houses were normal from the beginning of the new stone age wherever excavators' technique is adequate for their recognition . . . . (1949:77)

The purpose of this discussion is not to disparage Buttler's research. Despite his misinterpretation, his work at Köln-Lindenthal was pathbreaking in that it yielded such remarkable detailed evidence and also that it was published in a way that other scholars could readily scrutinize and reinterpret his finds. Moreover, through their broad dissemination throughout Europe, such as in the article Buttler published in *Antiquity* in 1936, the Köln-Lindenthal finds fired the imagination of the archaeological community about the potential for the study of Neolithic settlements that had previously seemed

---

[1] For more information on research described in this paper and for other publications by the author, visit http://www.princeton.edu/~bogucki/.

11

simple and boring.

In the hindsight of half a century, this debate seems humorous, yet it highlights the way in which analytical scale frames archaeological thinking. With small excavation areas, the primary unit of analysis was the individual feature, and no features were more visible archaeologically than the rubbish filled pits, which became the archaeologists' focus. Yet once the scale of analysis shifted to the community plan, as at Köln-Lindenthal and Brześć Kujawski, the fallacy of the "pits-as-houses, timber-structures-as-barns" concept became apparent. Subsequently, with the excavation of still-larger areas, the houses and pits have come to be seen to form household clusters or farmsteads, permitting new insights into Neolithic society.

Moral: Excavate sites, don't just clear features.

Neolithic Settlement Systems in Polish Lowlands

The next case is drawn primarily from my own field research. For nearly 25 years, I have been involved in the investigation of early farming sites in the lowlands of north-central Poland, in the Kuyavia region to be more exact. Between 1976 and 1984, Ryszard Grygiel and I continued the work begun by Jażdżewski at Brześć Kujawski (Bogucki 1982; Bogucki and Grygiel 1981, 1983, 1993). With nearly 80 houses, Brześć Kujawski has long been a highly visible locality in the regional archaeological record and in European archaeological literature. V. Gordon Childe (1949) and Grahame Clark (1952) referred to it in several publications during the 1940s and 1950s, and Grygiel and I have discussed various aspects of this site in many publications over the last two decades. Within 40 or so kilometers of Brześć Kujawski, however, no similar sites were known, save for one with two longhouses at Dobre that Jażdżewski also investigated in the 1930s. Instead, unsystematic excursions during the course of our 1970s research turned up a number of smaller sites, apparently without longhouses (although we should have learned something from Buttler's experience described above!). This led to my view that Brześć Kujawski was at the center of a regional settlement system, in which several small outlying special-purpose sites served this one main settlement (Bogucki 1982:133-135). Brześć Kujawski, as I imagined it, was the "navel of the Neolithic universe" in this area. How could any large contemporaneous settlements have existed nearby?

In 1985, however, survey work by Ryszard Grygiel turned up an interesting locality about 10 kilometers west of Brześć Kujawski, at a place called Osłonki on a low promontory next to an ancient lake basin. We were actually looking for a fairly simple site with only a couple of longhouses at which we could test ideas about Neolithic household organization that arose from our work at Brześć Kujawski (Bogucki and Grygiel 1981; Grygiel 1986). Our hope was to find a Neolithic settlement as uncomplicated as the one excavated in the early 1950s at Biskupin, not far from the famous Iron Age site, that seemed to have only a single longhouse and its associated features (Maciejewski et al. 1954).

Osłonki seemed fairly promising in this regard and in 1989, we

began to excavate, supported by funds from the National Geographic Society and the Wenner-Gren Foundation for Anthropological Research (Grygiel and Bogucki 1997). The first season was promising: only a few longhouses were separated by open space, although many adjacent clay pits complicated the stratification. Additional seasons in 1990 and 1991 brought several additional houses, and we were ready to call it a day. A sizeable grant from the Polish Committee on Scientific Research, however, allowed us to continue the excavations for another three seasons, and only then was the true extent of the settlement at Osłonki apparent. It just kept on going. Finally, we reached a massive ditch system that bounded the settlement on the landward edge of the peninsula on which it lies.

So, here at Osłonki we had a site of comparable magnitude, albeit with simpler superimposition of houses, to that of Brześć Kujawski, only 10 kilometers away. Moreover, most of the finds at Osłonki were exactly contemporaneous with the main phase of settlement at Brześć Kujawski. Suddenly, Brześć Kujawski did not look like the navel of the Neolithic universe between 4500 and 4200 BC anymore. Instead, we had to think of a regional system in which at least two—and who knows how many more?—large settlements co-existed, presumably with connections and interactions between them, and perhaps conflicts as well. Our view of the Neolithic landscape and land use had to be revised dramatically.

But there is more. In 1995, my colleague Grygiel began excavations about 500 meters to the northeast of Osłonki, on the other side of the old lake basin, in a locality called Miechowice. In several seasons of excavation there, he has found still more longhouses and graves, contemporaneous with Osłonki, indicating that several shores of this lake basin were intensively settled during these few centuries. Further work in 1999 at Konary just to the northwest of Osłonki revealed still more longhouses. This enormous settlement complex (**Figure 4**) was completely unknown prior to 1985. How many more such complexes await discovery in this area?

Moral: View your sites as elements of a cultural landscape that you are prepared to explore over an extended period. Don't quit prematurely.

Neolithic Colonization vs. Indigenous Agriculture in Central Europe

The assumption of a mobile Neolithic population in central Europe, conditioned by the pithouses and the *Brandwirtschaft* hypothesis mentioned above led very early to the general belief that the earliest farmers in central Europe were colonists who settled selectively on the loess soils of this region. The recognition that these farming communities were longer-lived than had been previously assumed did not really dislodge this view, although it made the search for a prime mover behind this colonization more difficult. But again, scales of analysis have entered the picture to complicate things.

When viewed on the scale of the subcontinent which I will call "riverine interior central Europe", the case for colonization is very clear (Bogucki 1995, 1996, 2000). Agricultural people selectively colonized habitats in the loess basins along second- and third-order streams. Their settlements with longhouses are distinctly different from anything seen among the indigenous foragers of this area, who also did not make pottery. The rapidity of their spread can be explained by noting similar phenomena in the dispersal of plant and animal populations. In many dispersals, the variation in the distance of movement does not form a normal diffusion which would result in a slow, steady spread. Instead, a few long-distance moves by some individuals establish a population throughout an area, followed by many shorter moves by other members of the population to fill in the gaps. The overall appearance of the dispersal, at a relatively coarse temporal scale such as that available to archaeologists, is of a rapid event, but at finer scales it may become evident that only a few members of the population are responsible for creating this impression.

Problems arise, however, when the evidence from smaller areas within this region are viewed in relative isolation, or even when individual categories of artifacts are considered in isolation from the larger corpus of comparative data. For example, in the western and southern parts of riverine interior central Europe, technological traits associated with the Late Mesolithic have been identified in Early Neolithic stone tool assemblages. Many researchers have suggested an involvement by local foragers in the establishment of farming communities in central Europe (e.g. Ehrich 1976; Newell 1970). There is nothing wrong with this position, for it seems entirely reasonable to accept that the farmers, even if they were colonists, engaged in some contact with the sparse indigenous foragers (Bogucki 1988; Gregg 1988). If one focuses on the lithic evidence to the exclusion of all other data, however, it is then possible to construct an argument that denies that an agricultural colonization of central Europe ever occurred.

Several German scholars have now taken up this "indigenist" position (Kind 1998; Tillmann 1993), arguing for a local development of early farming communities in parts of riverine interior central Europe, based largely on lithic evidence. Without going into all the details here, the indigenist case involves the selective identification of similarities in stone tool raw material, technology, and types in both late Mesolithic and early Neolithic sites in southern and south-central Germany. Were the earliest farmers of central Europe confined to the regions in which these similarities have been highlighted, the lithic evidence would be potentially a significant indicator of indigenous continuity. Yet the regions in which these similarities are found constitute only a small part of the approximately 750,000 km^2 extent of riverine interior central Europe. Over this entire area, we can observe discontinuities in house form and settlement pattern and the appearance of pottery and domesticates with no local antecedents (Limburg and La Hoguette wares constitute other localized anomalies). The more-comprehensive evidence for discontinuity overwhelms the localized lithic evidence for continuity over a much larger area.

Moreover, there are such scalar differences between the forager communities of central Europe and the earliest farmers of this area that rapid *in situ* transformation of indigenous societies is improbable. These differences are illustrated in

Figure 5, which graphs the spatial and temporal extent of Mesolithic and Neolithic activities, sites, and cultural groupings. It is clear that there is a substantial difference between the temporal and spatial scale of postglacial foraging society and that of the Linear Pottery farmers and their congeners. The apparent duration of Linear Pottery settlements—although Alasdair Whittle (1996) would disagree that they were so permanent—and their larger groupings forces the forager curve and the farmer curve apart, especially in the decadal range. Elsewhere in temperate Europe, such as in southern Scandinavia, these curves would probably not be so far apart, making indigenous transformation more likely. In central Europe, however, to go from seasonal camps to persistent households and hamlets is such a dramatic jump that minor similarities in stone tool style are misleading. Such transient similarities are possible, even expected, because the spatial and temporal dimensions of the stone tool production are so similar between foraging and farming societies.

Moral: Regional variability in one category of evidence does not necessarily contradict models operating at larger scales. In other words, while it is important to account for such variability, it does not in itself require revision of models based on evidence that embraces more data, space, and time.

The Hypothesized Black Sea Flood and Agricultural Dispersals

At the continental scale, the establishment of agricultural communities in Europe has been modeled as a "wave of advance" by Albert Ammerman and Luca Cavalli-Sforza, on a paradigm of dispersal of genes through populations. This model, articulated most fully in a 1984 book, explicitly does not consider individuals or communities, their motivations, or their history. Its focus is on the large-scale patterns behind the spread of agriculture. In viewing this process as continuous rather than punctuated and the adoption of agriculture as a local short-term event rather than a long-term process, the wave-of-advance model does seem to privilege colonization by farmers over the gradual adoption of agriculture by indigenous foragers. Ammerman and Cavalli-Sforza use the term "demic diffusion" in place of "colonization", but the idea is very much the same.

Looking at the establishment of agriculture in Europe in this way—on a continental scale at a fairly low level of resolution—can stir up some trouble, especially when it comes into contact with other big processes and events. A recent case in point is the attempt to connect the spread of agriculture in Europe with the breaching of the Bosphorus barrier around 5500 BC by seawater from the Mediterranean which flooded the Black Sea basin. The geoscientists who have documented this event, William Ryan and Walter Pitman, have proceeded to argue that the suddenness of the inundation of the Black Sea basin caused the people living there to flee to dryer land. In fact, these people seem to have been so traumatized by this event that they did not stop until they had reached the Paris Basin. In their 1999 book, *Noah's Flood*, Ryan and Pitman portray the earliest European farmers as having fled from the Black Sea up the Dniestr and Bug valleys, through southern Poland, and thence into central Europe. Another group exited up the Danube valley, oblivious to the Carpathian Mountains or the groups of foragers living in the Iron Gates.

Unfortunately, "God is in the details", as Mies van der Rohe used to like to say, and in this case, there has been too much attention to the forest and not enough to the trees. First of all, Ammerman and Cavalli-Sforza's 1984 wave-of-advance map has one important error (Ammerman and Cavalli-Sforza 1984: fig. 4.5). They accept the Soroca (formerly called Soroki) sites along the lower Dniestr in Moldova as being fully agricultural, although the evidence is certainly equivocal at best (Doluk-hanov 1997:64). It seems more likely that these sites represent indigenous foragers who acquired some domesticates in their later stages, much as took place in the Iron Gates, the Netherlands, and elsewhere in Europe. Counting the Soroca inhabitants as full farmers, however, produces a very early cline for agriculture north of the Black Sea, exactly where it enables Ryan and Pitman to identify an early farming population as candidates for their northern refuges. Ammerman and Cavalli-Sforza's inclusion of the Soroca sites as agricultural was subsumed into their large-scale wave-of-advance model, where it was simply noise and not particularly bothersome until Ryan and Pitman's own large-scale analysis incorporated this erroneous identification.

The other problem with connecting the Ryan and Pitman model to the spread of early European farming lies in the temporal scale of these processes. In their view, the rise of water in the Black Sea basin took about a decade to flood all parts of the basin, with most of the inundation occurring in the first two years. This surely would have displaced whoever lived along the shoreline and for dozens of kilometers inland. Yet this would have taken place in about half a generation. The agricultural settlement of Europe, however, took over a millennium, or over 50 generations. Surely there would have been ample time for the farming populations to adjust to this event in a short time without it having such a residual impact.

Figure 5 illustrates these scalar inconsistencies. Although the Black Sea flood may have had an impact over a substantial area, it is still at least an order of magnitude smaller than the spatial scale of agricultural dispersal in Europe. Temporally, the duration of this event is about two orders of magnitude smaller than that of the spread of agriculture. On both axes, there was ample space and time for the impact of this event to be "absorbed" before having the dramatic consequences claimed by Ryan and Pitman.

Ryan and Pitman say that this event was so dramatic that it remained ingrained in myth for thousands of years, but Occam's razor really starts getting dull here. The simplest explanation is that there is absolutely no connection between the hypothesized Black Sea flood and the spread of agriculture into Europe for the simple reason that the first was over in a decade and the second took place over a millennium. The dispersal of agriculture was already underway and proceeded for reasons unrelated to any localized displacement of peoples from the Black Sea continental shelf.

Moral: Establishing a causal relationship between two historical events is not so easy if they are operating at different spatial and temporal scales.

Conclusion

Archaeology is one of the few analytical disciplines in which most researchers are oblivious to scale factors, or they become aware of scale factors only in hindsight rather than in advance. It is important that archaeologists realize that their models are scale-dependent and that inferences drawn from studies at one scale and applied to another may be misleading. The case studies discussed in this paper highlight a few examples in which spatial and temporal scale are critical elements of excavation strategy, research design, and archaeological interpretation.

Biographical Sketch

Peter Bogucki received his B.A. from the University of Pennsylvania and his Ph.D. from Harvard University. Since 1976, he has studied early European farming society and conducted field research in north-central Poland. He currently serves as the Associate Dean for Undergraduate Affairs of the School of Engineering and Applied Science at Princeton University.

References Cited

Ammerman, Albert and L.L. Cavalli-Sforza 1984 *The Neolithic Transition and the Genetics of Populations in Europe* Princeton University Press (Princeton, NJ).

Bogucki, Peter 1982 *Early Neolithic Subsistence and Settlement in the Polish Lowlands* British Archaeological Reports, International Series 150 (Oxford).

Bogucki, Peter 1988 *Forest Farmers and Stockherders: Early Agriculture and its Consequences in North-Central Europe* Cambridge University Press (Cambridge).

Bogucki, Peter 1995 'The Linear Pottery culture of Central Europe: conservative colonists?' in W.K. Barnett and J.W. Hoopes (eds) *The Emergence of Pottery: Technology and Innovation in Ancient Societies* Smithsonian Institution Press (Washington, DC):89-97.

Bogucki, Peter 1996 'The spread of early farming in Europe' *American Scientist* 84:242-253.

Bogucki, Peter 2000 'How agriculture came to north-central Europe' in T.D. Price (ed) *Europe's First Farmers* Cambridge University Press (Cambridge):197-218.

Bogucki, Peter and Ryszard Grygiel 1981 'The household cluster at Brześć Kujawski 3: small-site methodology in the Polish lowlands' *World Archaeology* 13:59-72.

Bogucki, Peter and Ryszard Grygiel 1983 'Early farmers of the North European Plain' *Scientific American* 248(4): 104-112.

Bogucki, Peter and Ryszard Grygiel 1993 'Neolithic sites in the Polish lowlands: research at Brześć Kujawski, 1933-1984' in P. Bogucki (ed) *Case Studies in European Prehistory* CRC Press (Boca Raton, FL):147-180.

Buttler, Werner 1936 'Pits and pit-dwellings in southeast Europe' *Antiquity* 10:25-36.

Buttler, Werner and Waldemar Haberey 1936 *Die band-*

keramische Ansiedlung bei Köln-Lindenthal Römisch-Germanische Forschungen 11, Walter de Gruyter (Berlin).

Childe, V. Gordon 1949 'Neolithic house-types in temperate Europe' *Proceedings of the Prehistoric Society* 15:77-86.

Clark, J.G.D. 1952 *Prehistoric Europe: The Economic Basis* Methuen (London).

Dolukhanov, Pavel 1997 *The Early Slavs: Eastern Europe from the Initial Settlement to the Kievan Rus* Longman (London).

Ehrich, Robert W. 1976 'Anthropological theory and method: some applications to southeastern and central European prehistory' *Archaeologia Austriaca*, Beiheft 13:177-187.

Gregg, Susan A. 1988 *Foragers and Farmers: Population Interaction and Agricultural Expansion in Prehistoric Europe* University of Chicago Press (Chicago).

Grygiel, Ryszard 1986 'The household cluster as a fundamental social unit of the Brześć Kujawski Group of the Lengyel culture' *Prace I Materiały Muzeum Archeologicznego I Etnograficznego w Łodzi*, Archaeological Series 31:43-334.

Grygiel, Ryszard and Peter Bogucki 1997 'Early farmers in north-central Europe: 1989-1994 excavations at Osłonki, Poland' *Journal of Field Archaeology* 24:161-178.

Jażdżewski, Konrad 1938 'Cmentarzyska kultury ceramiki wstęgowej I związane z nimi ślady osadnictwa w Brześciu Kujawskim' *Wiadomości Archeologiczne* 15:1-105.

Kind, Claus-Joachim 1998 'Komplexe Wildbeuter und frühe Ackerbauern' *Germania* 76:1-23.

Maciejewski, Franciszek, Zdzisław Rajewski, and Franciszek Wokrój 1954 'Ślady osadnictwa kultury tzw. brzeskokujawskiej w Biskupinie, pow. Żnin' *Wiadomości Archeologiczne* 20:67-70.

Newell, Raymond R. 1970 'The flint industry of the Dutch Linear Bandkeramik' in P.J.R. Modderman (ed) *Linearbandkeramik aus Elsloo und Stein. Analecta Praehistorica Leidensia* 3:144-183.

Paret, Oscar 1942 'Vorgeschichtliche Wohngruben?' *Germania* 26:84-103.

Ryan, William and Walter Pitman 1999 *Noah's Flood: The New Scientific Discoveries about the Event That Changed History* Simon & Schuster (New York).

Tillmann, Andreas 1993 'Kontinuität oder Diskontinuität? Zur Frage einer bandkeramischen Landnahme in südlichen Mitteleuropa' *Archäologische Informationen* 16(2):157-187.

Whittle, Alasdair 1996 *Europe in the Neolithic* Cambridge University Press (Cambridge).

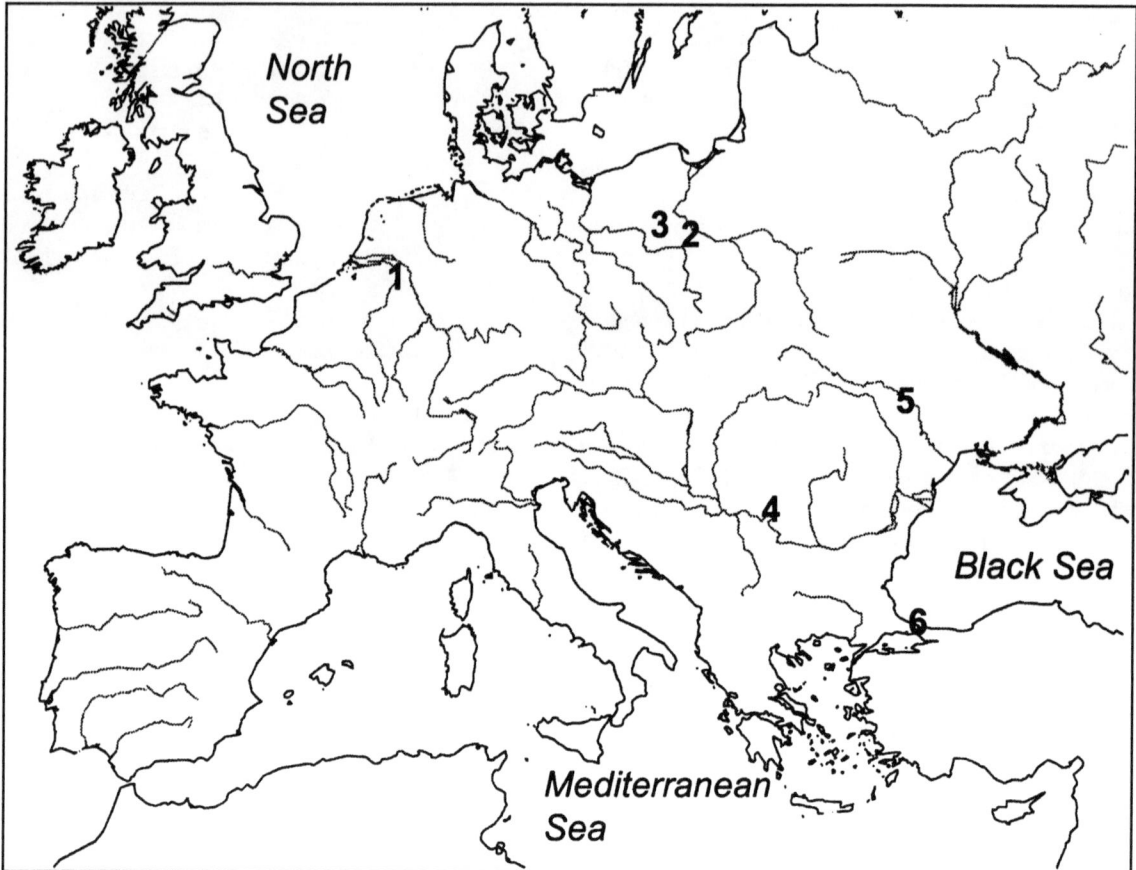

Figure 1: Map of Europe showing main localities discussed in text. Key: 1 - Köln-Lindenthal; 2 - Brześć Kujawski, Osłonki, Miechowice, and Konary; 3 - Biskupin; 4 - Iron Gates; 5 - Soroca (Soroki) sites; 6 - Bosphorus.

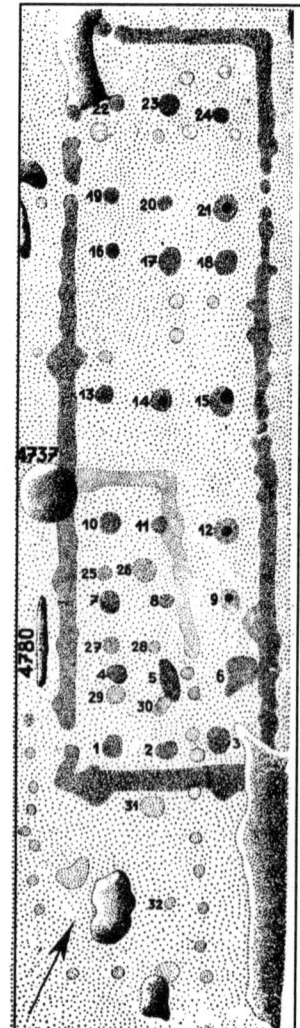

Figure 2: Outline of a longhouse at Köln-Lindenthal (after Buttler and Haberey 1936), interpreted as a barn or a granary by the excavators.

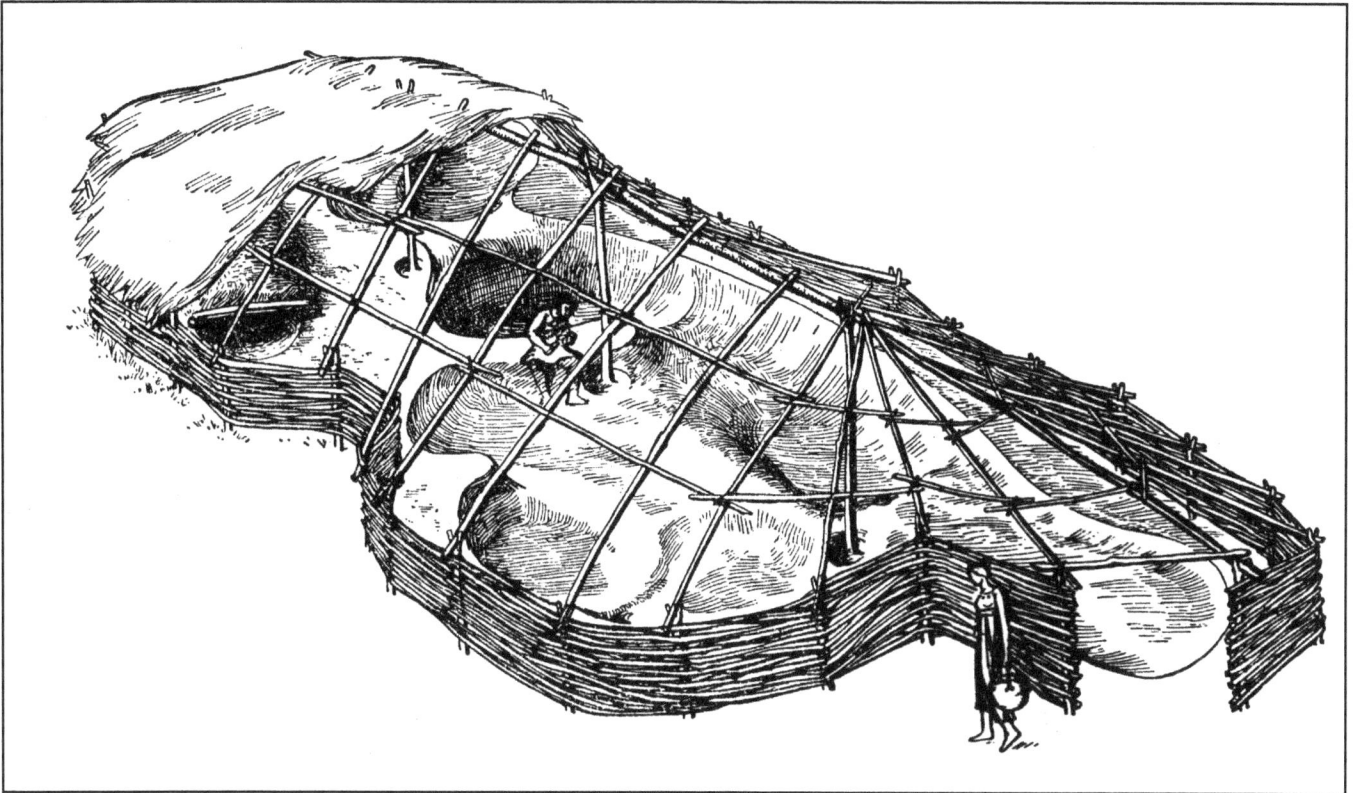

Figure 3: Buttler's reconstruction of a semi-subterranean dwelling showing conjectural structure over irregular pit, now known to have been a borrow pit for clay.

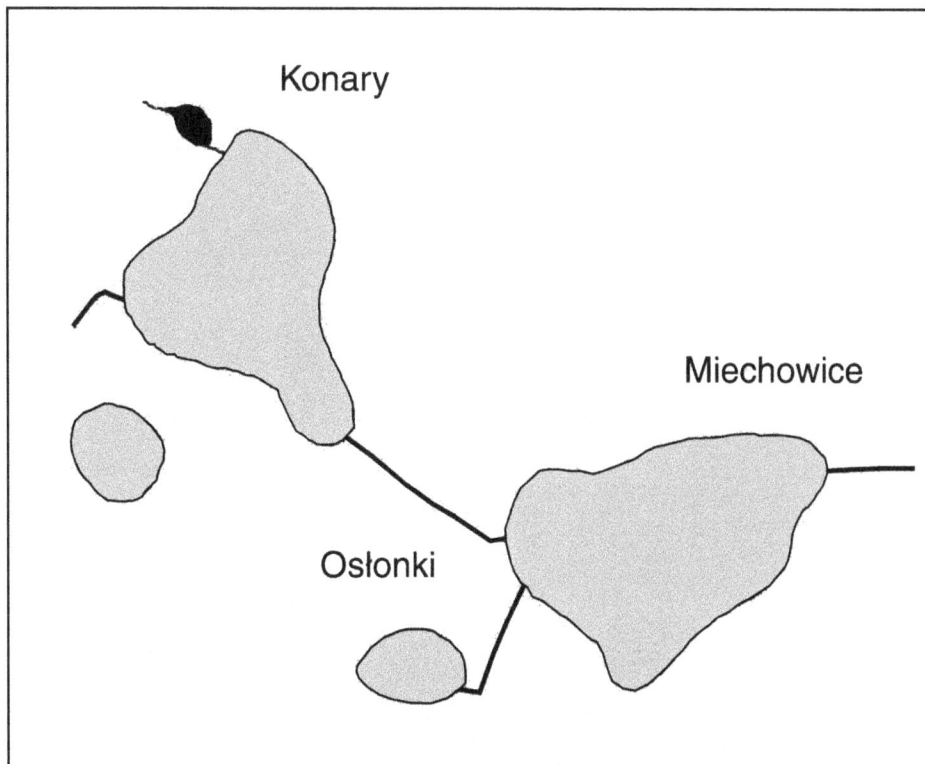

Figure 4: Neolithic settlement complex at Osłonki, Miechowice, and Konary, unknown prior to 1985. Black lines: drainage channels with surface water; shaded areas: ancient lake basins with deep accumulation of biogenic sediment.

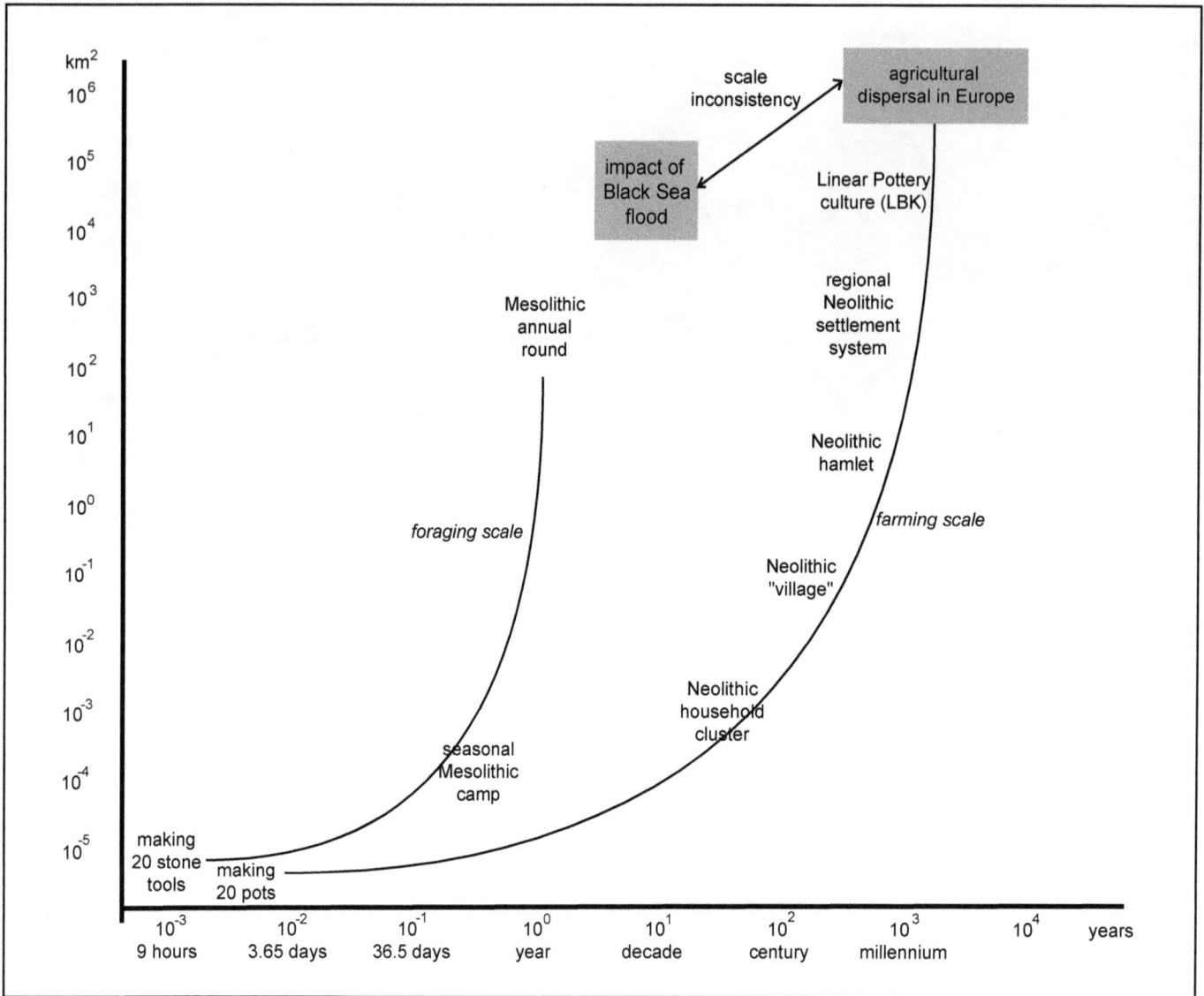

Figure 5: Spatial and temporal scales of early European forager and farmer behavior, analytical units, and processes.

Analytical Scale, Populations, and the Mesolithic-Neolithic Transition in the Far North-west of Europe

Timothy Darvill

Abstract

The Mesolithic-Neolithic transition from hunter/gatherer to farming economies in Europe has been heavily debated in terms of competing models of population continuity versus population change. Much of the debate has been at a theoretical level, in part because the kinds of sites expected to provide answers have not been found. However, another problem concerns the scale of research and the failure to find good methodologies to implement landscape-based approaches. It is argued here (using data from a project on the Isle of Man) that we have been looking for the wrong kinds of site, and that we should reframe our questions to allow geographically larger-scale analyses.

Introduction

Few topics in archaeology have engaged greater attention in recent decades than the sixth and fifth millennia BC in Europe, and this is especially true in relation to the archipelago off the Atlantic north-west coast of Europe that includes Britain and Ireland. Writing in 1940, the doyen of Euro-archaeology, V. Gordon Childe, was confident and precise about the nature, background, and result of events within the British Isles in what he believed to be the third millennium BC:[1]

> Agriculture and stock-breeding initiated an economic revolution; for they allowed population to expand beyond the narrow limits imposed for the naturally available supplies of game and wild fruits . . . . The Neolithic Revolution had to spread. Under the simple rural economy that at first prevailed, farming involved migration . . . . Immigrants from across the Channel brought, fully formed, the oldest Neolithic culture recognizable in the archaeological record. (1940:31-34)

Yet, 60 years on, we now believe that the changes Childe was referring to happened rather earlier in the backwardly projected extents of our own Christian calendars; and we are far less certain about why or how these changes happened. In 1996 Alasdair Whittle (1996:370) suggested that "the Meso-lithic-Neolithic transition itself was probably less momentous than our sense of social evolution has led us to suppose". And in 1999 Julian Thomas took us still further away from Childe's model in suggesting that:

> it is unhelpful to subsume the actual changes which took place in Britain around 4000 BC within a more large-scale or long-term process of either economic or ideological transformation. The archaeologically visible traces (monuments, pottery, stone tools) are not just a reflection of some more fundamental metaphysical process: they were integral to the particular kind of Neolithic which became established in Britain. (1999:16-17)

Just as The Beatles took us from their tightly syncopated *Revolution* of 1968 through to John Lennon's cacophony of sound bites, disconnected phrases, and real noises slowed down or speeded up in *Revolution Number 9*, so too Childe's ordered Neolithic Revolution of 1940 has become Thomas' web of idiosyncratic trajectories, local histories, and mosaics of unique circumstances in our Neolithic of 1999.

Yet, perhaps rather strangely, both Childe and Thomas, and many other authorities too, speak of a Mesolithic-Neolithic transition as something real, tangible, and meaningful within their own quite different understandings of the past. Indeed the concept of the Mesolithic-Neolithic transition has survived the turbulent waters created by the cross-cutting waves of successive theoretical perspectives, to become one of the truly BIG questions regularly addressed by archaeological research.

Uniting interest in the Mesolithic-Neolithic transition over the last 60 years or so has been a fundamental interest in change within the archaeological record and a concern with sequence insofar as it can be recognized archaeologically. As will be suggested later, an over-concern for the latter may have artificially obstructed alternative ways of looking at the accumulating evidence for the period. So far as change goes, it is certainly easy enough to see differences in the archaeological record representing the later sixth millennium BC and the mid fifth millennium BC even if there are considerable difficulties in understanding what exactly it all means, how the changes happened, when, and why. The evident variability in the picture across Europe, usefully summarized in a series of papers brought together by Zvelebil (1986b), should also caution against the continued application of rigid cultural-historic categorizations, unitary pan-European explanations, and still more the abandonment of notions of interface phases or transitional periods except with reference to closely defined geographical regions.

This is not the place to review the numerous individual contributions to the debate about Neolithic origins made to date, nor the various attempts that have been made to define what the Neolithic might be (but cf. Whittle 1996:4-9). It is, however, worth emphasizing that work on this period is marked by differences in intellectual tradition: scholars of the Mesolithic tend to project forward the trajectories of change represented in the things they study; while scholars of the Neolithic are seeking origins for the various raw materials they work with. Thus, for example, while Woodman (1976:300) talked of a "Mesolithic survival" in Ireland, Whittle (1977:238) noted that "the contribution to the emergence of Neolithic communities in southern Britain by indigenous late

---

[1] All the early dates referred to in this paper relate to calibrated radiocarbon ages expressed as calendar years BC.

nities in southern Britain by indigenous late Mesolithic communities seems to have been slight". Differences of intellectual tradition can also be seen in the range of insights offered to account for archaeological changes around 4000 BC. Three main groups can be distinguished. Traditional histories focus on events, for example migrations, invasions, and colonization (Case 1969; Clark 1965, 1966; Piggott 1954). Models based on cultural evolution place greater emphasis on acculturation, emulation, and social transformation (Case 1976; Zvelebil 1986a), while the sociological perspective focuses on social action and foregrounds the act of becoming and being in the world (Hodder 1990; Thomas 1999; Whittle 1996). Whether set within the positivist and processualist traditions of seeking explanations, or the post-processual interest in understanding, all of these approaches operate at a high level of abstraction, and at various levels of detachment from the archaeological data we actually have. While people, both as individuals and communities, are implicated in all these approaches, none of the models satisfactorily link the scale of action and human activity with what we conventionally find in the archaeological record. What we are presented with are essentially cover-models that can be drawn-down to particular cases as we think fit.

In this short paper I want to bring people back into the argument and examine briefly the changes seen in the archaeological record of the late sixth to early fourth millennia in a slightly different way. I would like to focus on issues of scale in social action and human behavior in the past and in the present, and suggest that to make any progress with the problem we need to be more concerned with issues of scale, especially spatial scale. As I will suggest, post-processual approaches to landscape archaeology hold one possibility of achieving this.

Scale

Within archaeological interpretation there are two issues of scale that need to be addressed—the social and spatial scale of our target populations, what we might call the "problem scale", and the scale at which we carry out our investigations, what might be called the "analytical scale".

The problem scale relates to the operational areas that we perceive to have been used by past societies in terms of the spatial extent, distribution, pattern, variety, and visibility of activities. In looking to find insights into the problems we pose, are we interested in the actions of individuals, the acts of a particular community, relationships between self-defining communities, or societies as a whole? The answer is probably that we are interested in all of these levels all the time.

Analytical scale refers to the size and nature of the windows we open up onto the past through the archaeological process. We might ask whether, for example, we are looking at a single piece of behavior, the summative result of repetitious actions by an individual, an established pattern of action by a whole community, or the accumulated residues from long-term sequences of actions at many different levels.

For much of the 1960s, 70s, and 80s, archaeological research

relating to the Mesolithic-Neolithic transition asked questions at a very general level—a wide problem scale—that were at least in part prompted by attempts to resolve conflicts between population replacement models and those which favored a major role for indigenous communities. Yet most research focused on the very detailed level of data gathering represented by the sample investigation of a small number of discrete sites. This can be seen crisp and clear in the succession of "Research Frameworks" offered up by various organizations since the end of the last war (e.g. CBA 1947:84). In one of the most expansive, *Exploring Our Past* published by English Heritage in 1991, we read that:

> The transition between the Mesolithic and Neolithic periods has proved persistently elusive, especially in areas of abundant, relatively thoroughly investigated evidence for established early farming communities. More light could be thrown on this period by targeting deposits which are likely to span all or part of it, and to preserve artefacts together with evidence for subsistence, fauna, vegetation and soils. (1991:36)

Here is exactly the heart of the problem: how can we match problem scale with analytical scale? Would we know the deposits that span the perceived transition if we saw them? And how should we approach them using available archaeological methods?

On the basis of present evidence there does not appear to be any deeply stratified settlements or shell middens in the British Isles except perhaps in the rather special environments of the north and west such as Newferry, Ireland (Woodman 1977).[2] Perhaps, however, the apparent scarcity of such sites in the British Isles is at least in part because an earlier obsession with vertical sequences has desensitized us to the value of horizontal stratigraphy.

Excavations at numerous sites suggest that, in the conventional terminology, Mesolithic people did not build monuments, while Neolithic people did not live in hunting camps. But is this right? What are monuments? What are hunting camps? And does the fact that our investigations of both kinds of site stop at what we traditionally see as their boundaries as a "site" or "monument" in any way restrict the size of our windows onto the past and our views of relationships and patterns? If we slacken off some of the categories and assumptions that are being applied here then some of the answers may already be staring us in the face. How many supposedly Neolithic sites have yielded substantial assemblages of late Mesolithic finds?

Take the case of Hazleton North on the Gloucestershire Cotswolds. Excavated by Alan Saville between 1979 and 1982, this provides a premier example of a Cotswold Severn long barrow and one of the relatively few completely excavated and

---

[2] In part these views were probably also influenced by continental sites, especially the shell middens and coastal sites of the Low Countries and Scandinavia. For example, the Ertebølle and Bjønsholm-Åle midden sites in northern Jutland both have deposits over 2 meters thick (Andersen and Johansen 1986; Andersen 1993), as do the Swifterbant culture sites at Brandwijk and Hazendonk in the Netherlands (Raemaekers 1999; van der Waals and Waterbolk 1976).

fully published (Saville 1990). However, the excavated area, centered on the surviving cairn, stops less than 5 meters from the edge of the mound (**Figure 1**). Sealed under the western end of the barrow is a midden and traces of a structure dated by a series of radiocarbon determinations to the early fourth millennium BC (Saville 1990:235-239). Beyond this to the west, partly outside the area of ground protected by the cairn, was a scatter of later Mesolithic flintwork which on typological analogy dates to the fifth millennium BC or later. The excavator concluded that the presence of this flintwork was probably fortuitous (Saville 1990:240). But was it? Elsewhere Saville (1990:175) accepts that two different but broadly contemporary populations could be individually responsible for the groups of flint. Sadly, no radiocarbon dates are associated with the Mesolithic assemblage to help gauge contemporaneity, and there does not appear to have been any sampling of the surrounding area to assess the possible extent of the flint scatter. It is possible, indeed very likely, that in scaling investigations to one objective (in this case the long barrow) we have restricted our view of another part of the picture.

The best evidence of later Mesolithic and early Neolithic land surfaces will be those trapped and preserved below middle Neolithic monuments, as at Hazleton. Indeed, associations of this kind have been noted at a small but growing number of other sites too, for example: Gwernvale, Powys (Britnell 1984:50), Ascot-under-Wychwood, Oxfordshire (unpublished but discussed in Case 1986:18), and Kilham, Yorkshire (Manby 1976). In all cases the mounds provide the preservation for rather broader patterns of activity, and might suggest a model of shifting focus as well as sequential replacement.

At the other end of the spectrum there are the regional and sub-regional studies in which the distribution of recorded finds, artifact scatters, and monuments are documented and analyzed. Here, too, there are issues of distributional bias every bit as relevant as the position and size of excavation trenches. Alasdair Whittle's (1990) examination of the Mesolithic-Neolithic transition in the upper Kennet Valley of Wiltshire employed careful categorization of the data to create a colonize and in-fill model. Yet, again, if the categories are slackened off a little, many of the places in the landscape from which these data come are actually the same in both stages. As **Figure 2** shows, a re-classification of the material suggests a core settlement area along the river valley, with monuments constructed around the headwaters at the western end from the fourth millennium BC onwards. Throughout the fifth and fourth millennia BC there was a scatter of short-lived and rather dispersed activity sites all around the core area. Holgate (1988) has documented a very similar pattern in the upper Thames Valley where many early core settlement areas comprise adjacent or overlapping scatters of flintwork that would traditionally be regarded as being either Mesolithic or Neolithic in date, and thus sequential in the landscape. Similarly in south-east Ireland, surveys and excavations suggest considerable co-existence of communities that would conventionally be characterized as Mesolithic and Neolithic (Green and Zvelebil 1990). This spatial overlap is supported too in chronological terms by available radiocarbon dates for traditionally Mesolithic and Neolithic deposits (Williams 1989),

and the recent recognition that the calibration of radiocarbon ages between about 7000 BP and 10,000 BP has the effect of closing what has for long been seen as a discrepancy in the clustering of determinations (e.g. Stuiver et al. 1998).

What all these examples suggest is that instead of thinking about long vertical sequences, which we just don't have, horizontal patterns may be just as relevant and potentially more revealing. People naturally operate in the horizontal plane rather than the vertical plane; the accumulation of evidence for sequential actions in the vertical plane is only one manifestation of recurrent patterns of social action. Putting the people back into the picture for the period around 4000 BC must surely mean looking at a problem scale and matching analytical scale above that of a single site or monument as conceptualized by conventional classifications, but below that of a region. Here again ways of thinking must adapt, and the theoretical perspectives used must be relevant.

One possible way forward is to draw upon some of the increasingly diverse but extremely exciting post-processual views of landscape as a socially constructed reality (cf. the papers in Ashmore and Knapp 1999; and Ucko and Layton 1999). This approach provides a useful set of overarching theory because it allows a recognition of the physicality of horizontal space in terms of the way it is finite and restricted, but at the same time emphasizes the critical role played by the social use of space that is culturally specific and three-dimensional. The social use of spaces can often be linked to cosmological referencing, sacred geographies, and land utilization through the structuration of action, the patterning of behavior, and the deployment of material culture (Darvill 1999a with earlier references). There are, of course, some uniformitarian assumptions underlying such thinking that serve to link the deep past with more recently observed understanding of cognition and physical expression—thinking and action—but these seem to hold up (e.g. Tilley 1994).

Billown Neolithic Landscape

In the final part of this paper I would like to look briefly at one case where such approaches are beginning to unfold new insights into events in the fifth and fourth millennium BC.

The study focuses on the area around Billown in the southern part of the Isle of Man, an area of coastal plain in and around which a certain amount of what might conventionally be termed Neolithic material has been known for many years (Cubbon 1945), although few major investigations of prehistoric sites have taken place here since the last war when Gerhard Bersu was interned on the island. Methodologically, the investigations at Billown are nested in analytical scale in the sense that general surveys involving extensive geophysics and geochemistry cover the entire valley system, while open area excavations and targeted trenches provide large and small samples respectively (Darvill 1996, 1997, 1998, 1999b). The work is just over half-way done, but already patterns can be seen, and I would like to touch on three of them: projectile points, pits, and quartz pebbles.

The sixth and early fifth millennium on the Isle of Man is

characterized by what Peter Woodman (1978a) has called the heavy flake industries. The Billown assemblage of this period is dominated by butt-trimmed flakes, basally retouched points, and tanged points of a type that is also widely found in Ireland. The exact purpose of these has been discussed in some detail by Woodman (1978b:93-97) who concludes that a range of functions could be undertaken with these tools hafted in different ways; some could well have been mounted as projectile heads or spear-tips (Woodman 1978b:fig. 35A). From the later fifth millennium BC onwards the lithic industries are certainly dominated by projectile points, especially leaf-shaped arrowheads. More than 300 of these have been recovered so far, many of them more or less complete. Again, their exact use is not known, but hunting, warfare, and execution are three of the most obvious applications; human deaths in particular are well represented amongst the small sample of injuries attributable to the use of flint arrowheads (Green 1980:178). Overall, it can tentatively be suggested that the leaf-shaped arrowheads represent comparable action sets to those involving the basally retouched points, carried out in the same spaces. Although work on the flint assemblage is still at an early stage, it is already clear that when looked at in this way the traditional categories of points and arrowheads overlap considerably.

The lithic material is loosely associated with the earliest structural evidence at Billown: pits and shafts. These pits were in some cases recurrently used for hearths, while in other cases they seem to have been dug simply as holes in the ground. One was nothing less than a massive shaft, 3 meters deep, capped by planks that have been radiocarbon dated to 4899-4719 BC (5910±70 BP Beta-110691). A shallower pit (F526), provisionally dated to 4542-4464 BC (5680±40 BP Beta-125767), contained a small amount of pottery, while another nearby (F472) contained similar pottery and a few grains of carbonized wheat and barley (**Figure 3**).

From the early fifth millennium BC through to the middle of the third millennium BC there is a continuous tradition of pit digging and the use of shafts. Conventionally such things would not be seen as monuments, but in a way they are, and it was in the same area that more substantial structures were placed which conform well to conventional understandings of monuments. These comprised a series of enclosures, culminating in a massive D-shaped structure with an open area to the west.

Closely associated with the pit digging and the early phases of the enclosures are white quartz pebbles. Hundreds have been found, in the bottom of pits and on the floors of the recut ditches of the enclosure boundaries. Bone does not survive on the site, but the placement of these pebbles strongly resembles the placement of human crania at contemporary sites in southern England, especially in the main enclosure at Hambledon Hill, Dorset (Mercer 1980:fig. 18). The open area west of the large D-shaped enclosure is dominated by a single large quartz standing stone that is still a visible feature of the landscape (**Figure 4**).

Conclusion

The investigations at Billown illustrate how important the linkages between problem scale and analytical scale really are, and how models based on the social use of space can help bring the two together. Space and action are critically important here. People are performing individual actions over and over again within certain spatial arrangements: the scale at which we are trying to understand them, the analytical scale we are using, focuses on the community rather than the individual—social action rather than personal behavior. Billown is not a Mesolithic site followed by a Neolithic site—what we are looking at here is a record of community presence and social action being acted out over a physically wide area and over a long period of time. Common threads run through the structuration of action: the use of projectiles, the digging of pits to look deep into the earth, and the role of quartz are just three. At the scale of the community there are new things that come into currency over the course of time that provide new foci and new dimensions to old practices: the use of enclosures and the erection of standing stones are just two.

In conclusion, it can be suggested that in thinking about the archaeological record of the fifth and fourth millennia BC, and the changes and variability that are represented in it, three points might be borne in mind. First, that in developing projects there should be more conscious efforts to match the problem scale with the analytical scale, preferably through the application of explicit archaeological theory. Second, that time and action are manifest horizontally as well as vertically, and that this horizontal dimension potentially has a great deal to offer. And thirdly, that the Mesolithic-Neolithic transition is as much about places and spaces as it is about sequence and succession.

Acknowledgments

This paper was first presented in the session "Peopling the Mesolithic in a Northern Environment" organized by Jenny Moore and Lynne Bevan at the Theoretical Archaeology Group Meeting held in Cardiff between 14th and 16th December 1999. A modified version was also presented in the session "Continuity or Change: The Role of Analytical Scale in European Archaeology" organized by James Mathieu and Rachel Scott at the 65th Meeting of the Society for American Archaeology held in Philadelphia between 5th and 9th April 2000. In preparing the paper for publication I would like to thank Jeff Chartrand and Damian Evans for assistance in preparing the illustrations relating to the case study from Billown, Isle of Man.

Biographical Sketch

Timothy Darvill was born and brought up in Gloucestershire, England. He was educated in Cheltenham and at Southampton University where he obtained an honours degree in Archaeology. His postgraduate research focused on the Neolithic period in Wales and the mid-west of England. Between 1982 and 1985 he worked for the Western Archaeological Trust and the Council for British Archaeology. He has directed a number of excavations in the Cotswolds, was Secretary of the Committee for Archaeology in Gloucestershire between 1980 and 1985, and Secretary of CBA Group 13 from 1984 until 1988.

From 1985 to 1991 he was the director of Timothy Darvill Archaeological Consultants. Between October 1990 and September 1991 he was Chairman of the Institute of Field Archaeologists. In October 1991, he was appointed to the Chair of Archaeology in the Department of Conservation Sciences at Bournemouth University. Professor Darvill has published over 50 reports and papers in academic and popular journals and has written several books including: *The Megalithic Chambered Tombs of the Cotswold-Severn Region* (Vorda, 1982); *The Archaeology of the Uplands - A Rapid Assessment of Archaeological Knowledge and Practice* (Royal Commission on the Historical Monuments of England, 1986); *Prehistoric Britain* (Batsford, 1987); *Ancient Monuments in the Countryside: An Archaeological Management Review* (English Heritage 1987); *Prehistoric Gloucestershire* (Alan Sutton and Gloucestershire County Library, 1987); and *Glovebox Guide: Ancient Britain* (Automobile Association, 1988). In addition, Professor Darvill lectures widely to general and specialist audiences and has appeared on television in local news reports and on both local and national radio.

References Cited

Andersen, S.H. 1993 'Bjørnsholm: a stratified *køkkeenmødding* on the central Limfjord, north Jutland' *Journal of Danish Archaeology* 10:59-96.

Andersen, S.H. and E. Johansen 1986 'Ertebølle revisited' *Journal of Danish Archaeology* 5:31-61.

Ashmore, W. and A.B. Knapp (eds) 1999 *Archaeologies of Landscape: Contemporary Perspectives* Blackwell (Oxford).

Britnell, W.J. 1984 'The Gwernvale long cairn, Crickhowell, Brecknock' in W.J. Britnell and H.N. Savory (eds) *Gwernvale and Penywyrlod: Two Neolithic Long Cairns in the Black Mountains of Brecknock* Cambrian Archaeological Monograph 2, Cambrian Archaeological Association (Cardiff):43-154.

Case, H.J. 1969 'Neolithic explanations' *Antiquity* 43:176-186.

Case, H.J. 1976 'Acculturation and the earlier Neolithic of western Europe' in S.J. De Laet (ed) *Acculturation and Continuity in Atlantic Europe Mainly During the Neolithic Period and the Bronze Age: Papers Presented at the IV Atlantic Colloquium, Ghent 1975* Dissertationes Archaeologicae Gandenses 16, De Tempel (Brugge):45-58.

Case, H.J. 1986 'The Mesolithic and Neolithic in the Oxford region' in G. Briggs, J. Cook, and T. Rowley (eds) *The Archaeology of the Oxford Region* Oxford University Department for External Studies (Oxford):18-37.

CBA [Council for British Archaeology] 1947 *A Survey and Policy of Field Research in the Archaeology of Great Britain I: Prehistoric and Early Historic Ages to the Seventh Century AD* Council for British Archaeology (London).

Childe, V.G. 1940 *Prehistoric Communities of the British Isles* W R Chambers (Edinburgh).

Clark, G. 1965 'Radiocarbon dating and the spread of farming economy' *Antiquity* 39:45-48.

Clark, G. 1966 'The invasion hypothesis in British archaeology' *Antiquity* 40:172-188.

Cubbon, W. 1945 'The stone circle at Billown' *Proceedings of the Isle of Man Natural History and Antiquarian Society* 4(4):506-516.

Darvill, T. 1996 *Billown Neolithic Landscape Project, Isle of Man, 1995* School of Conservation Science, Research Report 1, Bournemouth University and Manx National Heritage (Bournemouth, UK).

Darvill, T. 1997 *Billown Neolithic Landscape Project, Isle of Man, 1996* School of Conservation Science, Research Report 3, Bournemouth University and Manx National Heritage (Bournemouth, UK).

Darvill, T. 1998 *Billown Neolithic Landscape Project, Isle of Man: Third Report: 1997* School of Conservation Science, Research Report 4, Bournemouth University and Manx National Heritage (Bournemouth, UK).

Darvill, T. 1999a 'The historic environment, historic landscapes, and space-time-action models in landscape archaeology' in P. Ucko and R. Layton (eds) *The Archaeology and Anthropology of Landscape* One World Archaeology Series, Routledge (London):104-118.

Darvill, T. 1999b *Billown Neolithic Landscape Project, Isle of Man: Fourth Report: 1998* School of Conservation Science, Research Report 5, Bournemouth University and Manx National Heritage (Bournemouth, UK).

English Heritage 1991 *Exploring Our Past* English Heritage (London).

Green, H.S. 1980 *The Flint Arrowheads of the British Isles* British Archaeological Reports, British Series 75 (Oxford).

Green, S.W. and M. Zvelebil 1990 'The Mesolithic colonization and agricultural transition of south-east Ireland' *Proceedings of the Prehistoric Society* 56:57-88.

Hodder, I. 1990 *The Domestication of Europe* Basil Blackwell (Oxford).

Holgate, R. 1988 *Neolithic Settlement of the Thames Basin* British Archaeological Reports, British Series 194 (Oxford).

Manby, T.G. 1976 'Excavation of the Kilham long barrow, East Riding of Yorkshire' *Proceedings of the Prehistoric Society* 42:111-159.

Mercer, R. 1980 *Hambledon Hill: A Neolithic Landscape* Edinburgh University Press (Edinburgh).

Piggott, S. 1954 *The Neolithic Cultures of the British Isles* Cambridge University Press (Cambridge).

Raemaekers, D.C.M. 1999 *The Articulation of a "New Neolithic"* Faculty of Archaeology, Univ. of Leiden (Leiden).

Saville, A. 1990 *Hazleton North: The Excavation of a Neolithic Long Cairn of the Cotswold-Severn Group* Historic Buildings and Monuments Commission for England Archaeological Report 13, English Heritage (London).

Stuiver, M., P.J. Reimer, E. Bard, W.J. Beck, G.S. Burr, K.A. Hughen, B. Kromer, G. McCormac, J. van der Plicht, and M. Spurk 1998 'Intcal 98 radiocarbon age calibration, 24,000-0 cal BP' *Radiocarbon* 40(3):1041-1164.

Thomas, J. 1999 *Understanding the Neolithic* Routledge (London).

Tilley, C. 1994 *A Phenomenology of Landscape: Places, Paths and Monuments* Berg (Oxford).

Ucko, P. and R. Layton (eds) 1999 *The Archaeology and Anthropology of Landscape* One World Archaeology Series, Routledge (London).

van der Waals, J.D and H.T. Waterbolk 1976 'Excavations at Swifterbant – discovery, progress, aims and methods' *Helinium* 16:4-14.

Whittle, A. 1977 *The Earlier Neolithic of Southern England and its Continental Background* British Archaeological Reports, International Series 35 (Oxford).

Whittle, A. 1990 'A model for the Mesolithic-Neolithic transition in the upper Kennet valley, north Wiltshire' *Proceedings of the Prehistoric Society* 56:101-110.

Whittle, A. 1996 *Europe in the Neolithic: The Creation of New Worlds* Cambridge University Press (Cambridge).

Williams, E. 1989 'Dating the introduction of food production into Britain and Ireland' *Antiquity* 63: 510-521.

Woodman, P. 1976 'The Irish Mesolithic / Neolithic transition' in S.J. De Laet (ed) *Acculturation and Continuity in Atlantic Europe Mainly During the Neolithic Period and the Bronze Age: Papers Presented at the IV Atlantic Colloquium, Ghent 1975* Dissertationes Archaeologicae Gandenses 16, De Tempel (Brugge): 296-308.

Woodman, P. 1977 'Recent excavations at Newferry, Co. Antrim' *Proceedings of the Prehistoric Society* 43: 155-199.

Woodman, P. 1978a 'A re-appraisal of the Manx Mesolithic' in P.J. Davey (ed) *Man and Environment in the Isle of Man* British Archaeological Reports, British Series 54 (Oxford):119-139.

Woodman, P. 1978b *The Mesolithic in Ireland* British Archaeological Reports, British Series 58 (Oxford).

Zvelebil, M. 1986a 'Mesolithic societies and the transition to farming: problems of time, scale and organization' in M. Zvelebil (ed) *Hunters in Transition* Cambridge University Press (Cambridge):167-188.

Zvelebil, M. (ed) 1986b *Hunters in Transition* Cambridge University Press (Cambridge).

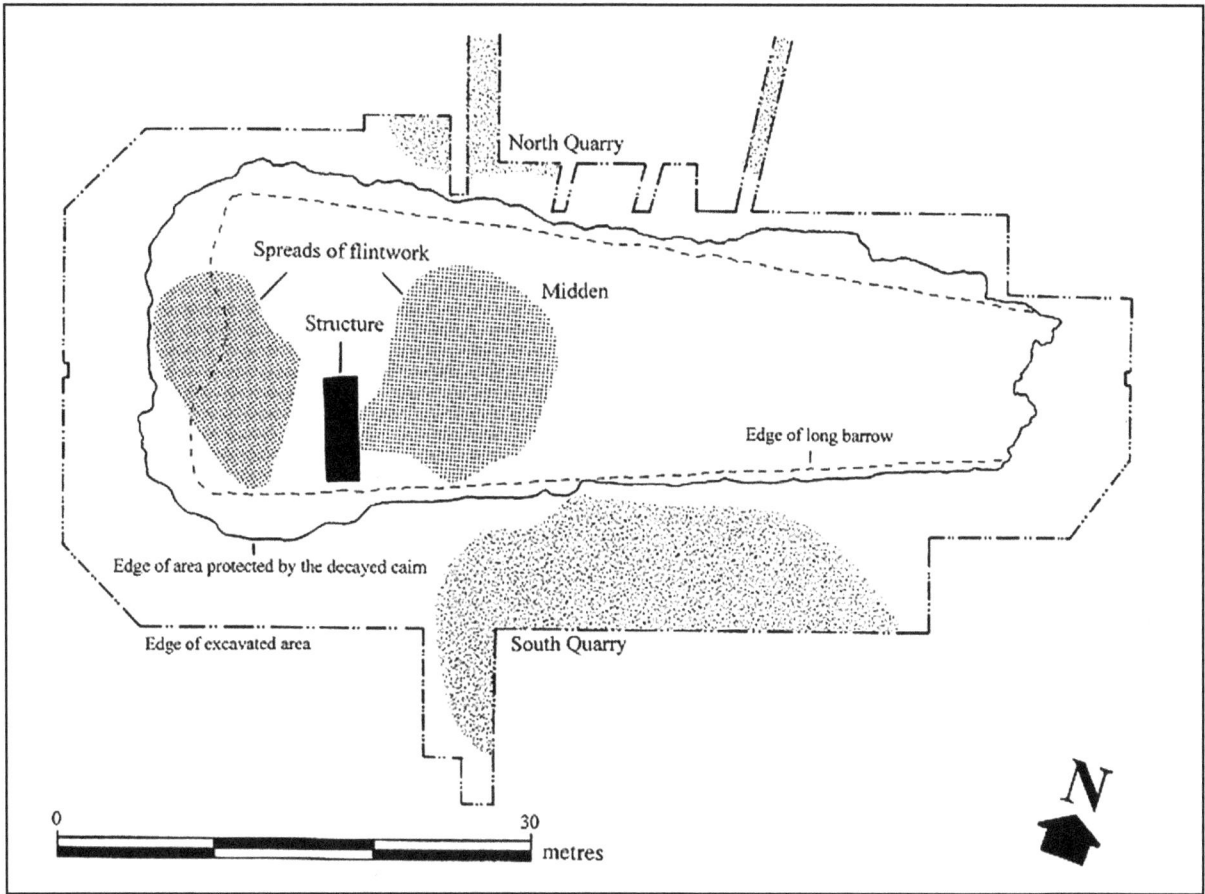

Figure 1: Plan of the Hazleton North Long Barrow, Gloucestershire, showing the extent of excavations and the limits of preservation in relation to the recorded pre-cairn later Mesolithic and early Neolithic activity areas (interpretations based on Saville 1990: figs. 13 and 170).

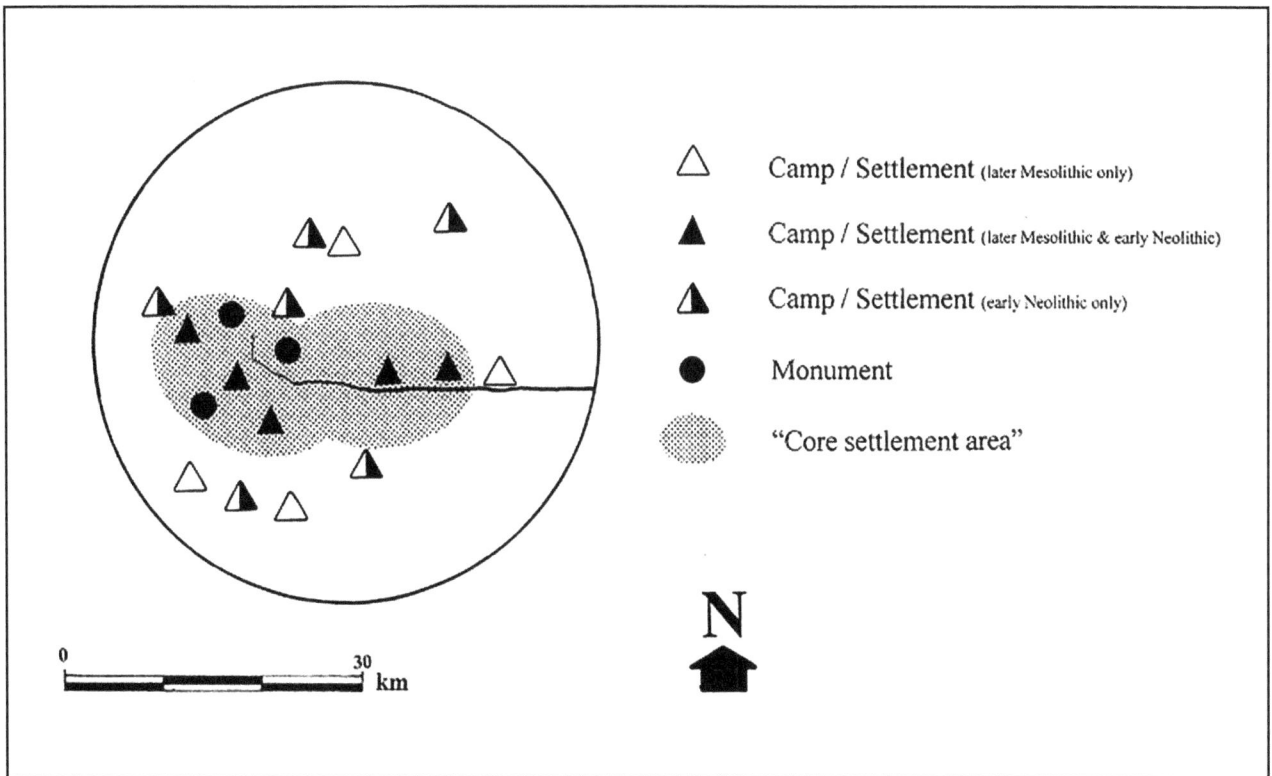

Figure 2: Schematic map showing an interpretation of the distribution of recorded later Mesolithic and early Neolithic sites in the upper Kennet Valley of Wiltshire (based on Whittle 1990: figs 1-3).

Figure 3: Two Neolithic pits at Billown, Isle of Man, excavated within Site K in 1998: F544 is in the foreground, F541 behind. [Photograph: T C Darvill. Copyright reserved]

Figure 4: Booilevane Stone, Billown, Isle of Man. A large quartz boulder situated west of the main D-shaped enclosure. The stone is 1.5m high and 2.3m wide. [Photograph: T C Darvill. Copyright reserved]

Scale and its Discontents

D. Blair Gibson

Abstract

To many modern social scientists, the necessity of referring to social scale in discussions of the social institutions of past societies would seem to be self-evident. However, there has always been a pervasive unease and downplaying of the importance of scale on the part of historians and some anthropologists. This paper examines some of the critiques and proposed alternatives to the use of scale, with an eye to evaluating the benefits and motivations of these. The paper further explores some of the challenges to the scale concept posed by the archaeological and historical record of Neolithic and Early Medieval Ireland.

> . . . the great questions . . . endure in and around archaeology because some of the subjects they touch on have (often unacknowledged) links to sociopolitical issues of more currently fashionable academic interest. Such issues concern the individual and totalitarianism, social justice, inequalities among nations and classes, and so forth. They are the issues that mobilize radical anti-evolutionist approaches—critical Marxism, post-structuralism, world systems (core-periphery) models, and structuration theory from sociology (Friedman and Rowlands 1977; Miller and Tilley 1984; Spriggs 1984; Hodder 1986; Giddens 1984, 1985). (de Montmollin 1989:2)

The Dimensions of Scale

Scale is one of those kinds of concepts that have existed largely in the vernacular language of the social sciences, a concept that is frequently invoked but, up until recently, was seldom defined or discussed. One encounters scale often as a compound adjective, as in "large-scale" or "small-scale". Analytical scale describes the geographical extent of the focus of research, as in "regional scale", or the size or ranking of the social entity under consideration, as in site or single-polity (de Montmollin 1989:7-8). Most often, scale is not qualified with terms to let one know whether geographical extent, or group size, or both is meant. A 1993 definition of the concept offered by Blanton, Kowalewski, Feinman, and Finsten conveys the ambiguities inherent in the concept when they define scale as ". . .the number of people incorporated into the society, and/or the size of the area involved" (1993:14; also Rothman 1994; Stein 1994).

The natural audience of the scale concept consists of those scholars with an interest in social evolution. Changes in the size of a group or polity have long been thought to be related to, or result in, changes in socio-cultural integration. This understanding has been axiomatic to all schools of evolutionary thought. However, all other indices of social evolution have been hotly debated, as have of course been the relative importance of various contributing factors, or "causes" of social evolution.

In the past, those of the neo-evolutionist school placed an emphasis on qualitative differences in societal organization as a way of assessing social complexity (Sahlins 1958, 1963; Service 1962; Steward 1979; White 1959). Since the 1970s this approach has been criticized as being clumsy, limiting, and rigidly essentialist. While some archaeologists, the present author included, see nothing wrong with working in the traditional neo-evolutionist vein, other archeologists have advocated that the neo-evolutionist paradigm's focus upon social integration be discarded in favor of superior evolutionist paradigms. Some alternatives that have been proposed are the

heterarchy model advocated by Carole Crumley and the selectionist paradigm advocated by Dunnell, Wenke, and others (Braun 1990; Crumley 1979, 1995; Dunnell 1980; Kosse 1994; Marquardt and Crumley 1987; Wenke 1981).

Political Economy vs. Cultural Ecology

Richard Blanton, Stephen Kowalewski, and Gary Feinman are the core players of yet another prominent evolutionist school of the past 20 years. They have been called the "political economy" school after their stated chief focus of investigation, though as this chapter will argue, perhaps neo-Boasian is a more apt sobriquet (Blanton et al. 1996a:3; Whitecotton 1988). The Blanton group advocates that social evolution should be examined through four dimensions: scale, integration, complexity, and boundedness (Blanton et al. 1993:13-18; Kowalewski et al. 1983). As the adherents of this school are exclusively archaeologists, it is unremarkable that they have abandoned the emphasis that neo-evolutionism's first generation had placed upon facets of social organization, in favor of variables more amenable to detection in the archaeological record. They further assert that no one dimension of a polity is by itself sufficient to chart the evolution of a society, as neither the outcome nor the pathway of evolution is preordained. "Culture change is not always linear, unvarying, or unidirectional" (Blanton et al. 1993:14).

At first glance, the position espoused by the political economy group might be aptly described as *gradualist* (Feinman 1994; Spencer 1990:2). Their many publications concerning prehistoric political developments in Oaxaca have been employed in a rancorous debate with a rival group of Mesoamerican scholars headed by William Sanders, and including Robert Santley (referenced in Flannery 1988:57), whom they term the "cultural ecology" group (Blanton 1980). In a later publication, the sobriquet "neoevolutionism" is substituted for cultural ecology (Blanton et al. 1996a:1, 14). The centerpiece of their assault on the cultural ecologists is a debunking of what they consider to be a key understanding of the cultural ecology paradigm: the causal link between population growth and social change in the form of increased centralization (Blanton 1980:146). Looking over the changes in the patterns of settlement in the Valley of Oaxaca over 3,000 years, the political economists conclude that social evolution there did not inevitably lead to state formation focused upon a single apical site. Instead their survey led them to conclude that in Oaxaca, and in the Valley of Mexico, periods of political centralization were followed by periods of decline or collapse characterized by less-centralized settlement patterns. During these latter periods, characterized by a population organized into more numerous, smaller-scale polities, horizontal economic integration through extra-local exchange, a "network strategy", supplanted vertical political integration (Blanton et al. 1996a:4; Kowalewski 1980:164). Further, their survey led them to conclude that the populations that produced Monte Alban and Teotihuacán did not approach the limits of the carrying capacity of their regions (Blanton et al. 1993; Feinman 1991:252; 1998; Kowalewski 1980, 1982). Therefore, what centralization that did transpire was not fueled by population pressure.

The objections of the political economy school against the perceived tenets of neo-evolutionism are difficult to objectively evaluate. Though their efforts are billed as a refutation of the causal effect of population pressure in the promotion of social change, they make scant effort at defining population pressure or searching for it in the archaeological record. Little archaeological data on subsistence economies in any region are offered in *Ancient Mesoamerica* or in any other publication, so one cannot determine whether or not food procurement strategies changed in response to stress. Indeed, in his discussions of population and land types in Oaxaca, Stephen Kowalewski explicitly assumes stasis in agricultural technology and resource utilization strategies (1980:152). Population pressure on food resources cannot be retroactively presumed not to have existed in Oaxaca or the Valley of Mexico in earlier phases when the model assumes that the subsistence strategy of the earlier periods was the same as that described in the first ethnohistoric sources, reflecting the last pre-Columbian cultural horizon. The Valley of Mexico is a case in point. The *chinampas* strategy of Late Aztec times did not exist to convert the lakeshore into a productive resource zone in prior phases. Key wild animal protein sources could have been diminished during these phases, leading to perceived scarcity and change in economic orientation and/or political organization, which would not be reflected in the presence of ample arable land (Sanders and Nichols 1988:42-44).

The Political Economy School and Social Scale

Gary Feinman has struggled specifically with the scale concept in two publications (1994, 1998). In "Scale and social organization", Feinman tries to apply his scale concept to the "archaic state". He notes the wide variability in the estimated sizes of archaic states, and goes on to demonstrate his thesis that demographic pressure is not a necessary precondition for the emergence of a state and that population density cannot be readily correlated with polity dimensions (1998). He is brought to the conclusion that states cannot be clearly demarcated from chiefdoms by scale alone, even when scale

and integration are viewed in tandem (1998:105-107).

Feinman's conclusions are hardly surprising. The work of cultural ecologists, beginning with Julian Steward in the 1930s, has demonstrated that the potential for demographic growth within regions varies with respect to both the ecological systems and the prevailing subsistence regimes (Carneiro 1961, 1967; Earle 1997; Harris 1977; Johnson and Earle 1987:3-4; Netting 1977; Steward 1979:35-45). A medieval Irish or East African Mandari chiefdom will exhibit population levels that are far lower than a comparably complex Indonesian or Hawaiian chiefdom due to a vast difference in the amount of land required for an economy premised upon cattle grazing vs. wet rice or taro agriculture, and the variation in the productive potential between these economies (cf. Earle 1997; Gibson 1988). For the same reason, it is probable that an agro-pastoral polity will have greater spatial dimensions than a comparably complex polity supported by intensive agriculture (Gibson 1995b:126).

The Efficacy of the Political Economy Challenge

It has yet to be determined whether a debunking of the role of population pressure could vitiate cultural ecology/neo-evolutionism as a paradigm. However, even if the challenge posed by the political economy school were to succeed and it was agreed that population pressure could not be regarded as an evolutionary prime-mover, for the political economy paradigm to successfully replace the cultural ecology paradigm of neo-evolutionism it would have to provide a superior explanation of social change.

Taking a wider perspective, as of 1993, the publication date of the latest edition of *Ancient Mesoamerica*, the approach Blanton, Kowalewski, and Feinman take to social evolution seems at first reading to be historical and particularistic. One is brought to the understanding that each region's evolutionary trajectory will be unique, due to the fact that constellations of the critical variables of scale, boundedness, complexity, and integration will ultimately be unique. Indeed, *Ancient Mesoamerica* sets as its chief task the rejection of ideas of monocausal evolution, and further, the discounting of the importance of prime movers (1993:207-208).

However, even though it would seem that *Ancient Mesoamerica* lacks a theory by which social change could be explained, its thesis of social evolution is presented almost as an afterthought in a section labeled "state dynamics" (1993:208-217). A contrast is made not between the four variables that are supposedly central to the book's thrust, but in a sense only two: the scale of the society and the degree to which the elites manipulated production and exchange, or what one may term social integration.

This position is elaborated in two publications from the late 1990s, the 1996 article in *Current Anthropology* "A dual-processual theory for the evolution of Mesoamerican civilization" (Blanton et al. 1996a) and Richard Blanton's chapter in *Archaic States* "Beyond centralization" (Blanton 1998). These articles set up binary oppositions with reference to polity organization, the expression and exercise of power, ideological underpinnings, and the strategies of goods production and exchange. These ideas are in essence extensions of concepts used by sociologists working in various Marxian traditions, the most prominent being the structural Marxist school (Frankenstein and Rowlands 1978; Friedman and Rowlands 1977; Godelier 1977; Hazelgrove 1982; McGuire 1992; Meillassoux 1981).

Though it seems like the tone of the various publications of the political economy group is to make a break with cultural ecology and neo-evolutionism, in several places the political economy paradigm is championed by its adherents as neo-evolutionism's future (Blanton et al. 1993:10-13; Blanton et al. 1996b:65). These claims seem incongruous if not outright ironic, as the multilineal evolutionism of Steward, and White's unilineal evolutionism, were rooted in a scientific paradigm.[1] In the work of Blanton and his colleagues, this approach has been supplanted by an inductive, interpretative methodology akin to those of European humanist scholars.

The contradictions surrounding the political economy school are not limited to the overarching theoretical orientation of its practitioners. Take for instance the contrast made by Blanton et al. between types of polities in which power was either corporate or exclusionary in nature (1996a:2-3). These two contrastive organizational modes have a lengthy intellectual heritage, going all the way back to the distinction made between the *polis/ethnos* modes of organization of Classical Greek communities by Aristotle (Champion et al. 1984:259-262; Fergusson 1991). One may also detect the contrast Marx made between the Asiatic and Feudal modes of production, and echoes of Wittfogel's Oriental despotism as well (Hindess and Hirst 1977: chs. 4 & 5; Wittfogel 1957).

The problem with Blanton's dichotomy, a problem which it shares with its more immediate ancestor, Colin Renfrew's (1974) distinction between group-oriented and individualizing chiefdoms, is that the organization of polities typified by exclusionary power is historically attested (e.g. Tenochtitlan, Classic Period lowland Maya polities), while the examples that Blanton et al. offer of corporate organization (Teotihuacán, Pre-Classic Maya lowland polities, and Chichén Itzá), are shrouded in an alliterate past. One cannot simply assume that an absence of images of leaders and self-aggrandizing texts indicates the dominance of systemic power. As Michael Kolb (1996:59) has recently pointed out in criticism of this school, one may be inclined to assume from an absence of images of leaders and the presence of communal gathering places in the form of *marae* in the aboriginal Sandwich Islands that the society was organized on a corporate basis, but the ethnographic record proves the opposite to have been true. Prior to the 1980s the cultures of Late Neolithic Ireland that constructed the immense communal passage grave burial mounds were also assumed to have been "group oriented" or "corporate" communities, integrated by a religion revolving around sun and fertility symbolism and by a communal burial ritual. However, the

discovery of two "maceheads" at Knowth in 1982 and the limited number of interments in this tomb suggested to the excavator the possibility of what would amount to "exclusionary" power and the existence of an elite social stratum (Eogan 1986:177-180). Ultimately, one must conclude that the interpretations of the political economy school rest on untested and unreliable assumptions. As a cover, the political economy school has advanced statements that both forms of organization would always have been present in all polities (Blanton 1998:148; Blanton et al. 1996b:66). If this is true, however, one may wonder at the worth of this approach in the first place.

The Legacy of the Grab-bag

Within American anthropology, some of those who disdain the evolutionist paradigm embrace the technique of unstructured cross-cultural comparisons of cultural institutions. One may view George Peter Murdock and his exhaustive synchronic examinations of social institutions as the progenitor of this approach (Murdock 1949). Many cultural anthropology textbooks are offspring of this legacy, especially Ember and Ember (1999). Chapters and sections are constructed around an institution, say marriage, the cross-cultural permutations of which are then detailed.

This approach was utilized in a critique of neo-evolutionism's reliance on stages of socio-cultural integration in a well-known paper by Feinman and Neitzel examining "middle-range" societies in the Americas (1984). "Too many types" begins with an attack on social typologies. The variation in a century's worth of typologies is offered up as proof that they have no objective reality. Feinman and Neitzel specifically discredit the chiefdom concept by repeating criticisms of redistribution voiced by Peebles and Kus (1977) and Earle (1978).

As an alternative to the stages of socio-cultural integration of the neo-evolutionists, Feinman and Neitzel offer contingency table examinations of a sample of American societies against select social attributes. The outcomes of these contingency table examinations fulfill the expectations of Feinman and Neitzel that differences in complexity between different societies are a matter of degree, not kind, as "modal" differences or groupings could not be detected.

The critique by Feinman and Neitzel of the use of social typologies by neo-evolutionists is efficacious if one accepts that redistribution is the *only* aspect of the chiefdom that sets it apart from other levels of socio-cultural integration. Even a superficial perusal of the literature, including their own, will reveal that the chiefdom concept subsumes a number of attributes, such as ancestor veneration, conical clan or *ramage* organization, a permanent office of leadership, a primitive bureaucracy, etc. (Carneiro 1981; de Montmollin 1989:14; Earle 1987; Sahlins 1958; to name just a few of many sources). Even if redistribution was a central and critical concept to the chiefdom level of socio-cultural integration, Feinman and Neitzel look away from the fact that neo-evolutionists have independently critiqued and modified it without calling into question the viability of the chiefdom concept (D'Altroy and

---

1 The immediate descendants of Steward and White—Lewis Binford, Kent Flannery, James Hill, and others—became advocates of testing evolutionary explanations in the material record of past societies.

Earle 1985; Earle and D'Altroy 1982; Peebles and Kus 1977).

Turning now to the alternate methodology used by Feinman and Neitzel, they don't bother to establish the link of many of the attributes that they selected for comparison to social complexity, nor do they defend their importance or necessity. There is no literature that makes a case that house size, prominence, and elaborateness are inexorably tied to social complexity. Ethnohistoric sources indicate that despite the presence of complex chiefdoms with up to four administrative levels, Irish chieftains of the Early Middle Ages lived in houses that were not markedly larger or more elaborate than those of commoners. Similarly no defense is offered for the importance of any of the functions of leadership that were chosen for comparison by Feinman and Neitzel.

Finally, the effect of cross-cutting dimensions, such as variability in ecological adaptations and subsistence strategies, which might well be expected to muddy their comparisons, is not controlled for. Such an unstructured grab-bag comparison should have been expected to reveal a paucity of modal differences in social complexity.

Carole Crumley and Heterarchy

Like Blanton and Feinman, Carole Crumley is a product of the University of Michigan, and like Blanton, an archaeologist who has chosen to focus on power and its role in societal organization. For the past two decades she has forcefully argued that archaeologists looking at complex societies have been too enamored of their hierarchical structure, to the exclusion of other dimensions of organization.

The concept she has posed as a useful addition to hierarchy is heterarchy—which describes the organization of a system in which the parts which compose it are not necessarily ranked. Crumley has discussed this concept in relation to her examination of the organization of the Late Iron Age Gaulish polity of the Aedui. With reference to the distribution of power in this polity, she argues that it was vested in several factions, including the aristocracy and the priesthood (Crumley 1987; Crumley and Marquardt 1987:613-615).

Her focus on heterarchy has also impelled her and William Marquardt to advocate an expansion of the scale concept beyond its usual demographic usage. They advocate the employment of multiple scales in regional analysis, depending upon the physical or behavioral dimension of a polity under examination. *Effective scale* is therefore a situational concept, applicable to environmental as well as cultural variables, such as religious practice (Crumley and Marquardt 1987; Marquardt and Crumley 1987). The scales under examination in a region should be measured at different points over a span of time in order to appreciate and study the dynamic changes to the various scale dimensions under view (Marquardt and Crumley 1987:5).

It is indeed useful to look beyond hierarchy in the study of political systems, or any other systems for that matter. It is becoming increasingly obvious that the proto-historic Celtic polities of Europe frequently constituted themselves into

confederate political systems (Gibson 1995b). In the absence of primogeniture or strict succession rules, within the Celtic chiefdoms and states, political power was negotiated, often violently, between factions. Celtic chieftains and kings were truly *primus inter pares*, whose tenure depended on the collusion of power brokers and the support of priests.

However, though Crumley's emphasis on heterarchy is an aid to thinking about the organization of political systems, the potential of the concepts of heterarchy and effective scale is limited to the realms of research planning and analytical methodology. One may use these concepts to study change to polities, but not to *explain* change. Not only are these concepts not likely to lead to the framing of evolutionary hypotheses, but also one is left wondering which questions are appropriate to ask of the data. It is also clear that Crumley's motivations for embracing heterarchy are as much moral as they are scientific, as she explicitly associates hierarchy with racism, colonialism, and one may suppose from the cover illustration of *Heterarchy and the Analysis of Complex Societies*, sexism (Crumley 1995:4).

Back to the Past: The Roots of the Reaction Against Neo-evolutionism

Neo-evolutionism has been almost exclusively an American theoretical school, so it is perhaps surprising to come across American scholars who are aligned against it. However, shifting to the long view of the history of thought in American anthropology, it is not really surprising to find hostility directed towards evolutionism specifically, and scientific approaches in general. Hostility towards social evolution has a lengthy history in the American social sciences.

At the time of its foundation, American anthropology had a decidedly humanistic orientation. The anthropologist who founded the first academic department, Franz Boas, was openly hostile towards evolutionism, as he equated it with racism. Boasian historical particularism gave birth to the Culture and Personality field, whose workers such as Mead, Benedict, Bateson, and DuBois, championed various humanistic psycho-philosophical models which embraced a cultural, or more broadly, environmental determinism. In the context of early 20th century thought, the materialist evolutionism expounded by Julian Steward and Leslie White went against the mainstream. Its effect on American cultural anthropology was negligible and short-lived, with the field remaining preponderantly humanistic in orientation and cultural ecology persisting only as a minority school that has faded into the background in recent years. However, it did find an audience among the next generation of archaeologists who attended the Midwestern universities where the founders of neo-evolutionism taught.

The rise of the "New Archaeology" and its explicitly scientific perspective should not have been expected to have completely displaced the earlier humanistic bent of American thought, and I would argue it decidedly has not. Ironically, the same Midwestern schools that in the 1960s spawned archaeologists who propounded an "explicitly scientific" paradigm, in the 1970s produced a number of archaeologists, Blanton, Feinstein, Crumley, and de Montmollin, who were to lead a resurgence of humanism. This humanistic wave reacted against the evolutionism of White, Steward, Sahlins, and Service much in the same way as Boas did against Morgan and Tylor, making many of the same kinds of criticisms. However, as the writings of Crumley and Alice Kehoe indicate, at the core of the reaction against neo-evolutionism is a sense of moral outrage (Kehoe 1998: ch. 10). To humanistic scholars, evolutionism is an idea that is simply not good to think. Acceptance of evolution is tantamount in their eyes to accepting oppression and human inequality. However, accepting the humanist paradigm leads one into a position of either explaining social change via mystical forces like class struggle, regarding change as due to historically contingent factors, and thus not amenable to explanation via a scientific theory, and/or denying that social evolution occurs. In the following section I argue counter to the humanist position that social evolution is amenable to scientific theory building.

Contra-Scale: On the Reality of Stages of Socio-cultural Integration

One of the admitted weaknesses of the neo-evolutionary perspective is a lack of consistency in the choice of dimensions that are used to define stages of socio-cultural complexity. The critics of neo-evolutionism are correct that the welter of terminology used to define stages of social complexity reflects the choices of variable dimensions. Steward himself was inconsistent in his formulations, choosing different critical variables for different stages of socio-cultural integration.[2]

Primary to a consideration of social evolution should be social organization, as social evolution is primarily manifested in changes in household constitution, systems of kinship, and political systems. The organization of society is a primary dimension, while concomitant changes in behavior, such as are reflected in sumptuary rules and house size, are contingent. Adoption of this position is actually compatible with the Marxian position, and latterly the structural Marxist position, that social organization subsumes relations of production and exchange (Frankenstein and Rowlands 1978; Godelier 1977:18; Hazelgrove 1982).[3] An area of contention is whether relations of production and exchange are to be accorded primacy in causal explanations of change. The Marxian position with regard to production as personified by V. Gordon Childe's technological determinism has been, to the satisfaction of most social scientists, falsified. Attributing causality to the dimension of exchange, as initially proposed by Engels and latterly championed by the structural Marxists Rowlands and Blanton, is problematic (Blanton 1996; Blanton et al. 1996a; Engels 1978; Frankenstein and Rowlands 1978).

The thesis of the substantivist school (Dalton 1961, 1969; Gibson and Geselowitz 1988; Polanyi et al. 1957) that relations of exchange are contingent upon, and function in the service of, social structure has gained limited acceptance

(Brumfiel 1980; Gudeman 1986). The reason for the unpopularity of this position is due to the fact that social structure was argued dogmatically to have been determinative in all manner of social formations. This led substantivists to logically conclude that market exchange and mercantilism were non-existent or unimportant until the emergence of capitalism (Polanyi 1944, 1957). This dogmatic position was a useful counterpoise to the projection of modern economic behavior onto pre-modern peoples. However, the dogmatic rejection of the importance of markets and mercantilism in ancient societies has been justly criticized (Cook 1966). Modern research has shifted to exploring the character of markets in pre-modern societies, and explaining their emergence or absence without entailing a rejection of the substantivist paradigm (Brumfiel 1980; LaLone 1982).

A reformulation of the substantivist position should enable the retention of the preponderant good aspects of this paradigm, primarily the focus on the study of social organization, while discarding its dogmatic aspects—the downplaying of social behaviors not embedded in the political system. Substantivism should lead a researcher to investigate when and to what degree social organization is determinant with respect to systems of production and exchange, and when it is not. This position is preferable to the humanist alternatives with their concomitant moral imperatives, economic causality, and historical particularism.

Levels of socio-cultural integration should override scale as a gross measure of complexity, as scale has been demonstrated to vary according to the type of prevailing subsistence economy. I would therefore agree with Blanton, Kowalewski, and Feinman that changes in the dimensions of scale, boundedness, complexity, and integration are critical indexes of evolution in political systems. However, I do not hold these dimensions to be equal in importance. Meaningful comparisons and analysis are only forthcoming if the three-dimensional *organizational* factors of societies, such as complexity and integration, are accorded primacy over two-dimensional variables such as scale and boundedness.

The approach advocated here begins with the acceptance as fact that levels of socio-cultural integration generate qualitative attributes which are direct outgrowths of the social structure of societies at that level (**Table 1**). To take the segmentary level as an example, societies at this level of development possess sodalities such as lineages, clans, and moieties. These sodalities employ totemic symbols and sacerdotal objects as a means of maintaining sodality solidarity. Therefore, paraphernalia such as the decorated screens, rattles, boxes, masks, and totem poles of the aboriginal cultures of the pacific Northwest are predicated upon the existence of the segmentary system.

Due to the variation in the organization of societies within a given level of socio-cultural integration, that is explainable at least in part by the variation that exists in ecological adaptations, but which is also due to historical circumstances, the possession of the complete range of qualitative attributes should not be viewed as a necessary precondition for inclusion. Hence Hawaiian or Danish Bronze Age chiefdoms may lack a

---

[2] Compare the emphasis Steward places on ecology and social organization in chapters 6-9, with the checklist approach in chapters 11-12 in the *Theory of Culture Change* (1979).

[3] This is as it is with Leslie White's (1959) theory that social structures expand in scale to capture energy.

central place pattern of settlement, but would still be considered to be chiefdoms due to evidence of ancestor veneration, ascribed status, corporate labor projects, elite sponsorship of religion, sumptuary patterns of consumption, etc. (Earle 1997). Likewise, one should not expect chiefly or royal burials to have been the norm within an Irish medieval state, due to the introduction of Christianity with its attendant notions of humility and equality before God.

The Utility of the Substantivist Approach

There is a wealth of social information contained in ethnohistorical documents of the Irish Early Middle Ages (AD 200-1200). So rich and varied is this information that one may conclude with absolute certainty that the social landscape of Early Medieval Ireland consisted exclusively of complex chiefdoms. These chiefdoms apparently extended back to the beginning of the Irish historical record, though most of the texts describing these chiefdoms, like the law texts and cycle of the kings, date to after the 8th century. The data of these documents reveal several levels of chieftains within a complex chiefdom or chiefdom confederacy, the roles of their followers like rechtaire and judges, the existence of attached craft specialists, and a system of staple finance through a complex patron/client system (Gibson 1995b; Kelly 1988; Patterson 1981, 1991). They further attest to the fact that lineages were the basic corporate group, and these were ranked on the basis of descent from a common ancestor—in other words into a ramage system (Charles-Edwards 1993; Gibson 1988, 1995b; Mac Niocaill 1972:49-54; Patterson 1990).

In Thomond, an indigenous medieval province roughly coterminous with present-day County Clare in the west of Ireland, it has proven possible to identify boundaries and pinpoint elite residences and religious centers of Irish chiefdoms from the 9th century onwards with a measurable degree of certitude (Gibson 1990, 1995b). Complex chiefdoms were roughly round in outline. The territories of cadet ramages surrounded the territory of the ramage of the chieftain. The subordinate capital sites were positioned with respect to the chieftain's capital commensurate with the expectations of the central place model of Vincas Steponaitis (1978; Gibson 2000). Each aristocratic center was paired with a religious center, a monastery, or in the later Middle Ages a church. Ancestor veneration was personified in the genealogies of aristocratic ramages, in the heroic biographies contained in medieval legends and sagas, in the names of the territories, and in the inauguration mounds that were held to be the resting places of apical ancestors.

The Configurations of the Burren's Ancient Fields: The Social Landscapes of the Neolithic

Establishing a polity's level of socio-cultural integration is relatively easy when copious ethnohistorical documents containing relevant information exist. Extension of the substantivist approach into earlier prehistoric periods is not only made more difficult by the lack of historic records, but also by an often patchy archaeological record. To take the Neolithic period of Northern Europe as an example, many more burial sites dating to this period have been excavated

than have settlements due to the greater prominence of the former. On top of that, it is now uncertain whether or not many of the Neolithic houses that have been excavated were indeed truly residential structures, and not ritual gathering places (Thomas 1996). These difficulties notwithstanding, few areas with anything near complete settlement patterns have been excavated, and as the various well-known archaeological surveys of the New World have demonstrated, regional surveys are an important first step in making assessments of the level of social complexity of a polity.

Though the Cahercommaun Project that worked in the Burren region of County Clare was focused upon the recovery of Early Medieval settlement patterns, archaeological landscapes from earlier periods were recorded as well. In the Burren, remnants of extensive systems of field boundary walls dating to the Neolithic and Bronze Ages[4] have survived in addition to the medieval systems. These were first revealed by the pioneering studies undertaken by Emma Plunkett Dillon (1983, 1985) and David Drew (1982, 1994). The landscapes are best preserved in the higher areas of the Burren where the soil cover is thin to non-existent and plowing has been historically absent. A program of survey and excavation of prehistoric field systems, settlements, and ritual structures, directed by Carleton Jones, has been underway in an uplands Burren locale, Roughan Hill, since 1994 (Jones 1998).

The earliest of the Burren's field boundary wall systems may be contemporaneous with the earliest ritual monuments, the court tombs of the Early Neolithic and the portal dolmens of the Middle Neolithic. Like the Neolithic field boundary wall systems that have been recorded at Céide, County Mayo, the Burren's early walls were constructed of the local limestone (Caulfield 1978, 1983, 1988; Caulfield et al. 1998).[5] Unlike the Céide walls, however, the field boundary walls of the Burren were not subsequently buried beneath bog. Instead, they remained exposed on the surface where they decayed to become linear limestone pedestals and heaps of stone. The fact that they lay relatively undisturbed throughout four millennia is probably attributable to a demise of the worth of the upland portions of the Burren for cultivation in subsequent periods. Studies carried out by Drew of soil preserved in fissures in the limestone bedrock and under the ancient walls and monuments indicate a loss of the Burren's original soil cover through erosion. The most likely cause of the erosion was the clearance of the Burren's vegetative cover by its ancient inhabitants (Crabtree 1982; Drew 1982, 1983).

The surviving portions of mound-type field boundary wall layouts in Tullycommon/Teeskagh townlands, at the core of the Cahercommaun Project's survey region, consist in part of smaller fields centering upon a cluster of circular huts (**Figure 1**). These small fields consist of walls that curve to intersect the straight sections of others. Some walls that originate within the small fields of the settlement cluster extend out from this nucleus to become a part of a system of sinuous walls running the length of the available land area (**Figure 2**). As was the

---

[4] Early Neolithic 4000–3600 BC, Middle Neolithic 3600-3100 BC, Late Neolithic 3100-2500 BC, Final Neolithic/Early Bronze Age 2500-2000 BC (Cooney 2000:14-17).

[5] Absolutely everything in the Burren of all ages is built of the local limestone.

case with some Final Neolithic/Early Bronze Age settlements on Roughan Hill, some habitation sites on the plateau in Tullycommon/Teeskagh would seem to have been more elaborate, enclosed by concentric perimeter walls of varying diameter (Jones 1998). The differentiation of settlements into enclosed and unenclosed during the Neolithic seems to have been a trend in the west of Ireland (Cooney 2000:46-47; Grogan and Eogan 1987). One prehistoric settlement surveyed by the Cahercommaun Project, C-361, was a hut surrounded by a perimeter wall consisting of a double row of large slabs. A smaller enclosure, also of a double row of slabs was encountered at a settlement excavated by the project, C-221, described below (**Figure 3**). Larger enclosures appear in aerial photographs taken of this section of the plateau, but it is unknown whether these were contemporary with the unenclosed huts (**Figure 2**), or even whether they were settlements.

A boundary wall layout of these configurations was mapped in detail around a settlement cluster located upon a narrow section of a plateau in Teeskagh townland (**Figure 1**). This settlement cluster consists of what were apparently a number of circular huts situated inside of karst depressions within the broken plateau surface. This settlement cluster is located just across the townland boundary wall to the south of the large 9th century AD cashel settlement of Cahercommaun.

A small portion of the midden adjacent to one hut circle of this complex, C-221 B, was test-excavated (**Figure 3**) (Gibson 1995a). Radiocarbon dates from this site (**Table 2**) suggest that C-221 B could date to the 32nd century BC—a date that would place at least one phase of this habitation at the end of the Middle Neolithic. This may mean that the site, or the pottery-producing level, was of an earlier date than the Roughan Hill system and possibly conterminous with the second phase of use of Poulnabrone dolmen, as pottery similar to the ware encountered at C-221 B turned up there and the radiocarbon dates overlap (Brindley and Lanting 1992:17). However, a small piece of cupferous material from the same unit and level as the provenienced carbon sample, and a younger date from an unprovenienced carbon sample leaves open the possibility of a later dating, though no Beaker pottery turned up in the small ceramic sample from the site as it did from settlement 1 on Roughan Hill (Jones 1998:33-34).

Only a small area of the settlement was investigated. The animal teeth from the excavation were sorted into species. These data are presented in **Table 3**. If the sample of animal teeth can be taken as any way representative of the livestock kept by the inhabitants of C-221, then it would seem from the proportions of the domestic animals in the sample that approximately equal numbers of cattle and pigs were kept, followed by a lesser number of goats or sheep. The cattle of this time, though smaller than modern breeds, would still have been significantly larger than the pigs, and so this sample would be weighted towards cattle as having been the most important domestic animal. It is interesting that venison was a significant component of the diet, indicating that hunting played a prominent role in the subsistence strategy of this time.

The finds from C-221 include bits of broken pottery, numerous small scrapers of chert, irregularly shaped grinding stones, and a few broken stone hoes (Gibson 1995a). It is impossible to state at this juncture how important grain was to their domestic economy. Considering the probably thin soil cover of the Burren and its karstic uneven land surfaces, the local inhabitants were possibly compelled towards some form of horticultural economy, rather than an agrarian strategy with plowed fields.

This settlement cluster perhaps represents an aggregation of kinsmen. The distribution of curving field boundary wall segments around C-221 and the other hut sites would seem to indicate that small fields adjoined these habitations, and that these formed the point of origin for more extensive systems of field boundary walls that ranged to the (north) east and (south) west (**Figure 2**).

In the southern half of Teeskagh townland this pattern of settlement and field boundary walls is in clearer evidence (**Figure 4**). This portion of the townland consists of an expanse of limestone that is nearly void of soil. This shelf of limestone is tilted from southwest to northeast, the lower northern area near the cliffs possessing the greatest amount of soil and vegetation cover. The limestone shelf has been fractured into a series of parallel strips oriented northeast to southwest. These strips are of uneven elevation, resulting in arroyos with vertical faces several meters in height. Walls presumed to be of some antiquity consisting of piled limestone boulders run both underneath and along the edge of these arroyos.

The site C-114 consists of a number of hut foundations that are located adjacent to walls that curve and intersect either other walls or natural escarpments to mark out small irregular fields (**Figure 5**). This pattern is very reminiscent of the arrangement of habitations and walls at C-221. Near to wall XXI are a number of small cairns. Cursory examinations by Emma Plunkett Dillon (1985:87) have shown cairns of this type to cover human remains. The wall originating from the largest hut, Hut 3, eventually intersects at right angles with the field boundary walls XVII and XXI. Both of these walls run along the edges of limestone bedrock which rises in the same direction. What appear to be isolated huts are found at points along, and possibly at the terminal ends of, field boundary walls in Teeskagh townland (C-109, C-107, C-116; **Figure 4**).

It is very difficult to hazard conclusions or interpretations of any kind, given the ambiguous data at hand on the early field boundary wall systems of the Burren. The research so far undertaken shows the mound-type field boundary wall systems to have been pervasive in the Burren. Communities consisting of small residential clusters of 3-5 huts would seem to have been the norm from at least the Middle Neolithic to the Final Neolithic/Early Bronze Age. The field boundary walls at C-114 segregate each hut within its own yard. One could read a variety of interpretations into this—the huts may have been occupied by wives of the lineage patriarch with their children, or by the sons of the patriarch with their wives, etc. The only thing that is certain is that hut clusters were small, and so probably represented the residences of related individuals. Overall, the pattern of small, fairly closely spaced hamlets is one that is reminiscent of other areas of the world with low levels of political development and a horticultural economy (e.g. highland New Guinea).

The field boundary walls that radiate from these hamlets would seem to have taken in the available level land surrounding the residence cluster. It would seem that the strategy was to divide up available expanses of relatively level land into parallel strips of maximum length. The layouts, whatever their exact function, are evidence of planning, though not necessarily at a level higher than the small community that built them.

Andrew Fleming's work on the co-axial field boundary systems of Dartmoor has led him to postulate the existence of communities organized into discrete territories with three levels of community organization: the household, the neighborhood, and the community (Fleming 1984). Multiple levels of community organization must correspond to at least a segmentary level of socio-cultural integration. Enough has been preserved of the Dartmoor field boundary walls to distinguish discrete systems. The Burren's ancient field boundary wall systems occupy a more convoluted landscape, and boundary walls of various periods are intermingled, so discrimination is more difficult. Despite these limitations on our ability to reconstruct Neolithic and Bronze Age wall systems, one can attest to the existence of a 'household' level of organization, though the Burren evidence suggests something more extensive such as a polygamous family unit or lineage existed at the lowest level. A 'neighborhood' level of organization was also likely during the Middle Neolithic and Final Neolithic/Early Bronze Age. In the Burren this would consist of all contemporaneously occupied huts linked by a common field boundary wall system, such as the system emanating from C-114 or C-221, or the associated settlements on Roughan Hill. In Tullycommon/Teeskagh other huts are found scattered along the sinuous walls. It is not known whether these were contemporary with the household clusters, or whether they were something other than simple field huts or corrals.

Fleming's 'community' level is even more difficult to substantiate in the Burren on present evidence. However, I would be willing to entertain the existence of such a level of organization on the basis of two lines of inference. The Burren contains a profusion of prehistoric tomb types: cists, simple small cairns, large hilltop 'prestige cairns', wedge tombs, portal dolmens, and maybe even passage graves. The exact dating of these tomb types has not been worked out. To date, to my knowledge, one portal dolmen and two prestige cairns have been excavated, and one court tomb is currently under excavation (James Eogan pers. comm. 2001; Carleton Jones pers. comm. 2001; Lynch 1988). The Roughan Hill court tomb and Poulnabrone dolmen would seem to have been constructed during the Early Neolithic (Hedges et al. 1990; Carleton Jones pers. comm. 2001; Lynch 1988), though the latter monument received interments through the Middle Neolithic and Early Bronze Age. Of the two prestige cairns that have been excavated, Poulawack and Coolnatullagh, only the former has been radiocarbon dated at the time of this writing, though morphologically they are very similar. Poulawack was constructed during the Middle Neolithic, and

reused during the Final Neolithic/Early Bronze Age and Later Bronze Age (Brindley and Lanting 1992). Though no wedge tomb has been excavated in the Burren, they have been conventionally ascribed to the Early Bronze Age due to the frequent occurrence of Beaker pottery in examples that have been excavated elsewhere (see Herity and Eogan 1977:117-119). The small cairns are the most numerous type of burial monument, surpassing the wedge tombs in number. None have been subjected to a professional excavation, though a disturbed example was reported to have produced human remains and a bracelet of an Early Bronze Age type (Plunkett Dillon 1985:87).

The court tombs, portal dolmens, wedge tombs, and prestige cairns were utilized for communal burial and were located in prominent positions, such as the crests of ridges and hilltops. Though the small cairns were found to be thickly clustered on the edges of cliffs, as were some prestige cairns, they were encountered by the Cahercommaun Project in more variable settings. They are directly associated with the huts described above, and on the plateau number in the dozens. Their size would have limited their use to one or two interments. The wedge tombs are also likely to have been contemporary with the huts and field systems discussed here, and the earlier monuments were reused during the Final Neolithic/Early Bronze Age. This limited evidence seems to point to the region's population having peaked at this time.

The Burren's wedge tombs are highly variable in size, sometimes assuming massive proportions, built of large slabs weighing in excess of a ton. The more massive tombs would have required labor on a corporate scale to be erected. If they were all built during the Final Neolithic/Early Bronze Age and in contemporary use, given the relative scarcity of this tomb type and their prominent location, they may indicate a 'community' level of social organization. There are 2-3 small wedge tombs near the field systems described here, across the boundary wall in Tullycommon townland on the plateau. There are only 1-2 massive wedge tombs, located in Tullycommon townland beyond the areas indicated in **Figures 2** and **4**.

One would expect that boundaries between antagonistic communities would consist of unmodified no-man's land. It is probably safe to assume that where field boundary walls are built and communities are in close proximity to one another, some ties of solidarity must exist. The Burren's ancient field boundary wall systems seem to substantiate the presence of ties within a social grouping. At the level of the lineage, they segregated households. The walls would have served further to mark off the land held by differing corporate groups within a group's territory. Although the final maps of mound-type field boundary walls recorded during the 1993 season of survey have yet to be completed, single walls were observed to run snake-like from hut cluster to hut cluster, reinforcing the impression that the field boundary systems were intended to link kin groups together within a larger polity. This may be what is indicated by the sinuous mound wall associated with C-361 in **Figure 2**. This wall was first spotted in an aerial photograph, and later confirmed on the ground. It continues in a beeline to the east up to the edge of a cliff. At the foot of the cliff, it continues its course on the same trajectory across the valley floor. Its primary purpose therefore does not seem to have been agricultural. Walls like this may be likened to the prehistoric roads in Chaco Canyon, New Mexico, which also ignore topography.

The integrated systems of field boundary walls, such as one finds in the Burren and elsewhere, testify to the existence of peoples at the fringes of Europe integrated into fairly large-scale groupings at an early age. To say that one may reach a definitive conclusion from such a dataset at this stage of investigation about the state of social development in the Late Neolithic/Early Bronze Age of the Burren is ridiculous. However, it is possible to use the substantivist approach to identify the kinds of data that should be obtained in future investigations to answer such questions.

The data described above do indicate that habitation sites are differentiated with respect to size, that communities were linked into systems exhibiting a scale of social organization above the level of the extended family. The court tombs, portal dolmens, and prestige cairn tombs point to ancestor veneration extending back to the Early Neolithic. Ancestor veneration has been viewed as a means of uniting, and in stratified societies ranking, lineage segments. Variation in tomb size and type would be seen as evidence of the ranking of some lineages above others. Large wedge tombs point to the mobilization of corporate labor above the capabilities and needs of a household. These data allow either segmentary societies or simple chiefdoms as possible levels of socio-cultural integration. Given the rarity of truly massive wedge tombs in the area, I am tempted to see simple chiefdoms during the Final Neolithic/Early Bronze Age. Given the even rarer occurrence of portal dolmens, and the occurrence of single interments in cists under prestige cairns, simple chiefdoms may even stretch back to the Early Neolithic.[6] To decide the matter one way or the other, one must search further for evidence appropriate to the social structure and dynamics of a chiefdom. Evidence, the discovery of which would constitute the fulfillment of test implications for this level of social integration, would include a central place pattern of settlement, attached craft specialization, and a high degree of warfare.

Conclusions

I would agree with the critics of 1960s neo-evolutionism, which could be termed the *transformationalist* perspective (Spencer 1990), that when societies are arrayed in order of ascending complexity, the social continuum appears continuous. Complex segmentary societies can be difficult to distinguish from simple chiefdoms, and complex chiefdoms bear striking resemblances to primitive states. However, when both scalar dimensions and qualitative attributes of social organization are placed simultaneously under scrutiny, one cannot escape the conclusion that though a simple chiefdom may share most of its attributes in common with a complex segmentary society, it will depart from it in a few key qualitative distinctions (e.g. a permanent office of leadership).

A close analogy may be made with the variation in living organisms. Phenotypically, most variation will appear to be continuously distributed, but at the genetic level, and also at the phenotypic level when closely analyzed, variation is discrete and discontinuous.

The political economy school has contended that their proposed new paradigm is still evolutionist and corrects the alleged deficiencies of the old neo-evolutionism. I would argue that their proposed paradigm is neither an evolutionist paradigm, nor much of an improvement on the older paradigm. The political economy paradigm lacks a mechanism by which social change can be explained. It instead seems predicated upon an analysis of political systems whereby they are matched against different modes of socioeconomic integration. The advocates seem to have little interest in the causes of change except to stipulate an expectation of cycles of political centralization and decentralization. This hardly goes beyond Steward's (1979:196) cyclical conquests model. Ultimately, the political economy paradigm is historical and Marxian. Instead of building upon and improving the work of Steward, Sahlins, and Service, it stands for a rejection of evolutionism in favor of a return to early 20th century (if not late 19th century) humanism. In a sense it embodies the "cycling" it describes in that it recapitulates the reaction against 19th century evolutionism by Boas and his students.

Contrary to the caricature of neo-evolutionism by the Blanton school and others, neo-evolutionism has not remained in a fossilized state since the 1960s. Evolutionist scholars such as Allen Johnson, Marvin Harris, Timothy Earle, and Colin Renfrew have moved on from the work of Steward, Service, and Sahlins, proceeding from the formulation of stages of socio-cultural evolution to the explanation of social change (e.g. Harris 1977; Johnson and Earle 1987; Renfrew 1984). It is informative that the critics of neo-evolutionism choose to attack older models rather than their modern descendants, possibly because they are easier to caricature. The attack on older neo-evolutionism amounts to a straw man strategy by means of exhumed anachronisms.

The present evolutionist school follows a scientific paradigm, and thus embodies a concern for the confirmation of its assumptions through testing. It proposes a framework for the study of social change that is universally applicable, in contrast to the Marxian construction of historical archetypes. It has an interest in the causes of social change, not merely the manner in which people reorganize their economic activities in the face of social change.

In spite of the lip service paid to the dimension of scale by the practitioners of the political economy group, their writings make clear that it is not of great significance to them. I would have to agree with them on this point—that scale, meaning the spatial dimensions of a polity or the size of its population, is not of great analytical consequence. Scale is not a significant measure of social complexity as the variation in subsistence regimes and productive potentials of different regions is so great that polities of equal complexity may be vastly different in size. Scale is clearly a dependent variable, and so is of questionable analytical value, at least by itself. However the

---

[6] Some of the objects found in Poulnabrone, such as a green polished stone axe and bone pendant, could be construed as primitive valuables.

dimension of *social* scale is indispensable to the study of social evolution. Social scale is as close as one can come in the social sciences to an independent variable, and one that is dangerous to ignore when seeking to understand the variance in other social and cultural dimensions.

Acknowledgments

The author gratefully acknowledges the funding and volunteer field assistants provided by Earthwatch, which made possible the 1985-6 field seasons of the Cahercommaun Project. The University Research Expeditions Program, associated with the University of California, supported the 1993 field season of this project. I would like to extend thanks to the crew chiefs Michael Geselowitz, Keith Johnson, Judith Carroll, Una MacDowell, Ellen McCallig, Kevin McGimpsey, Maura Smale, Mary Ann Murray, and the late Wade Richards. The author would also like to extend his gratitude to Tom and Jane Gutherie and Eamon McMahon for permission to survey and excavate upon their land, and to Carleton Jones and James Eogan for providing up-to-date information on their research.

References Cited

Blanton, Richard E. 1980 'Cultural ecology reconsidered' *American Antiquity* 45:145-151.

Blanton, Richard E. 1996 'The basin of Mexico market system and the growth of empire' in F.F. Berdan, R.E. Blanton, E.H. Boone, M.G. Hodge, M.E. Smith, and E. Umberger (eds) *Aztec Imperial Strategies* Dumbarton Oaks (Washington, DC): 3-84.

Blanton, Richard E. 1998 'Beyond centralization: steps towards a theory of egalitarian behavior in archaic states' in G.M. Feinman and J. Marcus (eds) *Archaic States* School of American Research Press (Santa Fe, NM):135-172.

Blanton, Richard E., Stephen A. Kowalewski, Gary M. Feinman, and Laura M. Finsten 1993 *Ancient Mesoamerica* 2nd ed. Cambridge University Press (Cambridge).

Blanton, Richard E., Gary M. Feinman, Stephen A. Kowalewski, and Peter N. Peregrine 1996a 'A dual-processual theory for the evolution of Mesoamerican civilization' *Current Anthropology* 37:1-14.

Blanton, Richard E., Gary M. Feinman, Stephen A. Kowalewski, and Peter N. Peregrine 1996b 'Reply' *Current Anthropology* 37:65-68.

Braun, David P. 1990 'Selection and evolution in nonhierarchical organization' in S. Upham (ed) *The Evolution of Political Systems* Cambridge University Press (Cambridge):62-86.

Brindley, A.L. and J.N. Lanting 1992 'Radiocarbon dates from the cemetery at Poulawack, Co. Clare' *The Journal of Irish Archaeology* 6:13-17.

Brumfiel, Elizabeth 1980 'Specialization, market exchange, and the Aztec state' *Current Anthropology* 21:459-478.

Carneiro, Robert 1961 'Slash-and-burn agriculture among the Kuikuru and its implications for cultural development in the Amazon Basin' *Anthropologica*, Supplement No. 2:47-67.

Carneiro, Robert 1967 'On the relationship between population size and complexity of social organization' *Southwestern Journal of Anthropology* 23(3):234-243.

Carneiro, Robert 1981 'The chiefdom as precursor to the state' in G. Jones and R. Kautz (eds) *The Transition to Statehood in the New World* Cambridge University Press (Cambridge):39-79.

Caulfield, Séamus 1978 'Neolithic fields: the Irish evidence' in H.C. Bowen and P.J. Fowler (eds) *Early Land Allotment* British Archaeological Reports, British Series 48 (Oxford):137-144.

Caulfield, Séamus 1983 'The Neolithic settlement of north Connaught' in T. Reeves-Smith and N. Hammond (eds) *Landscape Archaeology in Ireland* British Archaeological Reports, British Series 116 (Oxford): 195-215.

Caulfield, Séamus 1988 *Céide Fields and Belderrig Guide* Morgan Book Company (Killala, Ireland).

Caulfield, Séamus, R.G. O'Donnell, and P.I. Mitchell 1998 'Radiocarbon dating of a Neolithic field system at Céide fields, County Mayo, Ireland' *Radiocarbon* 40:629-640.

Champion, Timothy, Clive Gamble, Stephen Shennan, and Alasdair Whittle 1984 *Prehistoric Europe* Academic Press (San Diego, CA).

Charles-Edwards, T.M. 1993 *Early Irish and Welsh Kinship* Oxford University Press (Oxford).

Cook, Scott 1966 'The obsolete "anti-market" mentality: a critique of the substantive approach to economic anthropology' *American Anthropologist* 68:323-345.

Cooney, Gabriel 2000 *Landscapes of Neolithic Ireland* Routledge (London).

Crabtree, Keith 1982 'Evidence for the Burren's forest cover' in S. Limbrey and M. Bell (eds) *Archaeological Aspects of Woodland Ecology* British Archaeological Reports, International Series 146 (Oxford):105-113.

Crumley, Carole L. 1979 'Three locational models: an epistemological assessment for anthropology and archaeology' in M.B. Schiffer (ed) *Advances in Archaeological Method and Theory, Vol 2* Academic Press (New York):141-173.

Crumley, Carole L. 1987 'Celtic settlement before the conquest: the dialectics of landscape and power' in C.L. Crumley and W.H. Marquardt (eds) *Regional Dynamics: Burgundian Landscapes in Historical Perspective* Academic Press (San Diego, CA):403-429.

Crumley, Carole L. 1995 'Heterarchy and the analysis of complex societies' in R.M. Ehrenreich, C.L. Crumley, and J.E. Levy (eds) *Heterarchy and the Analysis of Complex Societies* Archaeological Papers of the American Anthropological Association No. 6 (Arlington, VA):1-5.

Crumley, Carole L. and William H. Marquardt 1987 'Regional dynamics in Burgundy' in C.L. Crumley and W.H. Marquardt (eds) *Regional Dynamics: Burgundian Landscapes in Historical Perspective* Academic Press (San Diego, CA):609-623.

Dalton, George 1961 'Economic theory and primitive society' *American Anthropologist* 63:1-25.

Dalton, George 1969 'Theoretical issues in economic anthropology' *Current Anthropology* 10:63-102.

D'Altroy, Terrence and Timothy K. Earle 1985 'Staple finance, wealth finance, and storage in the Inka political economy' *Current Anthropology* 26:187-206.

de Montmollin, Oliver 1989 *The Archaeology of Political Structure* Cambridge University Press (Cambridge).

Drew, David 1982 'Environmental archaeology and karstic terrains: the Burren, County Clare, Ireland' in S. Limbrey and M. Bell (eds) *Archaeological Aspects of Woodland Ecology* British Archaeological Reports, International Series 146 (Oxford):115-127.

Drew, David 1983 'Accelerated soil erosion in a Karst area: the Burren, western Ireland' *Journal of Hydrology* 61:113-124.

Drew, David 1994 'Ancient field boundaries, Ballyelly-Coolmeen area, Slieve Elva,' in M. O'Connell (ed) *Burren, Co. Clare* Irish Association for Quaternary Studies No. 18 (Dublin):22-28.

Dunnell, R. 1980 'Evolutionary theory and archaeology' in M.B Schiffer (ed) *Advances in Archaeological Method and Theory, Vol. 3* Academic Press (New York):35-99.

Earle, Timothy K. 1978 *Economic and Social Organization of a Complex Chiefdom: The Halelea District, Kaua'i, Hawaii* Museum of Anthropology, University of Michigan Anthropological Papers, Vol. 63 (Ann Arbor, MI).

Earle, Timothy K. 1987 'Chiefdoms in archaeological and ethnohistorical perspective' *Annual Review of Anthropology* 16:279-308.

Earle, Timothy K. 1997 *How Chiefs Come to Power* Stanford University Press (Palo Alto, CA).

Earle, Timothy K. and Terrence N. D'Altroy 1982 'Storage facilities and state finance in the Upper Mantaro valley, Peru' in J.E. Ericson and T.K. Earle (eds) *Contexts for Prehistoric Exchange* Academic Press (New York): 265-290.

Ember, Carol L. and Melvin Ember 1999 *Cultural Anthropology* Prentice Hall (Upper Saddle River, NJ).

Engels, Friedrich 1978 [1884] *Der Ursprung der Familie, des Privateigentums, und des Staats* Verlag für Fremdsprachige Literatur (Beijing).

Eogan, George 1986 *Knowth* Thames and Hudson (London).

Feinman, Gary 1991 'Demography, surplus, and inequality: early political formations in highland Mesoamerica' in T. Earle (ed) *Chiefdoms: Power, Economy, and Ideology* Cambridge University Press (Cambridge): 229-262.

Feinman, Gary 1994 'Social boundaries and political change: a comparative perspective' in G. Stein and M.S. Rothman (eds) *Chiefdoms and States in the Near East* Monographs in World Archaeology No. 18, Prehistory Press (Madison, WI):225-236.

Feinman, Gary 1998 'Scale and social organization: perspectives on the archaic state' in G. Feinman and J. Marcus (eds) *Archaic States* School of American Research Press (Santa Fe, NM):95-133.

Feinman, Gary M. and Jill Neitzel 1984 'Too many types: an overview of sedentary prestate societies in the Americas' in M. Schiffer (ed) *Advances in Archaeological Method and Theory, Vol. 7* Academic Press (New York):39-102.

Fergusson, Yale 1991 'Chiefdoms to city-states: the Greek experience' in T. Earle (ed) *Chiefdoms: Power, Economy, and Ideology* Cambridge University Press (Cambridge).

Flannery, Kent V. 1988 'Comment on "Ecological theory and cultural evolution in the Valley of Oaxaca" by W.T. Sanders and D.L. Nichols' *Current Anthropology* 29:57-58.

Fleming, Andrew 1984 'The prehistoric landscape of Dartmoor: wider implications' *Landscape History* 6: 5-19.

Frankenstein, Susan and Michael J. Rowlands 1978 'The internal structure and regional context of Early Iron Age society in southwestern Germany' *Institute of Archaeology Bulletin* 15:73-112.

Friedman, Jonathan and Michael J. Rowlands 1977 'Notes towards an epigenetic model of the evolution of "civilization"' in J. Friedman and M.J. Rowlands (eds) *The Evolution of Social Systems* Gerald Duckworth and Co. (London):201-206.

Gibson, D. Blair 1988 'Agro-pastoralism and regional social organization in early Ireland' in D.B. Gibson and M.N. Geselowitz (eds) *Tribe and Polity in Late Prehistoric Europe* Plenum (New York):41-68.

Gibson, D. Blair 1990 *Tulach Commáin: A View of an Irish Chiefdom* University Microfilms International (Ann Arbor, MI).

Gibson, D. Blair 1995a 'The excavation of a prehistoric habitation site, C-221, in the townland of Teeskagh, Co. Clare' Unpublished excavation report on file in the Office of Public Works, National Monuments Branch (Dublin, Ireland).

Gibson, D. Blair 1995b 'Chiefdoms, confederacies, and statehood in early Ireland' in B. Arnold and D.B. Gibson (eds) *Celtic Chiefdom, Celtic State* Cambridge University Press (Cambridge):116-128.

Gibson, D. Blair 2000 'Nearer, my chieftain, to thee: central place theory and chiefdoms, revisited' in M.W. Diehl (ed) *Hierarchies in Action, Cui Bono* Center for Archaeological Investigations, Occasional Paper No. 27 (Carbondale, IL):241-263.

Gibson, D. Blair and Michael N. Geselowitz 1988 'The evolution of complex society in late prehistoric Europe: toward a paradigm' in D.B. Gibson and M.N. Geselowitz (eds) *Tribe and Polity in Late Prehistoric Europe* Plenum (New York):3-37.

Giddens, Anthony 1984 *The Constitution of Society* Polity Press (Cambridge).

Giddens, Anthony 1985 *The Nation-state and Violence* Polity Press (Cambridge).

Godelier, Maurice 1977 *Perspectives in Marxist Anthropology* Cambridge University Press (Cambridge).

Grogan, Eoin and George Eogan 1987 'Lough Gur excavations by Sean P. Ó Ríordáin: further Neolithic and Beaker habitations on Knockadoon' *Proceedings of the Royal Irish Academy* 87C:299-506.

Gudeman, Stephen 1986 *Economics as Culture: Models and Metaphors of Livelihood* Methuen (New York).

Harris, Marvin 1977 *Cannibals and Kings: The Origins of Cultures* Random House (New York).

Hazelgrove, Colin C. 1982 'Wealth, prestige and power: the dynamics of late Iron Age political centralization in south-east England' in C. Renfrew and S. Shennan (eds) *Ranking, Resource and Exchange* Cambridge University Press (Cambridge):79-88.

Hedges, R.E.M, R.A. Housley, I.A. Law, and C.R. Bronk 1990 'Radiocarbon dates from the Oxford AMS system' *Archaeometry* 32(1):101-108.

Herity, Michael and George Eogan 1977 *Ireland in Prehistory* Routledge & Kegan Paul (London).

Hindess, Barry and Paul Q. Hirst 1977 *Pre-Capitalist Modes of Production* Routledge & Kegan Paul (London).

Hodder, Ian 1986 *Reading the Past* Cambridge University Press (Cambridge).

Johnson, A.W. and Timothy Earle 1987 *The Evolution of*

Human Societies Stanford University Press (Menlo Park, CA).

Jones, Carleton 1998 'The discovery and dating of the prehistoric landscape of Roughan Hill in Co. Clare' *Journal of Irish Archaeology* 9:27-43.

Kehoe, Alice Beck 1998 *The Land of Prehistory* Routledge (New York).

Kelly, Fergus 1988 *A Guide to Early Irish Law* Dublin Institute for Advanced Studies (Dublin).

Kolb, Michael J. 1996 'Comment' *Current Anthropology* 37:59-60.

Kosse, Krisztina 1994 'The evolution of large complex groups' *Journal of Anthropological Archaeology* 13: 35-50.

Kowalewski, Stephen A. 1980 'Population-resource balances in Period I of Oaxaca, Mexico' *American Antiquity* 45:151-165.

Kowalewski, Stephen A. 1982 'Population and agricultural potential: early I through V' in R.E. Blanton, S. Kowalewski, G. Feinman, and J. Appel (eds) *The Prehispanic Settlement Patterns of the Central and Southern Parts of the Valley of Oaxaca, Mexico* Memoirs of the University of Michigan, Museum of Anthropology 15 (Ann Arbor, MI):149-180.

Kowalewski, Stephen A., Richard E. Blanton, Gary Feinman, and Laura Finsten 1983 'Boundaries, scale, and internal organization' *Journal of Anthropological Archaeology* 2:32-56.

LaLone, M. 1982 'The Inca as a non-market economy: supply on command versus supply and demand' in J. Ericson and T. Earle (eds) *Contexts for Prehistoric Exchange* Academic Press (New York):292-316.

Lynch, Anne 1988 'Poulnabrone...a stone in time' *Archaeology Ireland* 2:105-107.

McGuire, Randall 1992 *A Marxist Archaeology* Academic Press (San Diego, CA).

Mac Niocaill, Gearóid 1972 *Ireland Before the Vikings* Gill and Macmillan (Dublin).

Marquardt, William H. and Carole L. Crumley 1987 'Theoretical issues in the analysis of spatial patterning' in C.L. Crumley and W.H. Marquardt (eds) *Regional Dynamics: Burgundian Landscapes in Historical Perspective* Academic Press (San Diego, CA):1-18.

Meillassoux, Claude 1981 *Maidens, Meals, and Money* Cambridge University Press (Cambridge).

Miller, Daniel and Christopher Tilley (eds) 1984 *Ideology, Power, and Politics* Cambridge University Press (Cambridge).

Murdock, George Peter 1949 *Social Structure* Macmillan (New York).

Netting, Robert McC. 1977 *Cultural Ecology* Benjamin/ Cummings (Menlo Park, CA).

Patterson, Nerys 1981 'Material and symbolic exchange in early Irish clientship' *Proceedings of the Harvard Celtic Colloquim* 1:53-61.

Patterson, Nerys 1990 'Patrilineal kinship in early Irish society: the evidence from the Irish law texts' *Bulletin of the Board of Celtic Studies*:133-165.

Patterson, Nerys 1991 *Cattle-Lords and Clansmen: Kinship and Rank in Early Ireland* Harvard Studies in Sociology (New York).

Pearson, Gordon W. and Minzi Stuiver 1986 'High-precision calibration of the radiocarbon time scale 500-2500 BC' *Radiocarbon* 29(2B):839-862.

Pearson, Gordon W., J.R. Pilcher, M.C.L. Baillie, D.M. Corbett, and F. Qua 1986 'High precision ^{14}C measurement of Irish Oaks to show the natural ^{14}C variations from AD 1840-5210 BC' *Radiocarbon* 28(2B):911-934.

Peebles, Christopher S. and Susan M. Kus 1977 'Some archaeological correlates of ranked societies' *American Antiquity* 42(3):412-448.

Plunkett Dillon, Emma 1983 'Karren analysis as an archaeological technique' in T. Reeves-Smyth and F. Hammond (eds) *Landscape Archaeology in Ireland* British Archaeological Reports, British Series 116 (Oxford):81-94.

Plunkett Dillon, Emma 1985 *Field Boundaries of the Burren, Co. Clare* Unpublished PhD. dissertation, Department of Geography, Trinity College (Dublin).

Polanyi, Karl 1944 *The Great Transformation* Holt, Rinehart, and Winston (New York).

Polanyi, Karl 1957 'Aristotle discovers the economy' in K. Polanyi, C.M. Arensberg, and H.W. Pearson (eds) *Trade and Market in the Early Empires* Gateway (New York):64-94.

Polanyi, Karl, Conrad M. Arensberg, and Harry W. Pearson (eds) 1957 *Trade and Market in the Early Empires* Gateway (New York).

Renfrew, Colin 1974 'Beyond a subsistence economy: the evolution of social organization in prehistoric Europe' in C.B. Moore (ed) *Reconstructing Complex Societies* Bulletin of the American School of Oriental Research 20:69-95.

Renfrew, Colin 1984 *Approaches to Social Archaeology* Harvard University Press (Cambridge).

Rothman, Mitchell S. 1994 'Introduction part I: evolutionary typologies and cultural complexity' in G. Stein and M. Rothman (eds) *Chiefdoms and States in the Near East* Monographs in World Archaeology No. 18, Prehistory Press (Madison, WI):1-10.

Sahlins, Marshall D. 1958 *Social Stratification in Polynesia* University of Washington Press (Seattle, WA).

Sahlins, Marshall D. 1963 'Poor man, rich man, big-man, chief: political types in Melanesia and Polynesia' *Comparative Studies in Society and History* 5:285-303.

Sanders, William T. and Deborah L. Nichols 1988 'Ecological theory and cultural evolution in the Valley of Oaxaca' *Current Anthropology* 29(1):33-80.

Service, Elman R. 1962 *Primitive Social Organization* Random House (New York).

Spencer, Charles S. 1990 'The tempo and mode of state formation: neoevolutionism reconsidered' *Journal of Anthropological Archaeology* 9:1-30.

Spriggs, Mathew (ed) 1984 *Marxist Perspectives in Archaeology* Cambridge University Press (Cambridge).

Stein, Gil 1994 'Introduction part II: the organizational dynamics of complexity in greater Mesopotamia' in G. Stein and M. Rothman (eds) *Chiefdoms and States in the Near East* Monographs in World Archaeology No. 18, Prehistory Press (Madison, WI):11-22.

Steponaitis, Vincas P. 1978 'Location theory and complex chiefdoms: a Mississippian example' in B.D. Smith (ed) *Mississippian Settlement Patterns* Academic Press (New York):417-453.

Steward, Julian 1979 [1955] *Theory of Culture Change* University of Illinois Press (Urbana, IL).

Thomas, Julian 1996 'Neolithic houses in mainland Britain and Ireland – a skeptical view' in T. Darvill and J. Thomas (eds) *Neolithic Houses in Northwest Europe and Beyond* Oxbow Monograph 57 (Oxford): 1-12.

Wenke, R. 1981 'Explaining the evolution of cultural complexity: a review' in M.B. Schiffer (ed) *Advances in Archaeological Method and Theory, Vol. 4* Academic Press (New York):79-119.

White, Leslie A. 1959 *The Evolution of Culture* McGraw-Hill (New York).

Whitecotton, Joseph W. 1988 'On ecological theory and the Valley of Oaxaca' *Current Anthropology* 29 (2):316-317.

Wittfogel, Karl 1957 *Oriental Despotism* Yale University Press (New Haven, CT).

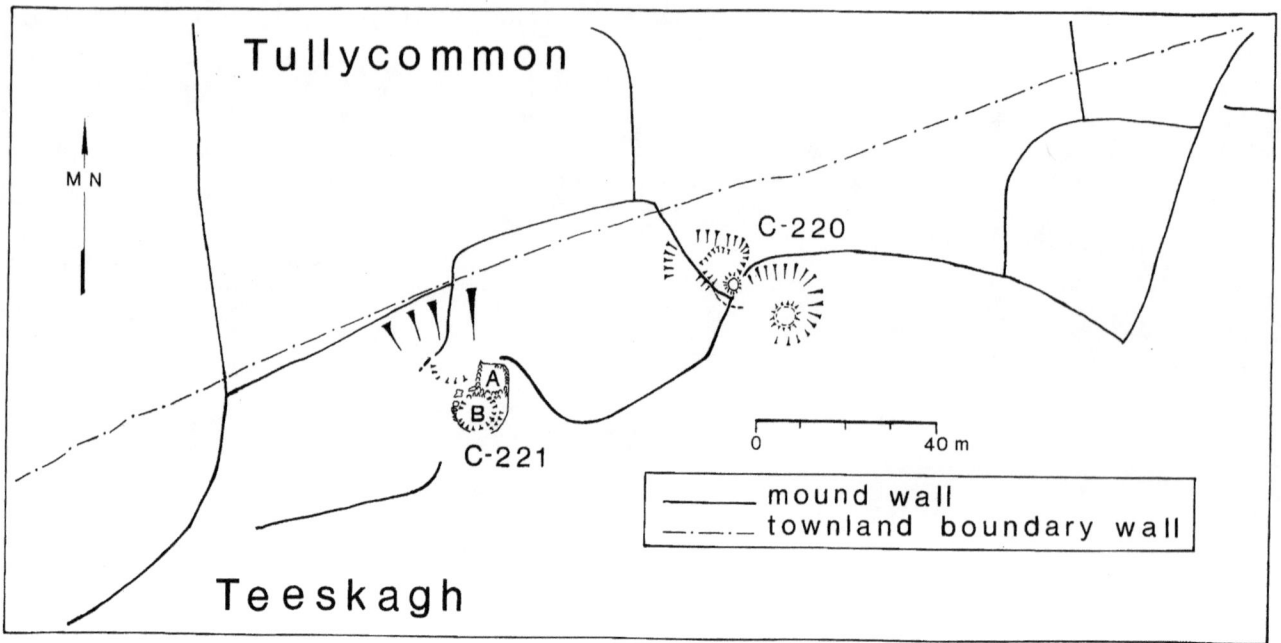

Figure 1. The LN\EBA hut sites of C-220 and C-221 and associated field system.

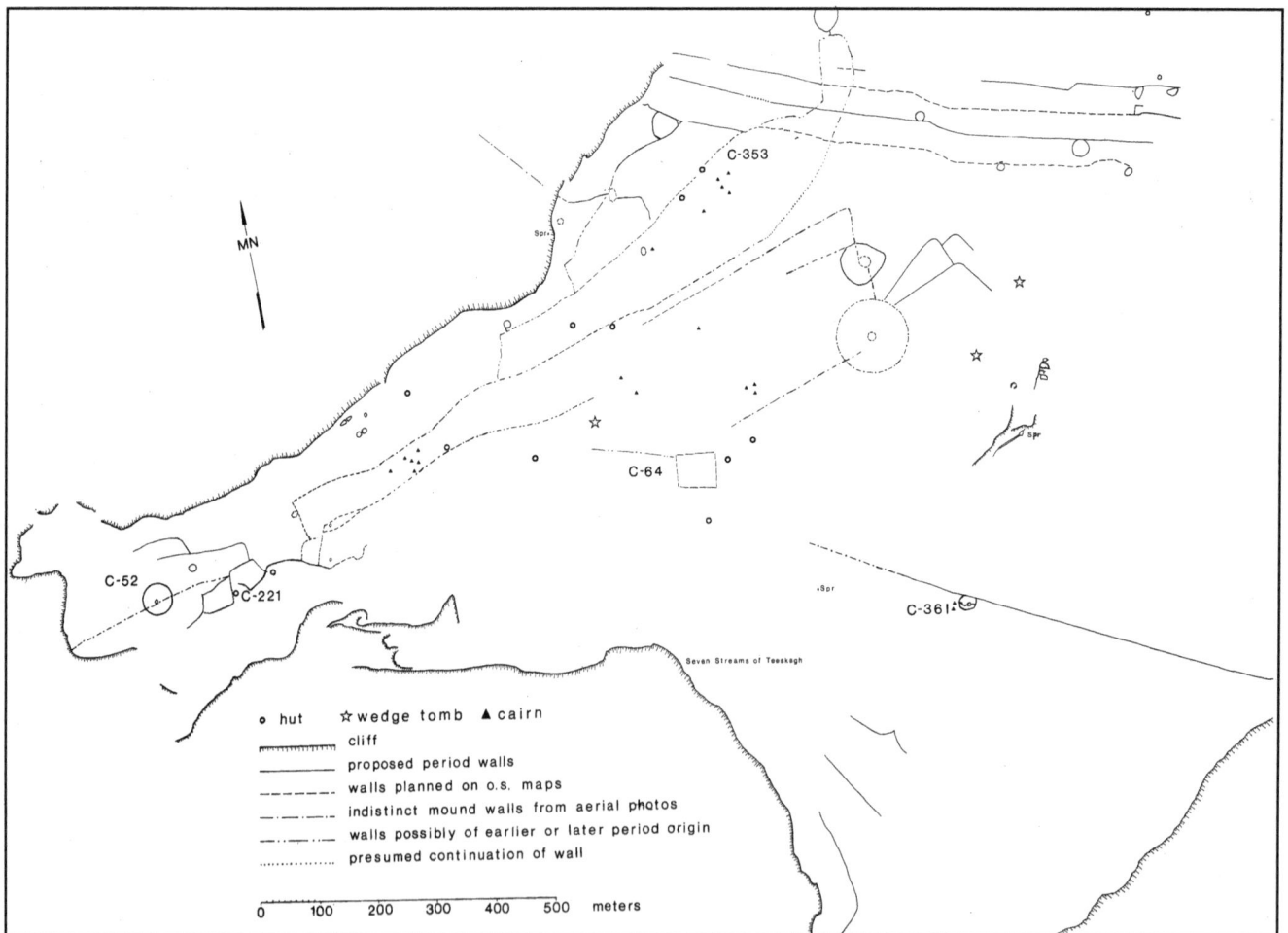

Figure 2. Map of a portion of Tullycommon and Teeskagh townlands, Co. Clare, presenting a somewhat conjectural reconstruction of mound-type field boundary wall systems from survey data and aerial photographs. It is likely that the various field systems depicted are not contemporary. Only a portion of the cairns noted by the Cahercommaun Project are indicated.

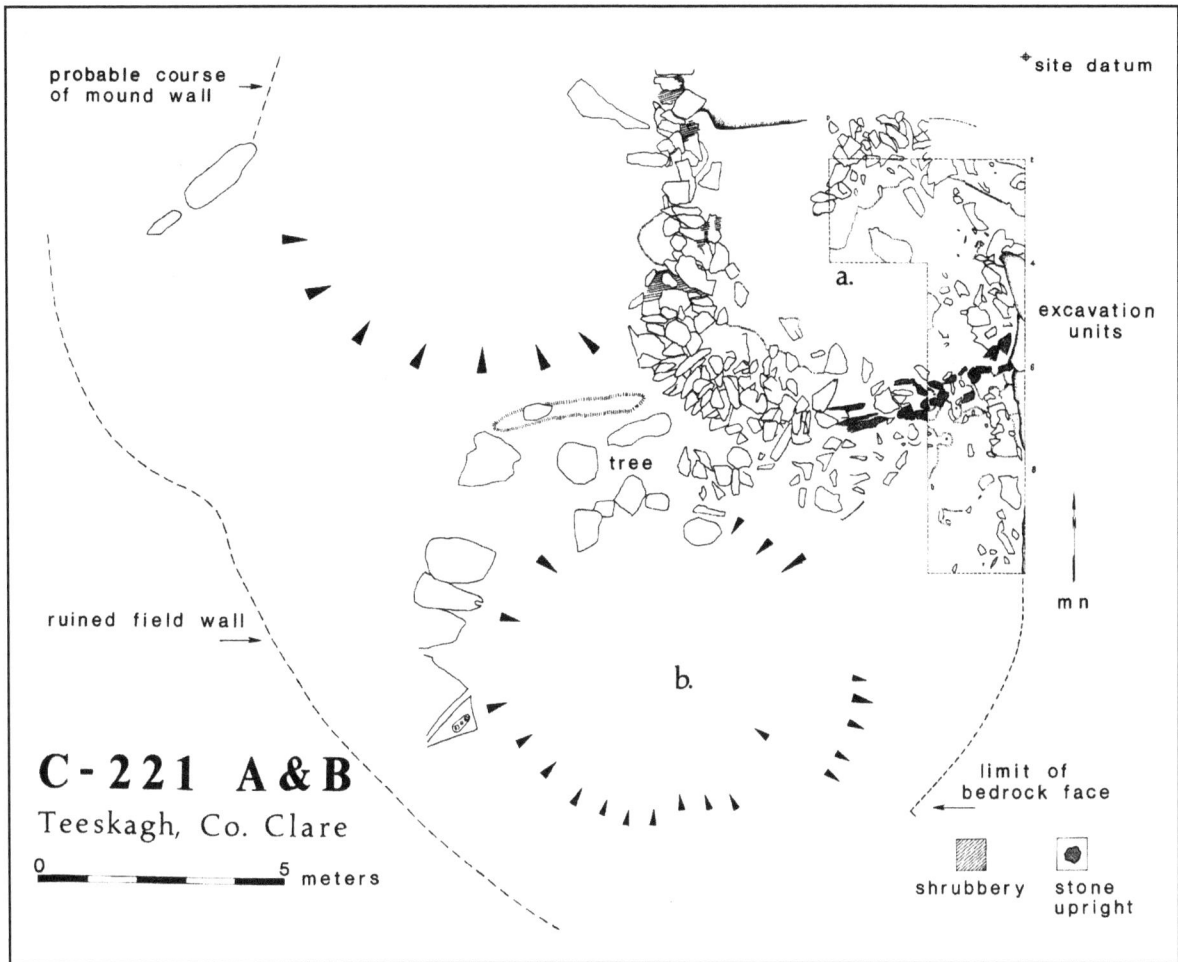

Figure 3. Site map of C-221, Teeskagh Townland.

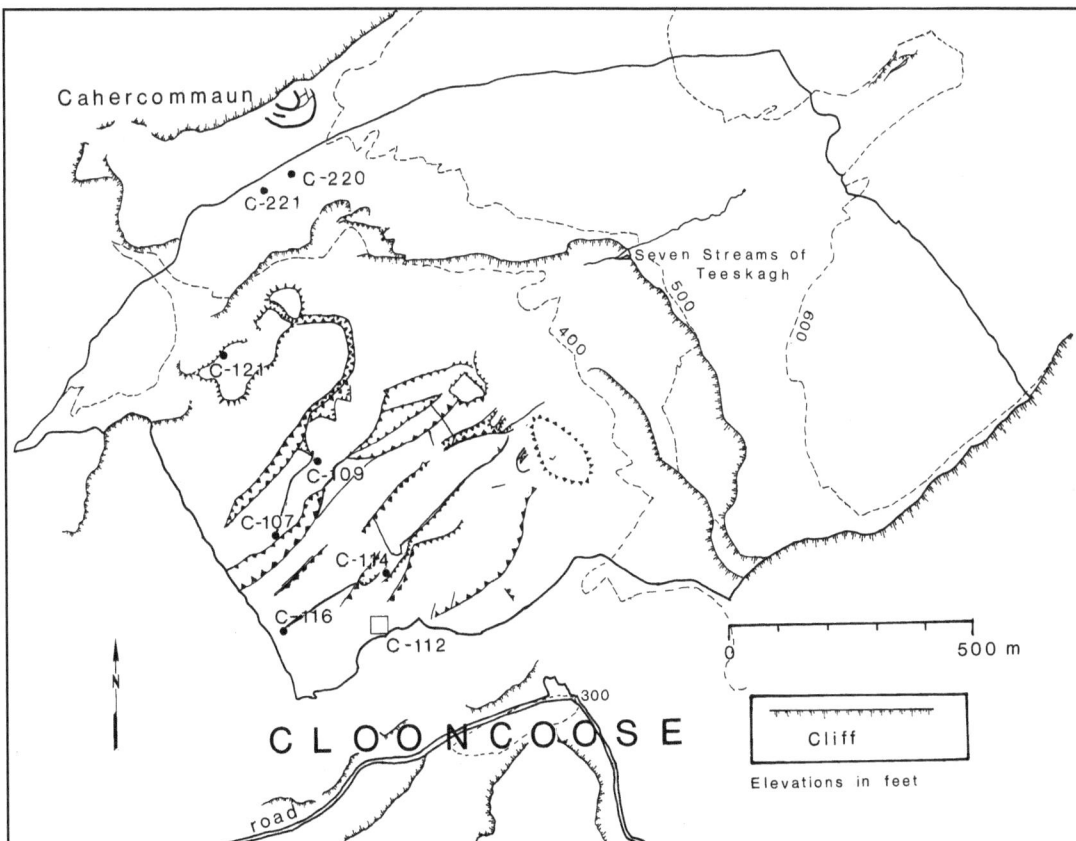

Figure 4. Map of mound and "scattered single stone" types of field boundary walls in the southern section of Teeskagh Townland, Co. Clare.

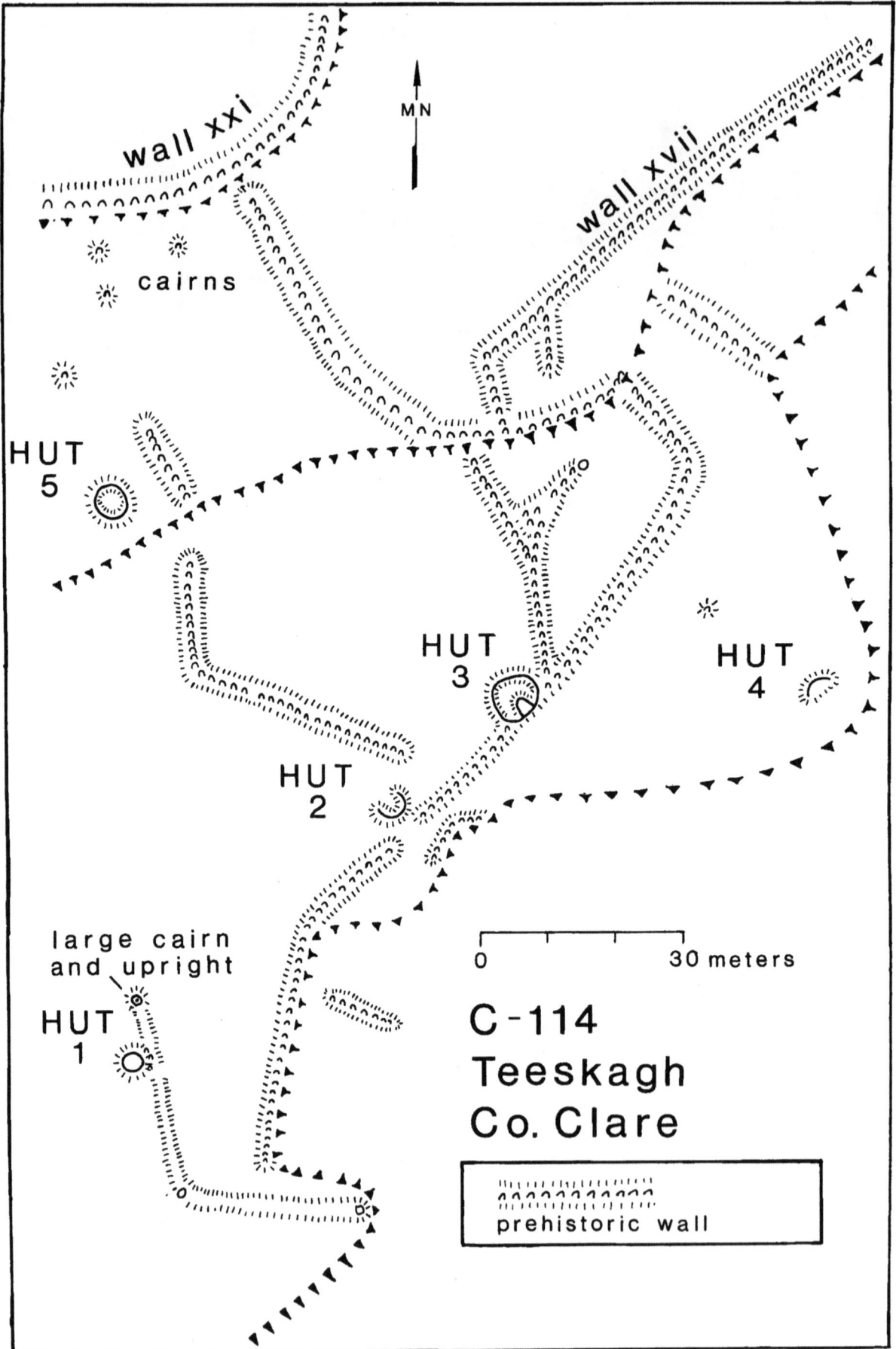

Figure 5. The hut, cairn, and field boundary wall complex of C-114, Teeskagh Townland, Co. Clare.

Table 1: Levels of Socio-cultural Integration and Associated Social and Qualitative Attributes

Level	Social Structure	Leadership	Form of Social Status
Segmentary	**Unranked Lineages**	**Headmen-Bigmen**	**Achieved**
		Prominent Killers	**Achieved**
		Shamans	**Achieved**

Qualitative distinctions:
Clan insignia/symbols, clan meeting houses, ancestor veneration including ancestral shrines/tombs, primitive valuables, community craft specialists.

Level	Social Structure	Leadership	Form of Social Status
Chiefdoms	**Ramage/Conical Clan**	**Chieftains**	**Ascribed**
		Aristocracy	**Ascribed**
		Section Leaders	**Ascribed**
		Judges	**Ascribed**
		Priests	**Ascribed**
		Master Craftsmen	**Ascribed**

Qualitative distinctions:
Lineages as basic corporate social grouping, 2-3 tiered administrative settlement hierarchy, chiefdom central place pattern of settlement, circular external boundary, wedge-shaped internal territories, set capital, ancestor veneration including ancestral shrines/tombs, professional genealogists, attached craft specialists, staple finance, sumptuary patterns of consumption, elite sponsorship of religion, elite-sponsored community-level corporate labor projects, primitive bureaucracy, chiefly demesne territory.

Level	Social Structure	Leadership	Form of Social Status
Primitive State	**Chiefdoms superceded**	**King**	**Ascribed**
	by administrators	**Royal Appointees**	**Achieved**
	and royal family	**Aristocracy**	**Ascribed**
		Chieftains	**Ascribed**
		Ranked Priesthood	**Ascribed**
		Head of Army	**Achieved**
		Judges	**Ascribed**
		Master Craftsmen	**Ascribed**

Qualitative distinctions:
4 tiered administrative hierarchy, royal capital, royal burials, ritual homicide, professional full-time army, taxes and rent, royal demesne territory, irregularly-shaped internal territories.

Table 2: Radiocarbon Dates for C-221

Site and Locus	Material	Laboratory Number	Uncalibrated Date	Calibrated Date
C-221 unit 8S-0W level 5 sample # 16	charcoal	GrN-14390	2530 ± 110 b.c.	3295, 3242, 3104 B.C. (F=3214 B.C.) 3360-2928 B.C.
C-221 unit 8S-0W level 5 general finds*	charcoal	GrN-14389	1800 ± 60 b.c.	2191, 2161, 2145 B.C. (F=2166 B.C.) 2284-2044 B.C.

*chunks of charcoal collected throughout the level

References for datasets [and intervals] used: Pearson and Stuiver 1986; Pearson et al. 1986

Table 3: Animal Teeth from C-221

N = 148 lots*

Bos.................................30.4%	[Cattle]	
Sus..................................29.05%	[Pig]	
Cervus...........................23.65%	[Deer]	
Capra/Ovis....................16.22%	[Goat/Sheep]	
Canis/Lupus.....................0.68%	[Dog/Wolf]	

*Excavated tooth or teeth believed to come from a single individual.

The Four Scales of Technical Analysis;
or, How to Make Archaeometry More Useful

Elizabeth Hamilton

Abstract

Archaeologists deal with the results of laboratory analysis every day, yet frequently ignore the wider cultural implications of the technical facts established by analysis. This paper argues that technical facts should be interpreted on four different scales: the individual actor/producer and his/her choices, the production group and its collection of knowledge and labor organization, the wider culture and the meanings ascribed to what and how artifacts are produced, and the greater interaction areas of cultures and transmission of technologies and values. These ideas are discussed in the context of the European prehistoric and early historic periods.

Archaeology is founded on technology, and that statement has more than one meaning. In the first sense, archaeology—at least good archaeology—cannot be carried out without tools that range from the trowel and tape measure to EDMs (electronic distance measurers), proton magnetometers, and special cameras used for aerial photography. We are accustomed to using tools, measuring things precisely, and welcoming new techniques and machines that we hope will give us more reliable data. Few of us, however, are expert at these things; most of us come from a humanistic background, and we frequently call in specialists in geomorphology, dating, elemental analysis and the like. The data they produce, the detailed laboratory analyses of materials, belong to the field of archaeometry. Though archaeologists use their data, and many archaeometrists are fascinated by the past, few of these specialists have much, if any, archaeological training.

In the second meaning of that initial sentence, the results of technology are what we as archaeologists study. We study objects of a physical nature that have been modified or created by human beings. These things were not created at random or by instinct, but in patterned ways governed by knowledge and technique, ways that can and do vary from culture to culture. The "things" can include artifacts, postholes, butchered bones; we all know what our raw material of study is. From the presence and patterning of these things, this archaeological stuff, we draw conclusions about subsistence, economy, social groups, and the complexity of society.

The small and relatively recent subfield of the "anthropology of technology" is the only movement that tries to integrate these two aspects of archaeology, though it has never been formulated quite that way. But if we as archaeologists have always dealt with technology, then why do we need a special new subfield? Because for most of the history of anthropology, we have operated on an implicit and inadequate definition of "technology". For us, technology has usually meant the artifact and the narrow set of techniques by which it is produced, and the assumption has frequently been that the constraints of the laws of physics are the main determinant in any given technology. Furthermore, there has been a strong strand of technological determinism, the assumption that changes in technology have been autonomous variables that when introduced or discovered, produce social change. Reflective of this is the number of anthropological studies assessing the effect of the introduction of Western technology into various cultures or social groups.

What is a better definition? Technology is comprised of three parts: a system of knowledge, a set of techniques, and the material product. The system of knowledge is held in one or more human heads, and includes not only the rules for the physical manipulation of materials to produce a desired result, but also the rituals, secret knowledge, and forbidden activities that are, in the culture's view, equally necessary for a successful result. The possession of this knowledge also has social consequences. Technique is behavior, the physical activities that produce the result, often called the "know-how". Anyone who has tried to put together a complicated toy just by following the written directions can testify that knowledge and know-how are not the same thing, and anyone who has learned to play a musical instrument knows the difference between knowledge of the mind and bodily competence.

But technology is more than knowledge and bodily action. It is labor organization, raw material procurement, invention and transmission of new techniques and knowledge, and even the disposal of the waste materials and finally the product. And above all, it is the system of values and meanings attached to the knowledge, the activities, the producers, and the products. Does the knowledge give special status? How are knowledge and techniques transmitted to others, and who is forbidden to participate? How is the technology congruent with other technologies and cultural assumptions about the world? What about how the product was valued? Western societies do and have for millennia valued metal for its hardness, durability, sharpness, and ability to be shaped, and we assume this is universal. But Heather Lechtman's (1993) work on the Andes demonstrates that the Inca valued metal, especially gold and silver, primarily for its color, for these colors reflected—and may have contributed to—their iconography of the sun and moon. Many of the utilitarian tasks assigned to metal in the Old World were in the Andes assumed by stone and fiber technology: weapons were maces and woven slings, armor was made of cloth, foot plows were of cord and stone (Lechtman 1993:252-256).

The point is, as Pfaffenberger (1988:241) says, that "technology is not an independent, non-social variable that has an 'impact' on society or culture. On the contrary, any technology *is* a set of social behaviors and a system of meanings".

So all this talk is fine, but how do we tease out information about labor organization, status, and especially values and meanings, especially in prehistory? The answer lies in archaeometry, the detailed laboratory and field analysis of materials and processes. This is necessary because only at this level can we discover what Sackett (1990:33) terms "isochrestic variation", the range of functionally equivalent ways of manufacturing or using a material object. While physical laws constrain technological practices, they do not dictate them, for there are usually many ways to achieve any given result. While you need 1083 ^{0}C and a reducing atmosphere to smelt copper, there are innumerable ways to design your furnace and treat your ores to achieve this result. In the first millennia BC and AD, Westerners made steel by forging, producing at low heat a bloom of pure iron and slowly infusing it with carbon. The Chinese used a completely different technology. From high heat furnaces they made cast iron, which has too much carbon, and carefully de-carburised it to make usable steel. These are two radically different methods, requiring different knowledge, labor organizations, and techniques, but ending in the same product. "Isochrestic variations" are all the possible ways to achieve a given physical result, and these variations are *culturally* chosen. The smelting temperature of 1083 ^{0}C is required; the furnace shape, number of laborers, choice of fuel, rituals, and virtually anything else is subject to choice. Detailed laboratory analysis, plus equally necessary replication experiments that throw light on the required gestures and know-how, is the only way to establish what aspects of the technology are subject to culturally significant variation. It is also the detailed laboratory analysis that can establish not only what can be done to the material, but what was done: the alloy compositions, the conditions of ceramic firing, the efficacy of two different axe designs.

Why Archaeologists Don't Fully Use Archaeometry

For archaeologists, opening a journal of archaeometry can be an intimidating experience. Few of us come from scientific backgrounds, and these articles, filled with esoteric bits of chemistry and physics and mineralogy, are largely incomprehensible to us. So we turn quickly to the conclusion and discover that, for instance, glass made at one Irish site had a tin oxide additive. The question now comes, what do we do with this information? It used to be that technical information could safely be left in an appendix of our site report, but now we know that we are supposed to integrate these findings into our conclusions, that somehow we are supposed to use data about alloy compositions and kiln temperatures and isotope analyses to answer interesting archaeological questions about culture and meaning and society. The question is, how?

The archaeometrists themselves will give us little help. Though the situation is changing, and more archaeometrists are using their own data to answer archaeological questions (see Sillar 2000; Sillar and Tite 2000; Smith 2000), few have

any archaeological training, and they rarely display any awareness that there are archaeological questions to be answered beyond "how and where was this artifact made?" Indeed, the viewpoint of many archaeometrists can be found in the introduction to the 872-page *Materials Issues in Art and Archaeology II*, published in 1991, where the editors write

> Our point of view is that the understanding of how, why, and from what objects were made involves a study of behavior which is a corollary to the empathetic understanding and sense of wonder derived from viewing the objects. (Vandiver and Wheeler 1991:xxii)

As Robert Dunnell (1993:164) points out, these scholars appear to be attracted mainly to "the non-scientific archaeology of the Sunday newspaper's feature section," with no understanding of the kind of evidence that would be useful in answering questions about culture.

So this leaves quite a gulf, with archaeologists on one side largely without training in physical science and archaeometrists on the other largely without training in modern archaeology. Since most of the archaeometrists seem to be perfectly happy doing technical history, it is up to archaeologists to determine how archaeometrical data can be made more useful to us.

As I see it, there are four levels of analysis possible. You can, if you wish, construct levels of scale of the analysis itself, from microscopic to macroscopic, but the levels of analysis I refer to deal with the levels of culture that one can explicate with the help of archaeometrical data. To begin with, artifacts are the products of individuals. They can be skilled or unskilled, careless, inventive or simply unlucky. The individual is most clearly seen in the flawed and unsuccessful products that were frequently discarded as trash after they were made. So, artifacts are records of individuals with varying levels of skill, care, and special knowledge. An example is Ehrenreich's (1985) discovery that in the Late Iron Age of Britain, knowledge of carburizing and quenching iron to make good steel was confined to only a very few sites, suggesting that this was proprietary knowledge passed down in families.

The second level is that of the production group, which is the collection of people that possess pieces of the knowledge and technique. They are the raw material procurers, the charcoal-makers, the kiln designers, the masters of workshops, the smelters, the specialists who perform the necessary rituals. Sometimes one person will have all the knowledge, know-how, and access to the raw materials necessary; more often the finished artifacts are the result of the collaboration of discrete groups, all of whom have some idea of the goal but only a portion of the necessary knowledge and access.

The third level is that of the wider culture, which assigns status to the workers, the activities, and the final results and which, of course, uses the artifacts. The producers operate within a nexus of values that are attributed to their work; for the archaeologist, these values can sometimes be discerned by examining how the artifact was made and the uses to which it was put. For instance, Heather Lechtman (1993) was able to discover not just the high value the Inca placed on gold and silver, which was already known, but also the high value they put on the integrity of the metal: the Inca did not plate gold over a copper core, instead they developed techniques to make gold-copper alloys look like gold, insisting that the material actually contain gold. Epstein (1993) demonstrated the equally high value the Inca metalworkers put on using human breath rather than bellows to smelt metal.

The fourth level of analysis is what I would call the interaction area. In the case of Iron Age Europe, for instance, the interaction area would include the Celts, the Germans, and the peoples of the Mediterranean, the Middle East, and the steppes—the areas where ideas, artifacts, and people circulated. Here we can look at trade and technology transmission: what kinds of technological knowledge spread, how it spread, under what conditions and how the values assigned to the technology and products changed as the knowledge spread.

But can laboratory work really be used on these four scales, particularly at prehistoric sites? In a word, yes. Using elemental analysis and optical metallography, I studied 120 copper-alloy artifacts from the site of the Titelberg, a Late Iron Age to Late Roman period *oppidum* in the Duchy of Luxembourg (Hamilton 1996). The artifacts dated from *circa* 100 BC to AD 300, a period that covered the invasions of Julius Caesar and the incorporation of this area (Belgic Gaul) into the Roman Empire. I set out merely to see what changes in technology might have occurred during this time of enormous political and cultural change. But, using this laboratory technology, I was able to document not only the first known use of brass in transalpine Europe (possibly the result of a single coppersmith melting down brass coins derived from Asia Minor), but also the existence of not one but two sociotechnical systems that arose around this new alloy. By my own analyses and other published analytical work, plus excavated evidence from the Titelberg and Bibracte (an *oppidum* in central France), and a small amount of written evidence, I was able to show that the new alloy was derived from different ore sources than contemporary bronze alloys, had a specialized labor organization, and was accorded different values and meanings in Gaul than in Imperial Rome. I was also able to show that these new sociotechnical systems disappeared at the end of the first century after Christ, when brass lost its special significance and was melted down and mixed indiscriminately with other copper-based metal. In this case, archaeometry enabled me to capture not only changes in material artifacts, but also changes in labor organization, and even more interesting, the creation and disappearance of meanings and values attached to new materials. In addition, I could show the probability of contact between Belgica and Asia Minor and the transmission of artifacts and technological knowledge that was used to produce products very different from those of the donor culture.

Some might argue that this is possible only in a situation, such as the Gallo-Roman period, where we have a comparatively large amount of archaeological and textual evidence. But the value of archaeometry is that much of this can be done on prehistoric and protohistoric sites; our use of archaeometrical data has been limited simply because we have not asked enough of the right questions. For an example of the kinds of questions that can be asked, I offer an article by Henderson and Ivens that appeared in the March 1992 issue of *Antiquity*. The article concerned the excavation and analysis of a small, probably monastic, early medieval site in Northern Ireland called Dunmisk. In addition to some evidence of metalworking, analysis of glass artifacts and crucibles indicated that glass making, as opposed to glass working, was practiced there. This is the earliest evidence for glass making found in Ireland, where most glass working was assumed to be done with recycled glass brought in from abroad. Analysis of the additives in the glass also suggested the survival of Celtic glass technological habits rather than imported Roman ones.

The authors have already gone well beyond the scope of the typical archaeometrical article to make broader conclusions about glass making versus glass working in medieval Ireland and the retention of pre-Roman technology. In that sense, they have done half our work for us, and their article is an excellent case study for those interested in society and technology in Ireland. Nonetheless, we can go further, using their technical data and conclusions as springboards for related but wider questions that touch upon all aspects of society. I hope the questions below can serve as examples of the kinds of questions, many answerable by purely archaeological or archaeometrical means, which can be asked of archaeometrical data.

According to the article, Dunmisk contained a cemetery with some 500 graves, a series of what seem to have been temporary residences, a church or shrine, and two industrial areas, one of which had slag and small furnaces probably used for iron smelting and the other containing remains of molds, crucibles, and debris resulting from the production of glass and copper alloy artifacts. The C^{14} dates suggest occupation from the 6th to the 10th centuries AD.

At the individual level: Who was making this glass? From study and replication experiments, do we know if a single individual could have produced it? What were the exact sequence of activities necessary to make this glass, the *chaîne opératoire*, and what isochrestic variations could exist? What was the status of a glass-worker? Did they work in a master-apprentice model? Were there mobile glassmakers and workers or did small sites have their own, as many seemed to have ironsmiths? Were they attached to monasteries and nobles? What did they eat? Did they have to supply their own food? If the residences were temporary, where did they live the rest of the time? Did they produce their own tools?

At the production group level: Where and how was the raw material procured? The raw materials were: silica, soda, lime, tin-oxide, sodium oxide, lead oxide, and calcium carbonate. Who controlled access to these? Where did each of these materials come from? Who mined/produced them and what was their industrial organization? Who controlled access to them? How much energy and organization was necessary to obtain the raw materials? Who produced the additives such as lead-tin oxide? Who made the crucibles and other tools? If some of the raw material was from recycled glass, where did that originate? What was the relationship between the glass-workers/makers and the metalsmiths, given that some artifacts were glass inlayed onto metal? What kinds of sites show evidence of glass working, as opposed to glass making?

How did the glass technology compare with metalworking and pottery making, since all three are pyrotechnological activities? All are malleable materials; were they worked in the same style and using the same techniques? Using similar tools? What distinguishes glass-working sites from other pyrotechnological sites? Was there a hierarchy of sites involved in making glass products in relation to other industries?[1] Where did the raw material for the furnaces come from? The charcoal? Who controlled access to forest wood? Was the wood coppiced (i.e. grown and managed to produce shoots of a small diameter)? How far away was the raw fuel? Did they use peat as fuel and if so, who cut it and controlled it?

At the societal level: What were the meanings and values attached to glass and various forms of glass in Early Christian Ireland? What was glass used for? Religious articles, cheap jewelry, expensive jewelry, bookbindings? Is there a difference in the use of glass between pagan groups and Christian groups? What is the distribution of glass at Irish sites and in what contexts are they found? Are there regional differences in use and context?

Henderson and Ivens (1992) indicate that there was some evidence of the preservation of specifically Celtic techniques (i.e. the use of lead-tin oxide to make the glass opaque). Were other aspects preserved, such as motifs or labor organization? How were the Celtic and Roman technologies combined? Did Celtic techniques appear in other areas, such as metalworking or ceramics? How long did this Celtic technique survive? Did it differ across Ireland? Was lead-tin oxide also used in Britain? How long was it used in Ireland?

At the level of the interaction area: What was the proportion of glass worked in early medieval Ireland that came from overseas?[1] Who organized and participated in the trading networks necessary to bring cullet glass (i.e. broken or scrap glass) across the sea? Did these trading networks work the same as other trading? Where did the cullet come from? Why make your own glass instead of just relying on imported recycled glass? Which is easier under which contexts? Was there a different valuation of imported glass and locally produced glass? Was there a different valuation of glass from the Mediterranean and glass from nearby lands?

Did Irish techniques spread later on? Where else was lead-tin oxide used? How did the Irish glassmakers acquire their knowledge of glass production? Did the valuation, use, and technology of glass in Ireland differ from elsewhere in Europe, especially in early Viking Scandinavia where Henderson and Ivens (1992) note that glass making was approximately contemporaneous with that in Dunmisk? What was the pattern of technological interaction in general in Western Europe?

Many of these questions, ranging from the individual to the interaction sphere, can be answered by archaeometry and most do not require any written sources. I hope this list of questions gives archaeologists some idea of the extraordinary potential usefulness of archaeometry to address wider archaeological problems.

Biographical Sketch

Elizabeth Hamilton received her doctorate from the University of Pennsylvania in 1995. Her dissertation dealt with changes in metallurgical technique, production, and ideology in Belgic Gaul during the period of the invasions of Julius Caesar and the subsequent incorporation of the region into the Roman Empire. She subsequently worked on a Viking period iron-smelting site in Iceland and is currently examining the use of bronze and iron materials from prehistoric Thailand.

References Cited

Dunnell, Robert 1993 'Why archaeologists don't care about archaeometry' *Archeomaterials* 7:161-165.

Ehrenreich, Robert 1985 *Trade, Technology and the Ironworking Community in the Iron Age of Southern Britain* British Archaeological Reports, British Series 144 (Oxford).

Epstein, Steven M. 1993 *Cultural Choice and Technological Consequences: Constraint of Innovation in the Late Prehistoric Copper Smelting Industry of Cerro Huaringa, Peru.* Unpublished Ph.D. dissertation, University of Pennsylvania (Philadelphia).

Hamilton, Elizabeth 1996 *Technology and Social Change in Belgic Gaul: Copper Working at the Titelberg, Luxembourg, 125 B.C. - A.D. 300* MASCA Research Papers in Science and Archaeology, Volume 13, University of Pennsylvania Museum of Archaeology and Anthropology (Philadelphia).

Henderson, Julian and Richard Ivens 1992 'Dunmisk and glass-making in Early Christian Ireland' *Antiquity* 66:52-64.

Lechtman, Heather 1993 'Technologies of power: the Andean case' in J.S. Henderson and P.J. Netherly (eds) *Configurations of Power in Complex Society* Cornell University Press (Ithaca, NY):244-280.

Pfaffenberger, Bryan 1988 'Fetishised objects and humanised nature: towards an anthropology of technology' *Man* N.S. 23:236-252.

Sackett, James R. 1990 'Style and ethnicity in archaeology: the case for isochrestism' in M.W. Conkey and C.A. Hastorf (eds) *The Uses of Style in Archaeology* Cambridge University Press (Cambridge): 32-43.

Sillar, B. 2000 'Dung by preference: the choice of fuel as an example of how Andean pottery production is embedded within wider technical, social, and economic practices' *Archaeometry* 42 (1):43-60.

Sillar, B. and M.S. Tite 2000 'The challenge of "technological choices" for materials science approaches in archaeology' *Archaeometry* 42 (1):2-20.

Smith, A. Livingstone 2000 'Processing clay for pottery in northern Cameroon: social and technical requirements' *Archaeometry* 42 (1):21-42.

Vandiver P.B. and G.S. Wheeler 1991 'Introduction to materials issues in art and archaeology' in P. Vandiver, J. Druzik, and G.S. Wheeler (eds) *Materials Issues in Art and Archaeology II* Materials Research Society Symposium Proceedings, V. 185 (Pittsburgh, PA):xvii-xxvi.

---

[1] Henderson and Ivens (1992:61) also ask this.

Faces in a Crowd or a Crowd of Faces?
Archaeological Evidence for Individual and Group Identity
in Early Anglo-Saxon East Anglia

Genevieve Fisher

Abstract

It has been argued that during the period of early Anglo-Saxon kingdom formation (circa AD 450-650), competition for power resulted in stylistic freedom, as vying groups attempted to express themselves through distinctive material culture. A multiscalar analysis of female dress ornaments derived from early Anglo-Saxon cemeteries in East Anglia indicates that differential patterning can be identified at the level of the individual, site, and region. Despite the heterogeneity evident in individual ensembles of dress fasteners, their overall composition is constrained, suggesting the existence of conflicting interests between the individual and the group during this period of political consolidation.

The social group has long been the primary unit of study for archaeologists. Whether defined archaeologically by material culture patterning, described in the historical record, or inferred from linguistic or biological affinity, social groups have provided archaeologists with an organizing structure and a set of analytical categories by which to address broader questions of the human condition. Because of the generalizing goals of archaeological inquiry, individuals have often been reduced to society writ small (Meskell 1998:152-153, 157-159; 2000:20).

However, increasing attention has recently been paid to the role of the individual in relations of power within and across social groups (e.g. Brumfiel 1992; Costin 1999; DeBoer 1990; Dobres 1999; Dobres and Hoffman 1994; Handsman and Leone 1989; Pauketat 2000). Although historically dependent and culturally variable (Dobres and Robb 2000:13; Meskell 1998:152-153, 157-159; 2000:18; Moore 1994:33-35; Tarlow 1999), the concept of individualism has deep roots in the European past (Childe 1958:162-173; Macfarlane 1978; Treherne 1995).

In this paper, one element of early Anglo-Saxon women's costume, brooches, will be explored to show how the tension between individual and group identities was articulated. Specifically, the conflicts and contradictions between individual and group interests will be elucidated through multiscalar analysis (Chapman 2000; Dobres 1999; Marquardt 1992).

The Anglo-Saxon Social and Political Landscape

Archaeological and documentary evidence indicate that in the 5th and 6th centuries AD, the political landscape of early Anglo-Saxon England was characterized by "broadly-equal, internally-ranked patrilineal and patrilocal descent groups farming or exploiting ancestral territories" (Scull 1999:21), with cemetery evidence, in particular, indicating the significance of age, gender, and lineage differences (Härke 1997; Scull 1993). Control of these popular groupings was administered through personal ties of obligation and domination (Scull 1992, 1999). Warfare, alliance, marriage, and population growth all contributed to the accumulation and control of territory and resources by individuals and affiliated kin-groups. Elites manipulated ideology, cultural identity, land organiza-

tion, and access to trading partners in order to create and legitimize new axes of authority (Scull 1999:22). Neighboring groups, sometimes retaining their folk-identity even as they forfeited their political autonomy, were absorbed into expansionist entities (Scull 1992).

By the early 7th century, these local affiliations, based in the extended family, were submerged by quasi-ethnic regional polities, presaging the formal kingdoms of the later Anglo-Saxon period. Archaeological and textual sources indicate that military success, strategic alliances with other polities, and effective royal administration endowed the East Anglian rulers of this period with exceptional power and wealth (Yorke 1990:58-71).[1]

East Anglian Dress and Identity

Among furnished inhumations, the types of dress ornaments and their positions on the body have been associated with ethnic differences among the traditional areas of the Angles, Saxons, and Jutes. Recently, changes in insular Anglian dress have been considered within the context of English nationhood (Carver 1989; Hines 1993: 90-93; 1994; 1999:141-143). The appearance of regional costume in East Anglia "can be seen as . . . acknowledgment of ideological allegiance to the supernatural nation to which these settlers believed they belonged" (Carver 1989:157). The emergence and spread of insular Anglian identity may be represented by the increasing popularity of certain dress accessories, such as small-long brooches (Hines 1994:52-53) and wrist-clasps (Hines 1993:90-93). The potency of these ornaments to articulate Anglian identity is indicated by the unwillingness of communities to the south or west to adopt them without translation into their own local idiom of dress. In Kent and Sussex, for example, wrist-clasps appear to have functioned on occasion not as sleeve-closures but rather, after re-fitting, as brooches or pendants (Craddock 1979:88; Hines 1984:103) and Anglian

---

[1] Note that the Anglo-Saxons themselves framed accounts of the dynastic foundations of their kingdoms within Germanic oral conventions, thereby obscuring the actual circumstances of political centralization (Yorke 1993). For example, written sources, such as Bede's *Ecclesiastical History* and Felix's *Life of St. Guthlac*, both dating to the first half of the 8th century, provide retrospective and occasionally fanciful genealogical and regnal details.

narrow-band annular brooches were remade into secondary functions as suspension rings (Down and Welch 1990:98, fig. 2.22, 15/1; Evison 1987:49; 1994:7). With no Anglian costume to adorn, these dress ornaments found new uses within other regional costumes. Thus, the invented traditions of women's clothing in the 5th and 6th centuries spoke to the political concerns of emerging kingdoms.[2] Furthermore, as will be discussed below, the selection of specific types of brooches worn by early Anglo-Saxon women and the combination of these brooches into idiosyncratic dress sets articulated a tension between individual expression and community conformity.[3]

Anglian Dress Style

During the 5th and 6th centuries, East Anglian women wore a Germanic-style costume adorned with beads and brooches (Owen-Crocker 1986:25-64; Vierck 1978). The primary garment was a tunic dress (*peplos*) secured at both shoulders by small, generally similar brooches. Although the classic *peplos* is sleeveless, the presence of wrist-clasps in early Anglo-Saxon England indicates that Anglian women wore either a long-sleeved version of this dress (Hines 1997:281) or a sleeved under-dress beneath its sleeveless variant (Vierck 1978). One or more strands of beads were often worn between, and occasionally strung from, the shoulder brooches. The presence of a third, often larger, brooch at the neck, shoulder, or chest of the woman either fastened the under-dress to the tunic or closed a heavier outer cloak. The tunic would usually have been cinched by a belt on or below the waist. Suspended from the waist, a woman may have carried an array of amuletic or scrap metal oddments, copper alloy girdle hangers, or iron or copper alloy keys.

The Burial Evidence

This study examines brooches from 106 undisturbed female inhumation burials from six East Anglian cemeteries in use primarily from the mid 5th to mid 6th century (**Figure 1**): Morning Thorpe (Green et al. 1987), Bergh Apton (Green and Rogerson 1978), and Spong Hill (Carr et al. 1970-1973; Hills 1977, 1989; Hills and Penn 1981; Hills et al. 1984; McKinley 1994) in Norfolk and Little Eriswell (Briscoe and Le Bard 1960; Hutchinson 1966), Westgarth Gardens (West 1985), and Holywell Row (Lethbridge 1931) in Suffolk (**Figure 2**).

Eight different types of brooches appeared singly, or in combination, in these East Anglian graves: annular, cruciform, disc, equal-armed, penannular, quoit, small-long, and square-headed (**Table 1**). Annular, cruciform, and small-long brooches were most frequently encountered, occurring in 70% (n = 74), 31% (n = 33), and 19% (n = 20) of the burials, respectively.

Analysis was undertaken at two distinct levels: the cemetery (or social/community group) and the burial (or individual).

The Crowd of Faces: The Community

Within the Anglian area of culture, the existence of localized dress styles (*pace* Hines 1992:86) and perhaps newly constituted cultural differences is suggested by the lack of co-occurrence of certain brooches. For example, wearing annular and small-long brooches was essentially mutually exclusive, as was wearing square-headed and cruciform brooches (**Tables 2** and **3**). In both cases, these forms of brooches—the lighter-weight annular and small-long brooches worn at the shoulders, and the heavier, more ornate square-headed and cruciform brooches generally worn on the chest—were functional equivalents. The rarity of dress sets combining annular with small-long brooches and cruciform with square-headed brooches implies a widely appreciated grammar of costume elements manifested as alternate dress styles.

At this larger scale of analysis, community preferences for specific brooch types were assessed using the Fisher exact test to compare frequencies between each pair of sites in this study (**Table 4**).[4] Site-level results for all brooch types were summarized as simple matching coefficients.[5] Only 7% of the 92 tests performed produced results statistically significant at the 0.05 level. In view of the 0.05 probability of Type I errors, these results must be interpreted conservatively. However, it should be noted that most of the significant results referred to annular brooches, comparisons of which proved significant in 33.3% of the site-level tests. The area of greatest discrepancy in preferred brooch types occurred between the River Lark cemeteries of Holywell Row, Westgarth Gardens, and Little Eriswell, on the one hand, and the other East Anglian cemeteries of Morning Thorpe and Bergh Apton on the other hand. The affinity of Spong Hill to both groups of sites may in some measure be related to Spong Hill's proximity to the Breckland, a sandy region that served as a corridor between the Lark valley and the East Anglia interior (West 1998:261). The Lark area grave repertoires less frequently included annular brooches and more often contained equal-armed brooches than did those recorded for the other East Anglian sites (**Table 5**).

These localized brooch preferences appear with greatest clarity in the burials of children furnished with single brooches. Although only six such graves were included in the sample, all three burials containing single small-long brooches belonged to the River Lark sites of Holywell Row and Little Eriswell and those furnished with single annular brooches were found at Morning Thorpe and Spong Hill. This distribution suggests that children could be perceived from birth as embodied

---

[2] Similarly, the inclusion of weapons in male burial deposits has been interpreted as a component in the creation of Germanic origin (Hedeager 1993) or conquest (Härke 1990, 1992) myths.

[3] For a literary presentation of this conflict, see Herschend (1992).

[4] The Fisher exact test calculates the probability of obtaining the observed frequencies of a selected variable under the null hypothesis of randomness. It has the advantage over the *chi*-square test of suitability to small samples and to moderate-sized samples with very small marginals (Blalock 1979:297). These factors were crucial to the selection of the Fisher exact test here, as many of the expected and marginal frequencies in the brooch data set were one or less. The more conservative Fisher exact test is less vulnerable to Type I errors, in which a significant relationship is claimed where one does not actually exist, than is the *chi*-square test (Blalock 1979:296-297).

[5] The simple matching coefficient, calculated as $^{s}sm = m/m + u$, where m = number of matched cells and u = number of unmatched cells, summarizes as a numerical value between 0 and 1 the amount of similarity between paired dichotomous samples (Sokal and Sneath 1963:133), here each group of sites.

members of a local community.

Faces in the Crowd: The Individual

By adjusting the scale of analysis to the individual burial, a more nuanced patterning in brooch frequencies was observed. Within individual burials, the structure of brooch sets was first examined by recording their composition in terms of like and unlike brooches, regardless of specific type. Nine differently structured sets were so identified.[6] No statistically significant associations between particular brooch sets and sites were evident.

Greater variability was encountered by next examining the combinations of types of brooches constituting these sets. Here, twenty-nine different combinations of brooch types were identified.[7] 57% (n brooch combinations = 17; n graves = 17) of these brooch ensembles were unique and another 21% (n brooch combinations = 6, n graves = 12) were encountered only twice. 21% (n = 22) of the burials in the study incorporated such idiosyncratic brooch combinations. The females buried with these unique brooch ensembles were, with one exception, all adults (p = 0.09, n = 50, *chi*-square = 2.94), suggesting that expressive freedom, perhaps marking social alliances, was considered appropriate with advancing age. While age appears to have been a constitutive factor of individual identity, wealth was of less significance. The burial assemblages accompanying these unique brooch ensembles did not differ significantly in the number of grave furnishings from those found with more common ensembles (p = .23, n = 106, *t*-test = -1.20), indicating that this freedom in brooch selection was not simply a prerogative of the elite.

The distribution of these unique brooch ensembles, localized at the individual, did not vary at the broader scale of site or area. This contrast between community conformity and individual autonomy suggests that the vocabulary and the grammar of costume voiced different social identities.

Shifting Fields of Vision

Within social groups, common cultural knowledge affords individuals the latitude to enjoy complex and ambiguous relationships which find their materialization in a personal idiom. The bounty of brooch combinations becomes understandable as the expression within the local language of costume of the interests of individual women and of the kin-group responsible for interment. This freedom to create new brooch ensembles may not be unconnected with the inventiveness and ambiguity expressed within the decorative metalwork designs themselves (Avent 1984) and echoed in the diversity of the costume assemblages outfitting female burials (Brush 1988:70; Stoodley

1999a:101; 1999b:79-82). Moreover, expressive variation need not have been restricted to the addition or subtraction of dress ornaments. Ethnographic analogy (Messing 1978) suggests that, through different arrangements of fabric, the un-fitted *peplos* garment and cloak may also have provided a rich source of communicative detail.

Despite the heterogeneity evident in the individual ensembles of brooches, their overall composition is clearly constrained, conveying an almost formulaic character to Anglian dress. The resulting tension between the apparent rigidity in the overall structure of the brooch sets and the apparent freedom enjoyed through the brooch combinations suggests the existence of conflicting interests between the individual or kin-group and the wider community. A desire to express diverse social affiliations through the incorporation of specific brooch types in the burial assemblage may have been more compelling for the mourners than compliance with a regional orthodoxy of dress. Through the number and variety of brooches interred with an individual woman, the living reinforced their links to the deceased as well as acknowledged her personal and familial relationships with a social community extending from the present into the mythic past.

The diversity of women's burial assemblages, which increased during the late 5th and 6th centuries, was replaced during the 7th century by simpler and more utilitarian grave furnishings (Stoodley 1999b:82-83). Group concerns, at least as mediated through dress and mortuary treatment, now extended across the Anglo-Saxon dominated area. This transition may be in some measure connected with structural changes which occurred in the political system (Carver 1989:158) and in the religious and economic authorities (Geake 1992:93) as sources of power shifted from kinship to kingship. The decline in furnished burial for women, followed by that among men, may indicate the changing importance of gender within the political arena. Of interest in this context is the suggestion that the suppression of ostentatious wealth or elaborate funerary rituals may serve to sublimate kin interests in favor of those promulgated by a centralized political authority (Coontz and Henderson 1986:152; Gailey 1987: 44-45).

The rise of political hegemonies is widely thought to affect gender relations. Remarks Elizabeth Brumfiel (1996:146):

> [T]he rulers of states will always make an effort to subordinate women because the control of women is both a metaphor and a mechanism for the state's control over kinship-based households.

Compliance is rarely embraced by those individuals who stand to lose their sovereignty. Areas of control may be contested (Hastorf 1991; Silverblatt 1988:452) or alternative routes to power sought (Gilchrist 1994; Pollock 1991). Moreover, while conforming to a gender ideology that limits female agency, women may use material culture to focus attention upon themselves (Gibbs 1987:88; Hodder 1982:69) or to elaborate a self-consciously feminine identity (Cohodas 1997:28-34; Gilchrist 1994:167-169; hooks 1991:41-43). The standardized grammar of brooch sets may have articulated interests in a shared regional identity. The multitude of idiosyncratic brooch

---

[6] Brooch Set Types: 1. Singleton; 2. Matched pair; 3. Unmatched pair; 4. Matched pair with unmatched singleton; 5. Matched triplet; 6. Unmatched triplet; 7. Unmatched triplet with different singleton; 8. Matched quartet; 9. Matched pair with different matched triplet.

[7] Brooch Ensemble Types, where A = annular, C = cruciform, D = disc, E = equal-arm, P = penannular, Q = quoit, L = small-long, and S = square-headed: 1. AA; 2. CL; 3. LCCC; 4. AS; 5. A; 6. AAC; 7. AAS; 8. L; 9. S; 10. C; 11. LLC; 12. LLP; 13. AAA; 14. CCCC; 15. LLCCC; 16. PP; 17. QQ; 18. CCS; 19. AAD; 20. LL; 21. P; 22. AP; 23. AAL; 24. LS; 25. CCC; 26. CD; 27. AC; 28. EE; 29. ECL.

combinations, then, may represent responses of women and their kin to attempts towards centralization. However, the variety displayed by these combinations suggests this discussion was conducted in diverse and even discordant voices.

Discussion

This study demonstrates how interpretation is consequent upon the scale of analysis. As the resolution of data is focused at different levels, contradictory patterns emerge. Although social practice must be viewed locally, its interpretation is facilitated only with the identification of the appropriate analytic scale. The use of the cemetery site as the sole unit of study assumes that each burying community enjoyed a cultural unity over time and, more problematically, that living communities distinguished between themselves in death on the scale of the cemetery. The unconsidered and exclusive use of the cemetery site as the unit of study assumes a functional equivalency between cemeteries and begs the question of in which community—or communities—the "rules of meaning" obtained. If these rules enabled the self-identification of wider groups, then burial practices must have assumed a universal meaning manifest over a larger region. Likewise, uniquely personal concerns may have found meaningful expression within the context of a single burial.

Although this "situated construction of difference" (Hodder 2000:26) facilitates an understanding of how large-scale transformations were experienced at the human level, questions remain. Were the political interests seeking authority and the process of political coalescence evident to the early Anglo-Saxons? To what extent did people act knowingly and in a goal-directed manner? Although resistance to political centralization appears feminist in a modern reading, was it so gendered, or gendered at all, for the observers and participants? Here, practice theory (Clark 2000; Pauketat 2000) offers an important approach.

The problem of how individuals lead collective lives presents a significant line of inquiry for archaeologists (Moore 1994:49). Different locations of variability speak to the factors which constitute identity and to the social arenas in which these identities are performed and experienced. Understanding the potentialities and constraints of subjective individual experience within the frame of collective social structures and ideologies remains a challenge. Counterbalancing the individual burial with the cemetery site as the unit of analysis provides a basic tool for this task.

Acknowledgments

I am grateful to Jim Mathieu and Rachel Scott for inviting my participation in the Society for American Archaeology session on analytical scale and for their editorial comments on the resulting paper. This work derives from doctoral dissertation research funded in part by the Wenner-Gren Foundation for Anthropological Research (Grant-in-Aid no. 4428) and the Department of Anthropology, University of Pennsylvania. Research access to the collections referenced in this study was generously provided by staff at the Castle Museum (Norwich), Moyses Hall Museum (Bury St Edmunds), Archaeology Sec-tion, Suffolk County Council (Bury St Edmunds), and Norfolk Archaeological Unit (East Dereham).

Biographical Sketch

Genevieve Fisher is Registrar, Peabody Museum of Archaeology and Ethnology, Harvard University. She received an M.Phil. in European Archaeology from Oxford University and a Ph.D. in Anthropology from the University of Pennsylvania. Her research interests include the social construction of domestic technologies in early medieval Europe and the dialectic of gender, identity, and the body.

References Cited

Ager, B. 1985 'The smaller variants of the Anglo-Saxon quoit brooch' *Anglo-Saxon Studies in Archaeology and History* 4:1-58.

Avent, D. 1984 'Ambiguity in Anglo-Saxon style I art' *Antiquaries Journal* 64:34-42.

Blalock, H. M. 1979 *Social Statistics*. 2nd ed. McGraw-Hill (New York).

Briscoe, G. and W.E. Le Bard 1960 'An Anglo-Saxon cemetery on Lakenheath Airfield' Archaeological Notes. *Proceedings of the Cambridge Antiquarian Society* 53: 56-57.

Brumfiel, E.M. 1992 'Distinguished lecture in archaeology: breaking and entering the eco-system – gender, class, and faction steal the show' *American Anthropologist* 94:551-567.

Brumfiel, E.M. 1996 'Figurines and the Aztec State: testing the effectiveness of ideological domination' in R.P. Wright (ed) *Archaeology and Gender* University of Pennsylvania Press (Philadelphia):143-166.

Brush, K. 1988 'Gender and mortuary analysis in Pagan Anglo-Saxon Archaeology' *Archaeological Review from Cambridge* 7(1):76-89.

Carr, R., C. Hills, and P. Wade-Martins 1970-1973 'First interim report of the excavations at Spong Hill, North Elmham (1972)' *Norfolk Archaeology* 35:494-498.

Carver, M. 1989 'Kingship and material culture in Early Anglo-Saxon East Anglia' in S. Bassett (ed) *The Origins of Anglo-Saxon Kingdoms* Leicester University Press (London):141-158.

Chapman, J. 2000 'Tension at funerals: social practices and the subversion of community structure in Later Hungarian prehistory' in M.-A. Dobres and J.E. Robb (eds) *Agency in Archaeology* Routledge (London): 169-195.

Childe, V.G. 1958 *The Prehistory of European Society* Penguin Books (Harmondsworth, UK).

Clark, J.E. 2000 'Towards a better explanation of hereditary inequality: a critical assessment of natural and historic human agents' in M.-A. Dobres and J.E. Robb (eds) *Agency in Archaeology* Routledge (London):92-112.

Cohodas, M. 1997 *Basket Weavers for the California Curio Trade: Elizabeth and Louise Hickox* University of Arizona Press (Tucson, AZ).

Coontz, S. and P. Henderson 1986 'Property forms, political power and female labour in the origins of class and state societies' in S. Coontz and P. Henderson (eds) *Women's Work, Men's Property: The Origins of Gender and Class* Verso (London):108-155.

Costin, C.L. 1999 'Formal and technological variability and the social relations of production: crisoles from San José de Moro, Peru' in E.S. Chilton (ed) *Material Meanings: Critical Approaches to the Interpretation of Material Culture* University of Utah Press (Salt Lake City, UT):85-102.

Craddock, J. 1979 'The Anglo-Saxon cemetery at Saxonbury, Lewes, East Sussex' *Sussex Archaeological Collections* 117:85-102.

DeBoer, W.R. 1990 'Interaction, imitation, and communication as expressed in style: the Ucayali experience' in M.W. Conkey and C.A. Hastorf (eds) *The Uses of Style in Archaeology* Cambridge Univ Press (Cambridge): 82-104.

Dobres, M.-A. 1999 'Of paradigms and ways of seeing: artifact variability as if people mattered' in E.S. Chilton (ed) *Material Meanings: Critical Approaches to the Interpretation of Material Culture* University of Utah Press (Salt Lake City, UT):7-23.

Dobres, M.-A. and C.R. Hoffman 1994 'Social agency and the dynamics of prehistoric technology' *Journal of Archaeological Method and Theory* 1:211-258.

Dobres, M.-A. and J.E. Robb 2000 'Agency in archaeology: paradigm or platitude?' in M.-A. Dobres and J.E. Robb (eds) *Agency in Archaeology* Routledge (London):3-17.

Down, A. and M.G. Welch 1990 'Apple Down and the Mardens' *Chichester Excavations* 7.

Evison, V.I. 1987 *Dover: Buckland Anglo-Saxon Cemetery* Historic Buildings and Monuments Commission for England, Archaeological Report No. 3 (London).

Evison, V.I. 1994 *An Anglo-Saxon Cemetery at Great Chesterford, Essex* Council for British Archaeology Research Report 91 (York, UK).

Gailey, C.W. 1987 'Culture wars: resistance to state formation' in T.C. Patterson and C.W. Gailey (eds) *Power Relations and State Formation* American Anthropological Association (Washington, DC):35-56.

Geake, H. 1992 'Burial practices in seventh- and eighth-century England' in M.O.H. Carver (ed) *The Age of Sutton Hoo: The Seventh Century in North-Western Europe* Boydell Press (Woodbridge, UK):83-94.

Gibbs, L. 1987 'Identifying gender representation in the archaeological record: a contextual study' in I. Hodder (ed) *The Archaeology of Contextual Meanings* Cambridge University Press (Cambridge):79-89.

Gilchrist, R. 1994 *Gender and Material Culture: The Archaeology of Religious Women* Routledge (London).

Green, B. and A. Rogerson 1978 'The Anglo-Saxon cemetery at Bergh Apton, Norfolk: catalogue' *East Anglian Archaeology 7* Norfolk Archaeological Unit and Norfolk Museums Service (Dereham, UK).

Green, B., A. Rogerson, and S.G. White 1987 'The Anglo-Saxon cemetery at Morning Thorpe, Norfolk' *East Anglian Archaeology 36* Norfolk Archaeological Unit and Norfolk Museums Service (Dereham, UK).

Handsman, R.G. and M.P. Leone 1989 'Living history and critical archaeology in the reconstruction of the past' in V. Pinsky and A. Wylie (eds) *Critical Traditions in Contemporary Archaeology: Essays in the Philosophy, History, and Socio-Politics of Archaeology* Cambridge University Press (Cambridge):117-135.

Härke, H. 1990 '"Warrior graves?" The background of the Anglo-Saxon weapon burial rite' *Past and Present* 126: 22-43.

Härke, H. 1992 'Changing symbols in a changing society: the Anglo-Saxon weapon burial rite in the seventh century' in M.O.H. Carver (ed) *The Age of Sutton Hoo: The Seventh Century in North-Western Europe* Boydell Press (Woodbridge, UK):149-165.

Härke, H. 1997 'Early Anglo-Saxon social structure' in J. Hines (ed) *The Anglo-Saxons from the Migration Period to the Eighth Century: An Ethnographic Perspective* Boydell Press (Woodbridge, UK):125-160.

Hastorf, C. 1991 'Gender, space, and food in prehistory' in J.M. Gero and M.W. Conkey (eds) *Engendering Archaeology: Women and Prehistory* Basil Blackwell (Oxford):132-159.

Hedeager, L. 1993 'The creation of Germanic identity: a European origin myth' in P. Brun, S. van der Leuuw, and C.R. Whittaker (eds) *Frontières d'Empire: Nature et Signification des Frontières Romaines: Actes de la Table Ronde Internationale de Nemours, 21-22-23 mai 1992* Mémoires du Museé de Préhistoire d'Ile-de-France 5. Ed. A.P.R.A.I.F. (Nemours):121-131.

Herschend, F. 1992 'Beowulf and St. Sabas: the tension between the individual and the collective in Germanic society around 500 A.D.' *Tor* 24:145-164.

Hills, C. 1977 'The Anglo-Saxon cemetery at Spong Hill, North Elmham, part I' *East Anglian Archaeology 6* Norfolk Archaeological Unit and Norfolk Museums Service (Dereham, UK).

Hills, C. 1989 'Spong Hill Anglo-Saxon cemetery' in C.A. Roberts, F. Lee, and J. Bintliff (eds) *Burial Archaeology: Current Research, Methods and Developments* British Archaeological Reports, British Series 211 (Oxford): 237-240.

Hills, C. and K. Penn 1981 'The Anglo-Saxon cemetery at Spong Hill, North Elmham, part II, *East Anglian Archaeology 11* Norfolk Archaeological Unit and Norfolk Museums Service (Dereham, UK).

Hills, C., K. Penn, and R. Rickett 1984 'The Anglo-Saxon cemetery at Spong Hill, North Elmham, part III' *East Anglian Archaeology 21* Norfolk Archaeological Unit and Norfolk Museums Service (Dereham, UK).

Hines, J. 1984 *The Scandinavian Character of Anglian England in the Pre-Viking Period* British Archaeological Reports, British Series 124 (Oxford).

Hines, J. 1992 'The seriation and chronology of Anglian English women's graves: a critical assessment' in L. Jørgensen (ed) *Chronological Studies of Anglo-Saxon England, Lombard Italy and Vendel Period Sweden, Arkaeologiske Skrifter 5* Institute of Prehistoric and Classical Archaeology, University of Copenhagen (Copenhagen):81-93.

Hines, J. 1993 *Clasps, Hektespenner, Agraffen: Anglo-Scandinavian Clasps of Classes A-C of the 3rd to 6th Centuries A.D.: Typology, Diffusion and Function* Kungl, Vitterhets historie och antikvitets akademien (Stockholm).

Hines, J. 1994 'Identity, material culture, and language in Early Anglo-Saxon England' *Anglo-Saxon Studies in Archaeology and History* 7:49-60.

Hines, J. 1997 *A New Corpus of Anglo-Saxon Great*

Square-Headed Brooches Reports of the Research Committee of the Society of Antiquaries of London 51 (London).

Hines, J. 1999 'The Anglo-Saxon archaeology of the Cambridge region and the Middle Anglian kingdom' *Anglo-Saxon Studies in History and Archaeology* 10:135-149.

Hodder, I. 1982 *Symbols in Action: Ethnoarchaeological Studies of Material Culture* Cambridge University Press (Cambridge).

Hodder, I. 2000 'Agency and individuals in long-term processes' in M.-A. Dobres and J.E. Robb (eds) *Agency in Archaeology* Routledge (London): 21-33.

hooks, b. 1991 *Yearning: Race, Gender and Cultural Politics* Turnaround Press (London).

Hutchinson, P. 1966 'The Anglo-Saxon cemetery at Little Eriswell, Suffolk' *Proceedings of the Cambridge Antiquarian Society* 59:1-32.

Lethbridge, T.C. 1931 'Recent excavations in Anglo-Saxon cemeteries in Cambridge and Suffolk' *Cambridge Antiquarian Society, Quarto Publications, New Series*, No. 3.

Macfarlane, A. 1978 *The Origins of English Individualism: The Family, Property, and Social Transition* Cambridge University Press (New York).

Marquardt, W. 1992 'Dialectical archaeology' in M.B. Schiffer (ed) *Archaeological Method and Theory Vol. 4* University of Arizona Press (Tucson, AZ):101-140.

McKinley, J. 1994 'The Anglo-Saxon cemetery at Spong Hill, North Elmham, part VIII' *East Anglian Archaeology 69* Norfolk Archaeological Unit and Norfolk Museums Service (Dereham, UK).

Meskell, L. 1998 'The irresistible body and the seduction of archaeology' in D. Montserrat (ed) *Changing Bodies, Changing Meanings: Studies on the Human Body in Antiquity* Routledge (London):139-161.

Meskell, L. 2000 'Writing the body in archaeology' in A.E. Rautman (ed) *Reading the Body: Representations and Remains in the Archaeological Record* University of Pennsylvania Press (Philadelphia):13-21.

Messing, S.D. 1978 'The non-verbal language of the Ethiopian Toga' in T. Polhemus (ed) *Social Aspects of the Human Body* Penguin Press (Harmondsworth, UK):251-257.

Moore, H.L. 1994 *A Passion for Difference: Essays in Anthropology and Gender* Polity (Cambridge).

Owen-Crocker, G.R. 1986 *Dress in Anglo-Saxon England* Manchester University Press (Manchester).

Pauketat, T.R. 2000 'The tragedy of the commoners' in M.-A. Dobres and J.E. Robb (eds) *Agency in Archaeology* Routledge (London): 113-129.

Pollock, S. 1991 'Women in a men's world: images of Sumerian women' in J.M. Gero and M.W. Conkey (eds) *Engendering Archaeology: Women and Prehistory* Basil Blackwell (Oxford):366-387.

Scull, C. 1992 'Before Sutton Hoo: structures of power and society in Early East Anglia' in M.O.H. Carver (ed) *The Age of Sutton Hoo: The Seventh Century in North-Western Europe* Boydell Press (Woodbridge, UK): 3-23.

Scull, C. 1993 'Archaeology, Early Anglo-Saxon society and the origins of Anglo-Saxon kingdoms' *Anglo-Saxon Studies in Archaeology and History* 6:65-82.

Scull, C. 1999 'Social archaeology and Anglo-Saxon kingdom origins' *Anglo-Saxon Studies in Archaeology and History* 10:17-24.

Silverblatt, I. 1988 'Women in states' *Annual Review of Anthropology* 17:427-460.

Sokal, R.R. and P.H.A. Sneath 1963 *Principles of Numerical Taxonomy* W.H. Freeman (San Francisco).

Stoodley, N. 1999a 'Burial rites, gender and the creation of kingdoms: the evidence from seventh century Wessex' *Anglo-Saxon Studies in Archaeology and History* 10:99-107.

Stoodley, N. 1999b *The Spindle and the Spear: a Critical Enquiry into the Construction and Meaning in the Early Anglo-Saxon Burial Rite* British Archaeological Reports, British Series 288 (Oxford).

Tarlow, S. 1999 *Bereavement and Commemoration: An Archaeology of Mortality* Blackwell (Oxford).

Treherne, P. 1995 The warrior's beauty: the masculine body and self-identity in Bronze-Age Europe' *Journal of European Archaeology* 3:105-144.

Vierck, H. 1978 'Zur angelsächischen Frauentracht' in C. Ahrens (ed) *Sachsen und Angelsachsen* Hamburgisches Museum für Vor- und Frühgeschichte (Hamburg): 255-261.

West, S.E. 1985 *West Stow: The Anglo-Saxon Village* 2 Vols. East Anglian Archaeology 24. Suffolk County Planning Department (Ipswich, UK).

West, S.E. 1988 *The Anglo-Saxon Cemetery at Westgarth Gardens, Bury St Edmunds, Suffolk: Catalogue* East Anglian Archaeology 38. Suffolk County Planning Department (Ipswich, UK).

West, S.E. 1998 *A Corpus of Anglo-Saxon Material from Suffolk* East Anglian Archaeology 84. Suffolk County Council Archaeology Service (Ipswich, UK).

Yorke, B. 1990 *Kings and Kingdoms of Early Anglo-Saxon England* Seaby (London).

Yorke, B. 1993 'Fact or fiction? The written evidence for the fifth and sixth centuries AD' *Anglo-Saxon Studies in Archaeology and History* 6:45-50.

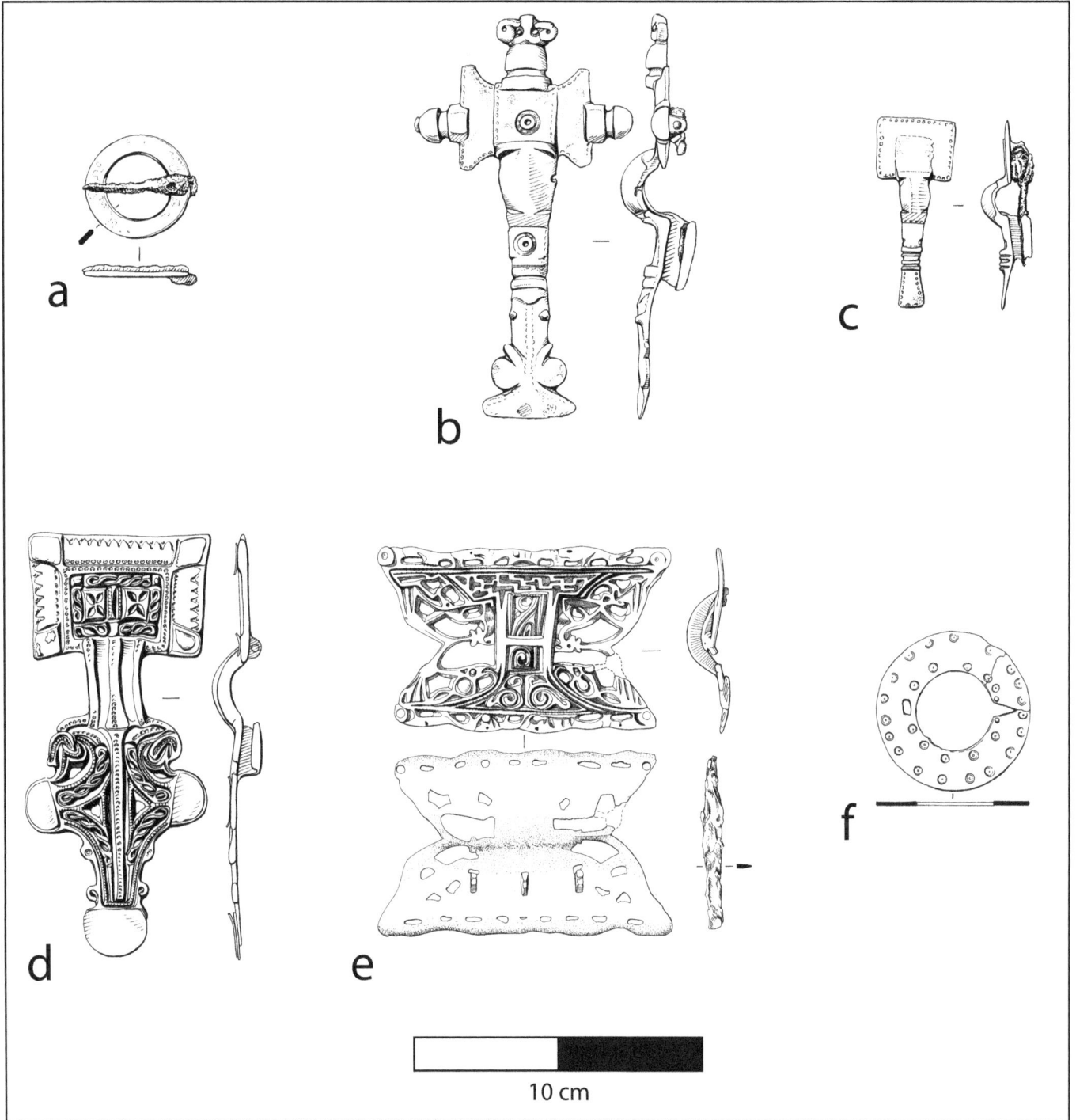

Figure 1: Some examples of the brooches studied (Ager 1985; West 1988): (a) Annular brooch, Westgarth Gardens, (b) Cruciform brooch, Westgarth Gardens, (c) Small-long brooch, Westgarth Gardens, (d) Square-headed brooch, Westgarth Gardens, (e) Equal-arm brooch, Westgarth Gardens, all reproduced by kind permission of Suffolk County Council; (f) Quoit brooch, Little Eriswell, reproduced by kind permission of Barry Ager.

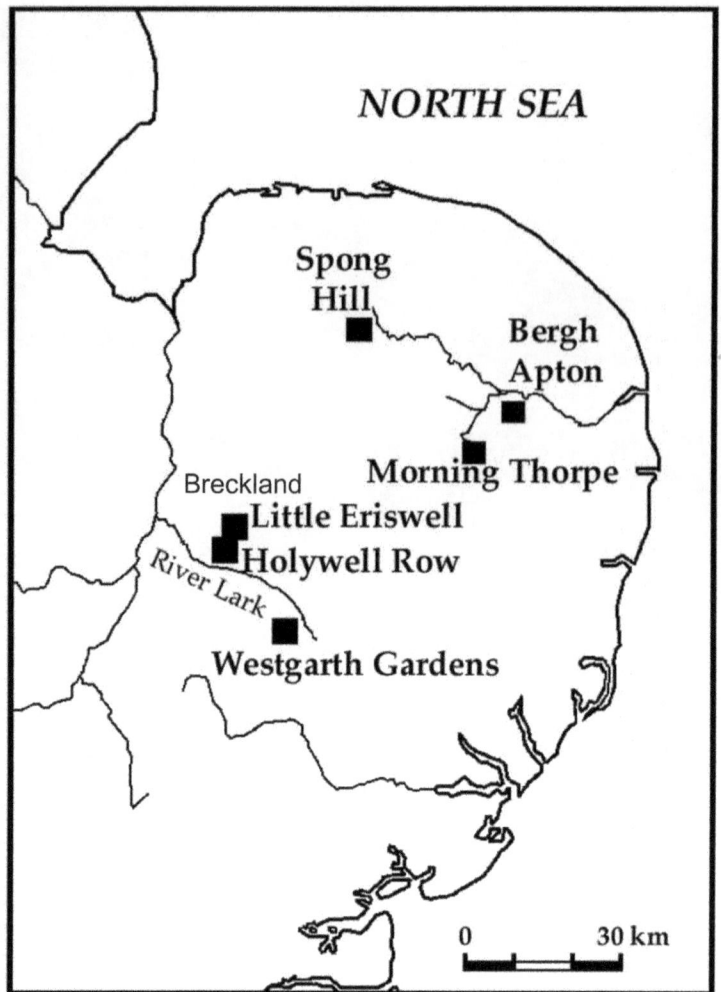

Figure 2: Map of East Anglia.

Table 1: Number of Graves Containing Specific Brooch Types.

Site	Annular	Cruciform	Disc	Equal-armed	Penannular	Quoit	Small-long	Square-headed
Bergh Apton n = 14	12	4	0	0	0	0	2	1
Morning Thorpe n = 35	30	11	1	0	2	0	4	0
Spong Hill n = 15	11	5	1	0	0	0	3	2
Westgarth Gardens n = 8	3	3	0	2	0	0	3	0
Holywell Row n = 24	12	6	0	0	2	1	6	3
Little Eriswell n = 10	6	4	0	0	1	0	2	1
Total Graves* n = 106	74	33	2	2	5	1	20	7

* Note: Graves furnished with more than one type of brooch have been scored for each brooch type. Consequently, the number of cases (n = 144) exceeds the number of graves (n = 106).

Table 2: Co-occurrence of Annular and Small-long Brooches.

	Graves without Annulars	Graves with Annulars
Graves without Small-longs	13	73
Graves with Small-longs	19	1

Table 3: Co-occurrence of Cruciform and Square-headed Brooches.

	Graves without Cruciforms	Graves with Cruciforms
Graves without Square-headed	67	32
Graves with Square-headed	6	1

Table 4: Simple Matching Coefficients Summarizing Frequencies of Brooch Types.

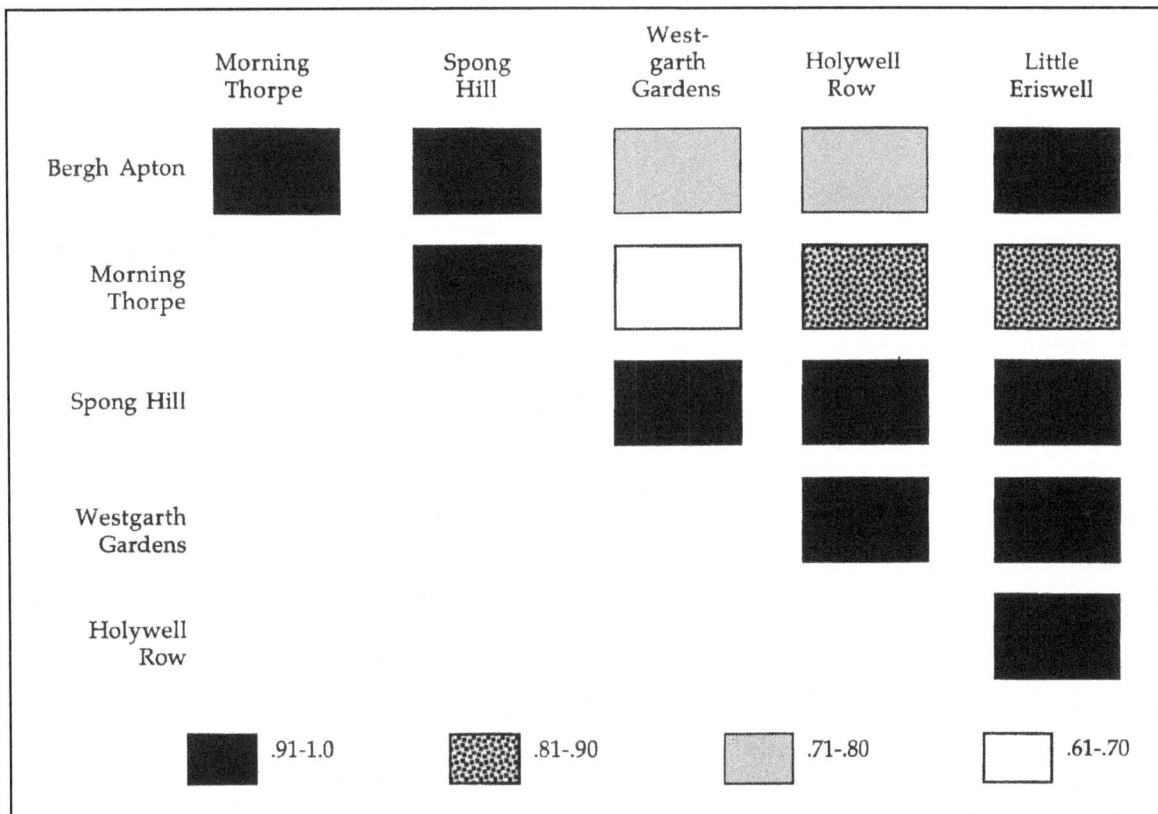

Table 5: Comparison of Frequencies of Brooch Types between the River Lark Sites and Other East Anglian Sites, Using the *Chi*-Square Test.

Brooch Type	River Lark Area/ Other East Anglia (Total n = 106)
Annular	$p < .01$ $n = 74$ $x^2 = 12.95$
Cruciform	$p = .97$ $n = 33$ $x^2 < .01$
Disc	$p = .25$ $n = 2$ $x^2 = 1.34$
Equal-arm	$p = .08$ $n = 2$ $x^2 = 3.11$
Penannular	$p = .34$ $n = 5$ $x^2 = .91$
Quoit	$p = .22$ $n = 1$ $x^2 = 1.54$
Small-long	$p = .12$ $n = 20$ $x^2 = 2.44$
Square-headed	$p = .37$ $n = 7$ $x^2 = .96$

Note: Total n (106) = number of burials containing brooches in East Anglia; n = number of burials containing specific brooch type.

The City and Complexity:
Change and Continuity in Late Antique Volterra

Rae Ostman

Abstract

Despite the great fascination that the collapse of past civilizations holds for the public, the process of decreasing social complexity has received surprisingly little attention from archaeologists. A brief examination of the history of archaeological scholarship on cities and complex societies reveals that our basic definitions of these phenomena have influenced both the object of study and the analytical scale employed. This paper presents a revised perspective for examining cities and complexity in the archaeological past, inspired in part by a consideration of the role of analytical scale in archaeological interpretation. I suggest that the individual city is the most meaningful context for examining the transformation of an urbanized, complex society, as well as the most convenient scale of analysis for examining the intersection of local and state interests. This perspective is elaborated for the case of late Antiquity, a period of decreasing social complexity in the ancient world dating from the late 2nd to the mid 6th centuries AD, focusing specifically on pottery production and consumption in the ancient center of Volterra in north-central Italy.

Despite the great fascination that the collapse of past civilizations holds for the public, the process of decreasing social complexity has received surprisingly little attention from archaeologists, especially when compared to the voluminous research on increasing complexity. Most studies of the process of decreasing complexity have been oriented toward understanding complexity by seeing how it fails, not toward understanding the different, "simpler" society that emerged (e.g. Yoffee and Cowgill 1988; see Yoffee 1988:2). But if there are specific motivations and particular processes for decreasing complexity, as Tainter (1988) has suggested—if "collapse" is a solution rather than a problem—then clearly there is much to be learned from examining the kinds of societies that emerge from the processes of decline.

Regardless of their theoretical perspective, most archaeologists define complex societies according to the constellation of factors articulated by V. Gordon Childe 50 years ago. Since Childe first emphasized urbanized settlement patterns, specialized craft production, and social stratification as essential elements in the definition of a complex society, social scientists have sought to describe and explain how these factors contribute to increasing social complexity. Although Childe's specific models outlining the process of increasing complexity in the ancient Near East and Europe have been revised and in some cases rejected, the overall utility of his perspective has been affirmed (see the literature review and studies in Brumfiel and Earle 1987 and the studies in Wailes 1996).

Childe believed that the development of complex societies, or civilizations, was directly related to a shift in their living patterns to incorporate nucleated population centers. The "urban revolution," as he considered it, necessitated profound changes in the economic organization of production. Primary producers supported a new administrative elite class residing in the urban centers, who in turn supported specialist craft producers. As technology advanced, the more productive economy could support a growing population (Childe 1950:4, 9-16). In Childe's model, cities stand for complexity, as the home of specialized producers and dependent consumers, the seat of administrators and rulers, and the link to the outside world, its goods and ideas. From this perspective, the breakdown of urban life seems a clear signal of decreasing social complexity, just as cities unambiguously seem to imply increasing complexity.

Recent research suggests, however, that the city is not simply an index for complexity, but that the relationship between urbanism and complexity is in fact much more complicated and interesting. In this paper, I present a research strategy to examine how one complex society reorganized to a relatively simple society, focusing on the response of a local pottery industry to much more extensive political, social, and economic processes. This research is currently being performed as part of my doctoral dissertation.

In my study, I propose to accept Childe's materialist approach to the examination of urbanism and complexity, but to turn his model inside out, viewing the problem from an opposing perspective: problematizing the relationship between city and complexity, rather than assuming their interconnectedness; focusing on the city during its period of decline rather than its development; examining the process of decline in order to understand the simpler society that emerged from it, not the more complex society preceding it; and analyzing the process through the social relations revealed through consumption as well as production. In order to indicate why this inversion of Childe's approach is both suitable and useful, the next section provides an introduction to previous scholarship on the problem of decreasing social complexity and urbanism.

This brief review of selected literature on decreasing social complexity is intended to define the topic of study, to outline important trends in recent research, and to situate the proposed study within existing thought on the problem. Based on this discussion, I will suggest that the most promising avenue for future research is one that approaches decreasing social complexity as a period of transition and transformation rather than decline and collapse, and that to do justice to this simultaneously constructive and destructive process, more focused and detailed analyses are required to complement recent systemic research.

In a recent study dedicated to the problem, Tainter (1988:6, emphasis in the original) provides a concise definition of collapse: *"A society has collapsed when it displays a rapid, significant loss of an established level of sociopolitical complexity"*. Another recent volume of collected studies (Yoffee and Cowgill 1988) also defines the collapse of complex societies as the fragmentation or discontinuity in the political institutions of formerly integrated states. Like Tainter, the editors of this volume emphasize that no state collapses in all parts equally, explicitly allowing for substantial cultural continuity following political collapse (Cowgill 1988:256; Yoffee 1988:14-15; cf. Tainter 1988:4). This definition is accepted for the proposed study.

Yoffee and Cowgill (1988) and Tainter (1988) take a processualist, generalizing approach to the problem, seeking to develop a comparative methodology for collapse and a model of collapse as a general phenomenon respectively (Tainter 1988:43; Yoffee 1988:2). Both studies view complex societies as systemic in nature, emphasizing that change in one aspect of a society affects all other aspects. They also argue that material phenomena (including economic, technological, demographic, and political aspects of social life) can be demonstrated to have had a primary or causal role in effecting the collapse, and that cultural or ideational factors had a secondary role and may be disregarded for the sake of clarity and objectivity (Tainter 1988:39-41; Yoffee 1988:6-11). As a result, the description of collapse in both studies emphasizes the profound disjunction and discontinuity between the earlier, more complex period and the later, less complex period (see especially Tainter 1988:4, 18-20).

Studies that have taken an alternative approach—examining decreasing complexity on a more focused scale and paying significant attention to the particularistic and continuous aspects of society and culture—reach quite different conclusions. In these studies, decreasing complexity is viewed as a process of transition and transformation rather than decline and collapse (Bowersock 1988:165), a process that occurs in a particular, meaningful context: the ancient city (Adams 1988:33-34, 37).

Bowersock (1988), examining the slow and complex dissolution of the Roman Empire, challenges the generalizing project of Yoffee and Cowgill (1988). He argues that even the Roman case (a classic example of decreasing complexity) defies typical definitions of collapse when it is examined in detail. He maintains that it is nearly impossible to locate exactly when and where the empire collapsed, due to the great variability in circumstance across time and space. Bowersock (1988:170) provocatively suggests that in the case of Rome there was no collapse, instead, a profound "social, political, and intellectual reorganization" occurred "entirely within the framework of what had been there before". He concludes that collapse "is intimately connected with continuity" (Bowersock 1988:175).

Adams (1988:33) returns to the problem introduced by Childe—the city as the *context* of complexity—and asks whether cities are "merely the locales of change", or whether they played "an autonomous role of their own, either hastening or resisting trends toward social disintegration". He points out that definitions of the city—whether by geographers or by materialist theorists such as Childe—make urbanization appear a "derivative, dependent phenomenon", a "secondary reflection of underlying forces such as productive, technological, or demographic growth" (Adams 1988:34). Adams (1988:34) argues instead that cities and the institutions they fostered "played a central part in the cognitive worlds of their inhabitants", and that "urbanism itself constituted an at least partly independent realm of meaning and motivation for action". Adams (1988:37) focuses on Mesopotamian civilization, arguing that it was "inseparable from groups and institutions that flourished only as cities flourished" and that "[t]he decline of Mesopotamian civilization, accordingly, also must have a vital urban dimension".

Finley's (1973) research into the ancient economy illustrates the value of examining decreasing complexity in the context of the city. By considering how the cultural ideology of the city in the Greco-Roman world was implicated in the collapse of Antiquity, Finley is able to demonstrate how urban-rural relationships affected the development of late Antique and medieval society. Finley's research also recommends that cities be examined from the perspective of consumption and status—a major shift in paradigm from Childe's materialist approach emphasizing production and class.

Finley (1973) argues that in the ancient mind, the city was absolutely essential to civilization. The city included both the urban center and its territory as one integral social, cultural, political, and economic unit. The urban center was the social, political, and cultural (religious) center for the region, while the agrarian countryside was its complementary source of wealth and "moral excellence" (Finley 1973:123, 131). Population size was insignificant to the definition of an ancient center, as was its economic function—as long as "the material goods indispensable for civic amenities" were available (Finley 1973:124). Trade effected through the center permitted it to support a greater population, brought in a greater variety of goods to circulate among its residents, and provided essentials that may have promoted a limited degree of specialization and efficiency in the agricultural landholdings. Specialized craft production also occurred in the center, but it served to satisfy internal urban needs, not to reach external markets. Craft production, no matter how lucrative, was not viewed to be morally enriching, as farming was, and specialized producers were invariably of low social status (Finley 1973:74, 138-139, 144-145).

In Finley's (1973:35-36) view, the urban center was unabashedly oriented toward acquisition, reflecting the attitude of its residents "that wealth was necessary and it was good; it was an absolute requisite for the good life". Nonetheless, this "strong drive to acquire wealth was not translated into a drive to create capital; stated differently, the prevailing mentality was acquisitive but not productive" (Finley 1973:144).

Medieval and early modern cities were different from ancient cities, according to Finley, because they no longer retained the conceptual identification of the city and the countryside as one unit comprised of two complementary parts. Finley points out that after the city and the countryside were divorced in late Antiquity, they came to have a different kind of economic relationship in medieval Europe. Most importantly, the agrarian world of medieval Europe, with the sociopolitical and ecclesiastical elite seated in country estates, provided medieval cities with the external markets that ancient cities lacked, encouraging production for external consumption (Finley 1973:140-141). In Finley's view, then, the processes leading to the decline of the ancient city directly affected the way that the city was reborn in medieval times.

By now it is clear that decreasing complexity is as interesting, variable, and complicated a process as increasing complexity. Although not comprehensive by any means, the discussion above provides some important indications of where to begin studying this less well-known aspect of the relationship between the city and complexity.

Two important comparative studies (Tainter 1988; Yoffee and Cowgill 1988) provide a useful general framework for examining decreasing complexity by establishing that substantial political and economic change as well as significant social and cultural continuity are characteristic of the problem. Whether one wishes to strengthen or challenge the premises, goals, and conclusions of these comparative and generalizing works, the next step is clearly to follow with more detailed analyses of particular case studies. As all of the studies discussed above recognize, the variability of the process of decreasing complexity across cultures requires that any efforts at examining the problem be based on strong empirical data.

The ancient city represents a convenient analytical point of intersection between large-scale and small-scale analyses, and is therefore an appropriate scale of analysis for new studies. The city may also be considered the primary unit of analysis for examining social complexity (Adams 1988:36), because if cities were essential to the creation and maintenance of complex societies, they certainly were essential to the transformation of complex societies.

My study examines one of the classic cases of decreasing social complexity—the development of late Antique society out of imperial Rome between the end of the 2nd and the middle of the 6th centuries AD—focusing on the ancient city of Volterra, Italy. Although it is not possible here to review the complex economic, social, and political processes involved in the formation of late Antiquity, a brief description of the case study will provide an introduction to the period.

Volterra, like many Etruscan city-states, remained a regional administrative center during the Roman Empire and beyond, into the late Antique and medieval periods. The urban center of Volterra is situated between the Era and Cecina rivers, at the heart of an extensive regional territory (**Figure 1**). Like most of the Etruscan city-states, Volterra was located inland with a separate port along the coast (Mansuelli 1985:111; Martelli 1985:175).

Many of the broad historical trends of late Antiquity are reflected in the settlement patterns of the Volterran area. Most

dramatic were the changes within the urban center that indicate a decline in elite investment in civic life. During both the Hellenistic and Roman periods, there had been continual investment in Volterra's civic institutions and public works, seen in ambitious building programs undertaken during the 3rd century BC and during the 1st centuries BC and AD. This investment continued in the late Roman period (the 3rd and 4th centuries AD) with the construction of two major bath complexes in the urban center (S. Felice and Vallebuona) and the systematic reworking of the *horrea* in the port of Vada Volaterrana. But after the 4th century, monumental construction was no longer attempted in Volterra. Existing monumental buildings gradually went out of use, a process complete by the 5th century AD. Areas previously occupied by civic buildings were reused or plundered for building material, often replaced by huts and cabins made of more perishable materials, resulting in the strata of Black Earth found in archaeological excavations throughout the heart of the former center. Burials were introduced within the city walls, even though existing cemeteries remained in use (Motta 1997:253-255; Munzi et al. 1994:644-646; Pasquinucci and Menchelli 1999:136).

In contrast to the urban center, settlement in the rural territory of Volterra appears relatively stable during the transition from the imperial period to late Antiquity, retaining the pattern established as far back as the Hellenistic period: a dense network of small farms interspersed with larger villages, practicing a consistent, traditional agricultural economy. Although some sites disappeared in the middle imperial period, those that survived remained through late Antiquity. This pattern held even in areas which previously had shown evidence of "Romanization." In the Val di Sterza, for example, during the Imperial Roman period middle-sized farms and numerous pottery kilns were introduced, perhaps as an attempt to maximize the use of this marginal agricultural area. These innovative settlement types were abandoned during late Antiquity, and the valley reverted to a pattern similar to the surrounding area. Some parts of the Volterran landscape, especially in coastal regions but also inland, were dominated by the large villas of rich landowners, with smaller farmsteads surrounding them. Significantly, many of these villas were renovated in the 3rd century, as elites made them their primary residences (Motta 1997:263-264, 250-251; Pasquinucci and Menchelli 1999:136; Terrenato 1998:109).

The core rural areas of the Volterra region, then, indicate great continuity of social and economic patterns from the Hellenistic Etruscan period up to the threshold of the Lombard conquest (AD 568)—in contrast to the conspicuous changes occurring in the urban center during these eight centuries (Motta 1997:250-51). This suggests that the resilience of the Volterran economy and society was located in its rural core, and that the urban center was less crucial to maintaining traditional social structures.

Motta (1997) and Pasquinucci and Menchelli (1999) have provided a convincing explanation for this pattern: Volterran elites, who often had longstanding local ties as well as impressive imperial connections, chose to divest in the urban center and invest in the countryside, a conscious and self-interested action intended to preserve the conservative social structures in Volterra. Beginning in the 3rd century AD and continuing through the 5th century, both the senatorial aristocracy and probably also the local elites abandoned the urban center together with the burdensome civic duties their offices required. Often the senatorial and local elites were one and the same, due to the Roman policy of leaving local power structures intact and incorporating local elites into the imperial government. The remarkable conservation of Volterran social structures is exemplified by the Caecinae family, who were active governing citizens from the earliest Etruscan times through the Roman Empire up to the reign of Theodoric (AD 498-526)—at least a millennium of prominence, still observed in the name of the river Cecina (Pasquinucci and Menchelli 1999:137).

When the elite were no longer committed to civic life and the burdens it placed upon them, there was a crisis in civic institutions. Especially quick to go were the aspects of civic culture introduced by the Romans, manifested materially in the ostentatious theater. There was no accompanying crisis in the fundamental social and economic structures of the countryside, because the elite classes chose to invest in their country properties and to move their economic activities to their country estates. Especially long-lasting were the traditional forms of the rural settlement, which for centuries formed the basis of Volterra's wealth (Motta 1997:263-264; Pasquinucci and Menchelli 1999:137).

Because of this marked and profound rural stability, Motta (1997) rejects the idea that late Antiquity was a period of crisis for Volterra, viewing it instead as a period of transformation which remains incompletely understood, due in part to a scarcity of archaeological data and an insufficiently detailed chronology. Certainly the Volterran data call into question the applicability of generalizing models for the period which envision a drastic disappearance of settlements, a concentration of the population into larger sites, and a regional administration significantly different from the imperial period. In Volterra, only the urban center is deconstructed, with a new kind of resident practicing new ways of living—more a cluster of poor hamlets within the city walls than a true city in the Childean or the classical sense. The countryside instead preserved both the traditional settlement pattern and the traditional social structures (Motta 1997:263-264; also Bintliff and Hamerow 1995; Ward Perkins 1997).

The results of recent research in the Volterra region support the proposal to turn Childe's approach to urbanism and complex societies inside-out. It seems necessary to evaluate critically rather than simply accept Childe's identification of complexity with urbanism. The decline of Volterra's center was not accompanied by a radical change in sociopolitical organization, but rather worked initially to preserve the traditional, local, sociopolitical structure, and ultimately may have had its most direct affect on the character of early medieval society. Surprising as this may seem, the decline of the great ancient cities and the fall of the Roman Empire simply do not appear to have been felt as strongly locally as we might expect viewing them from a global perspective. This in turn indicates the value of examining this transitional period not in order to understand how the preceding society fell, but rather in order

to understand how the succeeding society developed; that is, to examine how late Antiquity emerged, paving the way for early medieval Italy.

Comparing the life in the city during its period of development (the Hellenistic Etruscan period) to its period of decline (the late Antique period) seems the logical place to begin, as the most dramatic changes in late Antique Volterra took place in the former center, amounting to a profound social, political, economic, and cultural transformation. A new kind of urban living and a new kind of urban population developed, yet little is known about life in the city during this period. Finley's (1973) work suggests that life in Volterra's former urban center would most effectively be studied by examining both production and consumption patterns, rather than focusing primarily on the organization of production as Childe proposed.

It is argued here (following Adams 1988) that cities are not simply the most convenient locales in which we can observe these phenomena; rather, their very existence meant that the transformation of society occurred through the actions of people who conceived of the world in terms of city and countryside. There is no doubt that the appearance of cities in Italy coincided with the earliest complex societies; and there is no doubt that cities went through a period of transformation (or "crisis") during this first period of decreasing complexity. If cities stood for the existing imperial political, social, and economic structures (embodied in the majestic civic architecture of the imperial Roman period), the countryside stood for local political, social, and economic structures. Choosing between local and imperial, the elites also chose between countryside and city, investing in the former at the expense of the latter. Thus the decline and neglect of urban centers may be a specific, self-interested action of the elite, just as the decision to promote them may have been (cf. Brumfiel and Earle 1987).

In response to this revised perspective, using the case study of Volterra, my dissertation examines the ways in which a local, relatively self-contained city-state economy was affected by and adapted to incorporation into a much broader imperial economy—and how the choices made by local producers and consumers contributed to the creation of a new society, the late Antique world. The thesis of my study is that the adaptation (or maladaptation) of local craft industries to the imperial economy led to the integration of Italian city centers with other urban centers of the empire, at the same time loosening their economic ties with their hinterlands. This disruption in the traditional productive relations between Italian cities and their territories contributed to what has been termed the "provincialization" of Italy, as the former social, economic, and political center of the empire became increasingly reliant on its provinces. When long-distance relations faltered due to a variety of historical circumstances, Italy was left with an incomplete domestic economy and was unable to support its traditional civilized society (that is, a society based on city centers). At this point, both elite and non-elite actors chose (consciously or not) to develop a rural-based society, unseen since protohistoric times on the Italian peninsula (see the essays collected in Giardina 1986, especially the contributions by Carandini, Giardina, and Panella).

Specific hypotheses supporting this viewpoint posit that the local producers responded to "competition" from imported wares by restricting and reducing their range of goods to specialize in those products that were not easily transported from abroad. As a result, the local industry was no longer oriented toward supplying all of the pottery needed in the city and territory, but rather toward supplementing the goods available externally. The industry was therefore no longer prepared to provide the complete range of pottery required locally when the supply of imported goods dried up. This scenario is suggested and supported by findings in other studies (e.g. Anselmino et al. 1986; Carignani et al. 1986; Ciotola 2000; Del Rio and Cherubini 1994; Lupi 1998; Menchelli 1994; Panella 1986). If this view is incorrect, the study will instead find that the local industry developed independently, rather than responding to external influence. In addition to the specific hypotheses, a number of exploratory questions will be addressed which attempt to establish how local producers and consumers responded to incorporation into a broader economic network, and which will consider how their choices may have affected the transition from classical to late Antiquity.

The primary goal of the dissertation research is to contribute to the model for social, political, and economic transformation of late Antiquity produced by a comprehensive archaeological research program begun in the 1980s. Under the direction of Andrea Carandini and Edina Regoli, the research program included three phases: survey of the Volterra region, excavation within the city center, and excavation of rural sites (Carandini 1988; Cateni 1993; Motta et al. 1993; Munzi and Terrenato 2000; Regoli and Terrenato 2000; Terrenato 1992; 1996, 1998; Terrenato and Ammerman 1996; Terrenato and Saggin 1994). The decade of intensive archaeological research in Volterra has resulted in a remarkably coherent and consistent picture of how Volterra was affected by large-scale processes of change occurring in the late Roman and late Antique periods. The results of this program (summarized above) provide a unique opportunity to examine an Italian late Antique urban center on the basis of excavated materials from a well-defined archaeological and historical context.

The dissertation thesis will be examined on the basis of original field research performed on an existing collection of archaeological ceramics drawn from excavations in the Vallebuona quarter of Volterra (**Figure 2**). The excavations were performed during 1987 and 1989 under the field direction of Nicola Terrenato. Vallebuona is an exciting context for examining late Antiquity because the area manifests all of the changes characteristic of the period: a striking transformation of the built environment in the city, a new population living in these transformed spaces using a new material culture, and a new economy based on different productive and exchange relationships with the countryside and other centers. Research will be performed on material excavated from two contexts, one dating to the Hellenistic Etruscan period (3rd through 1st centuries BC) and one to the late Roman imperial and late Antique transition (late 2nd through mid 6th centuries AD)—corresponding to the period of greatest ancient urban development and decline, respectively.

The first phase of research (currently underway) provides a comprehensive field analysis of the ceramic deposit excavated from Areas I and IV, Vallebuona, Volterra. The primary objectives of the field analysis are: to classify the pottery according to fabric and form, to characterize the primary fabric groups that constitute the deposit, to document the technology used in pottery production in late Roman and late Antique Volterra, to provide a catalogue of the vessel forms and variants represented in each group, to quantify the deposit according to standard measures in order to permit intersite comparison, and to evaluate the utility of further materials analyses. In order to fulfill these objectives, the following studies and analyses will be performed: macroscopic visual examination of the entire deposit, microscopic visual examination of a selected sample, and the creation of a comparative collection of local clays potentially used in antiquity.

The corpus of data created by the field analysis will then be interpreted in order to consider the degree of social, economic, and technological continuity exhibited in the pottery corpus. This second portion of research addresses the thesis and specific supporting hypotheses summarized above. Patterns of change and continuity across time in the Vallebuona pottery collection will be identified, and the results will be compared with research results from other contemporary sites in central and northern Italy.

This paper has presented a research strategy to examine how one complex society reorganized to a relatively simple society, emphasizing the simultaneously constructive and destructive aspects of the process. The proposed study considers one of the classic cases of decreasing complexity: the development of late Antique society out of imperial Rome between the late 2nd and mid 6th centuries AD. It argues that the incorporation of local craft industries into the imperial Mediterranean-wide trade network disrupted the traditional productive relations between Italian cities and their territories, disintegrating the "basic unit" of Roman society (Dyson 1992:1-2). The economic disintegration of city and territory represents one of the earliest manifestations of the process known as the "provincialization" of Italy, wherein the former center of the empire saw its social, economic, and political functions scattered across its various provinces—a first step toward the famous fall of Rome. The theory and methods of this study are based on the Braudellian-materialist perspective of Italian scholars, as presented in a recent set of edited volumes on late Antiquity (Giardina 1986). In order to assess the dissertation thesis, an existing collection of pottery from the city of Volterra in north-central Italy will be examined.

This approach unites the classic approach to the city and complexity in archaeological thinking—typified by a big-picture analysis of the intertwined processes of urbanization, increasing complexity, and the social organization of production—with a new perspective gained by considering its complement—a more focused analysis of decreasing complexity and patterns of consumption. In developing my research proposal, exploring the concept of analytical scale helped me to consider explicitly how we (my colleagues and I interested in cities and complexity) defined our subject and devised research strategies to achieve our objectives. Most importantly, considering "scale" inspired me to think about how to integrate traditional concerns with new approaches to the cities and complex societies of the archaeological past.

The results of my research potentially will provide a significant contribution to anthropological research examining the relationship between urban centers, craft production, and social complexity; to archaeological methods for studying social reproduction and change on the basis of material culture; and to empirical knowledge of late Antique Italy. By focusing on a period of economic decline in an urban context, the study directly addresses the theoretical problem of urbanization, the specialized economy, and social complexity. By studying a common find category and using relatively simple methods of analysis, it will indicate how humble categories of material culture and modest archaeological resources can contribute important insights into the processes of social reproduction and transformation. And finally, by focusing on a newly excavated urban center, this research will contribute to an understanding of the particular processes of social change in late Antique Italy and will illuminate the character of urban settlement there.

Acknowledgments

I am grateful to Pam Crabtree, Alessandro Furiesi, Nicola Terrenato, and Rita Wright for their extensive and generous help with all phases of the larger research project partially described here. I would also like to thank Jim Mathieu and Rachel Scott for organizing the SAA conference session to which this paper belongs and for arranging its subsequent publication as a BAR volume. Finally, I would like to thank the discussants and my fellow presenters for an interesting and stimulating conference session.

Biographical Sketch

Rae Ostman received her BA degree from Cornell University in 1994. She received her MA from New York University in 1997, and is currently working toward her PhD at the same institution. She has excavated in Italy and Poland, and has worked in museum education and visitor services in Italy and the United States.

References Cited

Adams, Robert McC. 1988 'Contexts of civilizational collapse' in N. Yoffee and G.L. Cowgill (eds) *The Collapse of Ancient States and Civilizations* University of Arizona Press (Tucson, AZ):20-43.

Anselmino, Lucilla, Caterina Maria Coletti, Maria Luisa Ferrantini, and Clementina Panella 1986 'Ostia: Terme del Nuotatore' in A. Giardina (ed) *Società Romana E Impero Tardoantico: Vol. III: Le Merci, Gli Insediamenti* Laterza (Rome-Bari):45-81.

Bintliff, John and Helena Hamerow 1995 'Europe between late Antiquity and the middle ages: recent archaeological and historical research in western and southern Europe' in J. Bintliff and H. Hamerow (eds) *Europe between Late Antiquity and the Middle Ages: Recent Archaeological and Historical Research in Western and Southern Europe* British Archaeological Reports, International Series 617 (Oxford):1-7.

Bowersock, G.W. 1988 'The dissolution of the Roman empire' in N. Yoffee and G.L. Cowgill (eds) *The Collapse of Ancient States and Civilizations* University of Arizona Press (Tucson, AZ):165-175.

Brumfiel, Elizabeth M. and Timothy K. Earle 1987 'Specialization, exchange, and complex societies: an introduction' in E.M. Brumfiel and T.K. Earle (eds) *Specialization, Exchange, and Complex Societies* Cambridge University Press (New York):1-9.

Carignani, Andrea, Alberto Ciotola, Francesco Pacetti, and Clementina Panella 1986 'Roma: Il contesto del Tempio del Magna Mater sul Palatino' in A. Giardina (ed) *Società Romana E Impero Tardoantico: Vol. III: Le Merci, Gli Insediamenti* Laterza (Rome-Bari):27-43.

Carandini, Andrea 1986 'Il mondo della tarda antichità visto attraverso le merci' in A. Giardina (ed) *Società Romana E Impero Tardoantico: Vol. III: Le Merci, Gli Insediamenti* Laterza (Rome-Bari):1-19.

Carandini, Andrea 1988 'Un progetto archeologico per Volterra e il suo territorio' in A. Carandini (ed) *Volterra '88: Un Progetto* Accademia dei Sepolti (Poggibonsi): 107-111.

Cateni, Gabriele (ed) 1993 *Il Teatro Romano di Volterra* Octavo (Florence).

Childe, V. Gordon 1950 'The urban revolution' *Town Planning Review* 21:3-17.

Ciotola, Alberto 2000 'I materiali ceramici' in M. Munzi and N. Terrenato (eds) *Volterra: Il Teatro E Le Terme. Gli Edifici, Lo Scavo, La Topografia* All'Insegna del Giglio (Florence):163-176.

Cowgill, George 1988 'Onward and upward with collapse' in N. Yoffee and G.L. Cowgill (eds) *The Collapse of Ancient States and Civilizations* University of Arizona Press (Tucson, AZ):244-276.

Del Rio, Antonella and Linda Cherubini 1994 'Le produzioni ceramiche delle basse valli del Fine e del Cecina' in G. Olcese (ed) *Ceramica Romana E Archeometria: Lo Stato Degli Studi* All'Insegna del Giglio (Florence):217-223.

Dyson, Stephen L. 1992 *Community and Society in Roman Italy* Johns Hopkins University Press (Baltimore, MD).

Finley, M.I. 1973 *The Ancient Economy* University of California Press (Berkeley, CA).

Giardina, Andrea 1986 'Le due Italie nella forma tarda dell'impero' in A. Giardina (ed) *Società Romana E Impero Tardoantico: Vol. III: Le Merci, Gli Insediamenti* Laterza (Rome-Bari):1-36.

Giardina, Andrea (ed) 1986 *Società Romana E Impero Tardoantico: Vol. I-III* Laterza (Rome-Bari).

Lupi, Simonetta 1998 'La ceramica a vernice rossa nel Volterrano' in L. Saguì (ed) *Ceramica in Italia, VI-VII Secolo* All'Insegna del Giglio (Florence):625-628.

Mansuelli, G.A. 1985 'L'organizzazione del territorio e la città' in M. Cristofani (ed) *Civiltà Degli Etruschi* Electa (Milan):111-116.

Martelli, M. 1985 'I luoghi e prodotti dello scambio' in M. Cristofani (ed) *Civiltà Degli Etruschi* Electa (Milan): 175-181.

Menchelli, Simonetta 1994 'Le produzioni ceramiche della basse valle dell'Arno' in G. Olcese (ed) *Ceramica Romana E Archeometria: Lo Stato Degli Studi* All'Insegna del Giglio (Florence):205-215.

Motta, Laura 1997 'I paesaggi di Volterra nel tardoantico' *Archeologia Medievale* 24:245-267.

Motta, Laura, Lorenza Camin, and Nicola Terrenato 1993 'Un sito rurale nel territorio di Volterra' *Bolletino di Archeologia* 23/24:109-116.

Munzi, Massimiliano, Giovanni Ricci, and Mirella Serlorenzi 1994 'Volterra tra tardoantico e alto medioevo' *Archeologia Medievale* 21:639-656.

Munzi, Massimiliano and Nicola Terrenato 2000 *Volterra: Il Teatro E Le Terme. Gli Edifici, Lo Scavo, La Topografia* All'Insegna del Giglio (Florence).

Panella, Clementina 1986 'Le merci: produzioni, itinerari e destini' in A. Giardina (ed) *Società Romana E Impero Tardoantico: Vol. III: Le Merci, Gli Insediamenti* Laterza (Rome-Bari):431-459.

Pasquinucci, Marinella and Simonetta Menchelli 1999 'The landscape and economy of the territories of *Pisae* and *Volaterrae* (coastal North Etruria)' *Journal of Roman Archaeology* 12:122-141.

Regoli, Edina and Nicola Terrenato (eds) 2000 *Guida al Museo Archeologico di Rosignano Marittimo: Paesaggi e insediamenti in Val di Cecina* Nuova Immagine (Siena).

Tainter, Joseph A. 1988 *The Collapse of Complex Societies* Cambridge University Press (New York).

Terrenato, Nicola 1992 'La ricognizione della Val di Cecina: l'evoluzione di una metodologia di ricerca' in M. Bernardi (ed) *L'Archeologia Del Paesaggio* All'Insegna del Giglio (Florence):561-596.

Terrenato, Nicola 1996 'Field survey methods in central Italy (Etruria and Umbria): between local knowledge and regional traditions' *Archaeological Dialogues* 3(2): 216-230.

Terrenato, Nicola 1998 '*Tam firmum municipium*: the Romanization of Volaterrae and its cultural implications' *Journal of Roman Studies* 88:94-114.

Terrenato, Nicola and A.J. Ammerman 1996 'Visibility and site recovery in the Cecina Valley Survey, Italy' *Journal of Field Archaeology* 23:91-109.

Terrenato, N. and A. Saggin 1994 'Ricognizioni archeologiche nel territorio di Volterra' *Archeologia Classica* 46:465-482.

Wailes, Bernard (ed) 1996 *Craft Specialization and Social Evolution: In Memory of V. Gordon Childe* University of Pennsylvania Museum (Philadelphia).

Ward Perkins, Bryan 1997 'Continuitists, catastrophists, and the towns of post-Roman northern Italy' *Papers of the British School at Rome* 65:157-176.

Yoffee, Norman 1988 'Orienting collapse' in N. Yoffee and G.L. Cowgill (eds) *The Collapse of Ancient States and Civilizations* University of Arizona Press (Tucson):1-19.

Yoffee, Norman and George L. Cowgill (eds) 1988 *The Collapse of Ancient States and Civilizations* University of Arizona Press (Tucson, AZ).

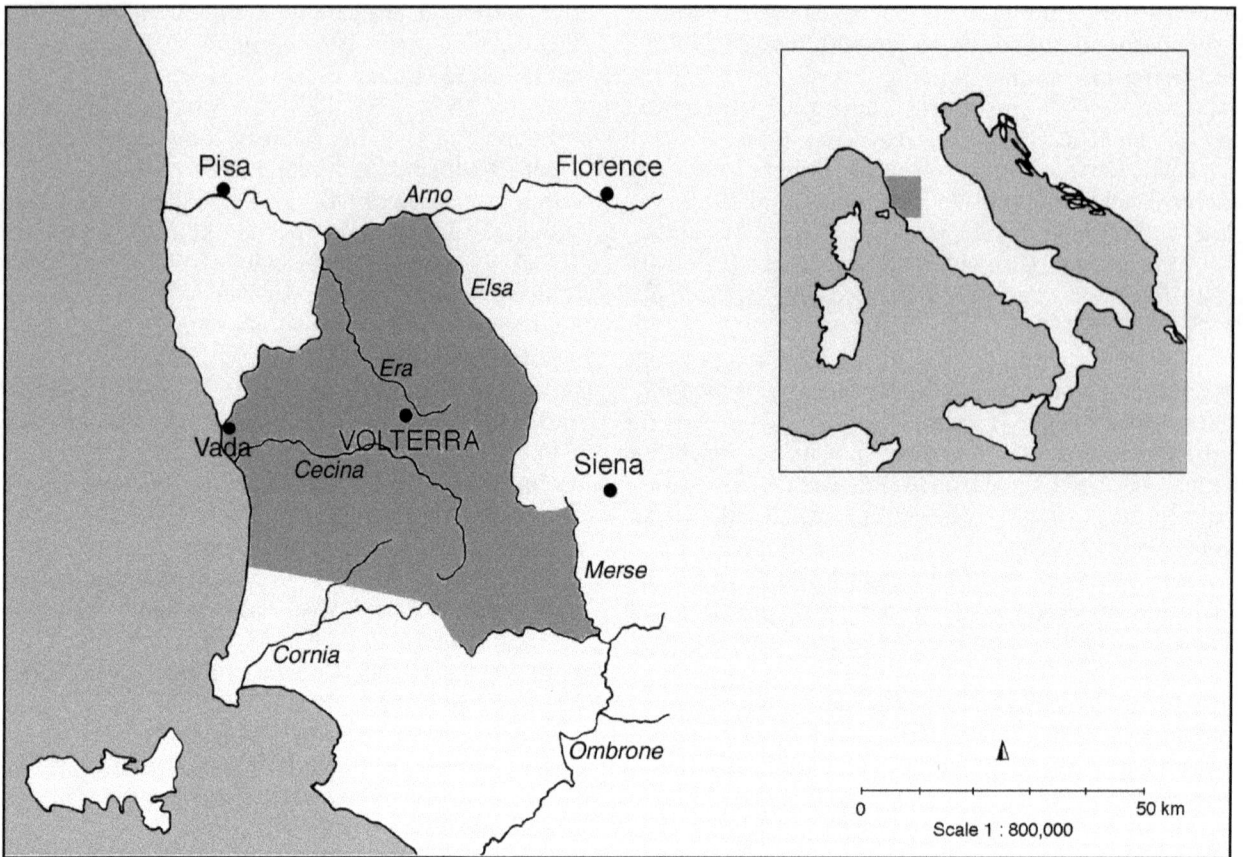

Figure 1: Map of north-central Italy, indicating the city of Volterra and its territory

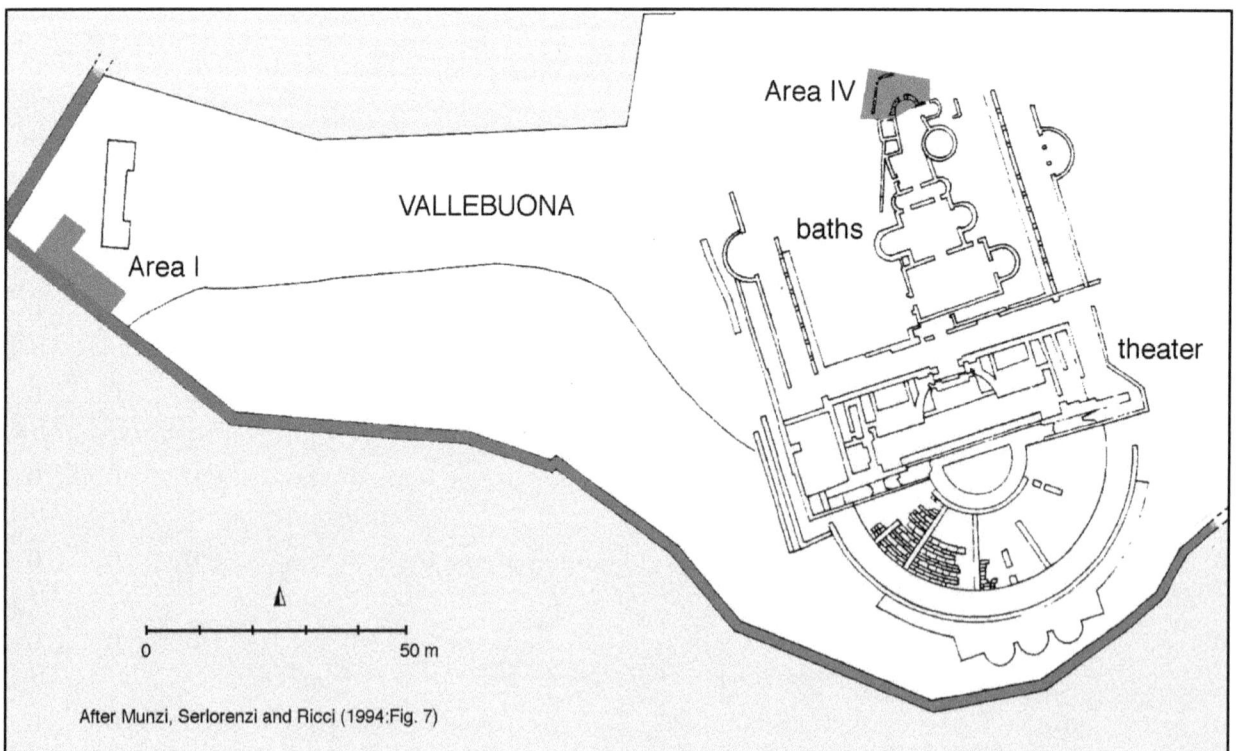

After Munzi, Serlorenzi and Ricci (1994:Fig. 7)

Figure 2: Plan of the Vallebuona area of Volterra, indicating two of the four recent excavation areas

Distinguishing the Local from the Regional:
Irish Perspectives on Urbanization in Early Medieval Europe

John Soderberg

Abstract

For several decades, approaches to social complexity have increasingly focused on "a complex of domination" (Graham 1987:3) as the fundamental cause of change worldwide. For medieval Europe, this orientation on elite control of resources as a spur to increasing complexity is often elaborated in terms of a regional scale of analysis in which long-distance trade for prestige goods fosters competitive market exchange and the creation of urban centres to fuel that exchange, developments which, in turn, extend elite control. The emergence of these regional social dynamics is characterized as dependent on supplanting earlier, localized dynamics that hinder change where they persist. Social complexity, then, becomes the process by which regional dynamics come to prevail at all levels of interaction. Medieval Irish monasteries provide key evidence that this regional orientation is insufficient. This paper presents evidence that one monastery, Clonmacnoise, had urban qualities by circa AD 700, a period lacking substantial evidence for the regional scale's "complex of domination". This evidence presents a significant challenge to the regional perspective and suggests that a distinct local scale of analysis must be reintegrated into conceptions of social complexity.

Introduction

Nearly two decades after its publication, Richard Hodges' *Dark Age Economics* (1982) remains a definitive work for archaeologists on early medieval urban centers in northwestern Europe. *Dark Age Economics* rejects the local scale of analysis advocated by earlier scholars and articulates a regional scale of analysis that still dominates archaeological approaches to the European Middle Ages. The regional scale of analysis found in *Dark Age Economics* gives precedence to long-distance or regional interaction in fostering social change. Hodges views that sort of interaction as distinct from localized interaction because he sees region-wide activity as less bound by social ties. For Hodges such external exchange is more oriented to individualistic and competitive behavior than local or internal exchange. Accordingly, elites seek foreign goods in order to enhance their own status and authority. As their authority grows, they become less bound by local social obligation and more able to extract enough surplus from dependents to found urban trade centers. In turn, these towns foster market exchange in that locality.

In adopting this regional perspective on European urbanism, Hodges participates in the establishment of prevailing approaches to social complexity and scales of analysis. As Johnson (1999:220-222) describes, agency and the individual as a willful actor have been major concerns in archaeological theory during the last twenty years. Johnson argues that this orientation fosters attention to local scales of analysis. While they may promote study of small areas, approaches such as Hodges'—which stress individual competition—also collapse distinctions between local and regional scales so that a distinct local scale of analysis ceases to exist. Local dynamics become subsumed into regional dynamics. From this perspective, individual competition drives elite power acquisition strategies, and the institutions of social complexity are essentially a by-product of that process. Consequently, questions about the validity of Hodges' view of northwestern European medieval urbanism are equally questions about prevailing notions of social complexity.

Medieval Irish monasteries provide key evidence that this regional orientation is insufficient. For heavily regional approaches, Ireland represents the danger that a city will appear in the wrong place: an area without a highly developed social hierarchy and an orientation to long-distance trade. Scholars have long considered the possibility that certain Irish monasteries developed into urban centers. Annals and hagiography provide tantalizing, but ultimately equivocal, references to monastic cities as early as the 7th or 8th century AD. Hodges flatly rejects the possibility of these monasteries being urban centers at that date. He argues that urban centers appeared in Ireland only after *circa* AD 900, several centuries after they appeared elsewhere in northwestern Europe. The explanation for this delay is that the essential social conditions were not sufficiently prevalent in Ireland until that date. Furthermore, Hodges associates these monasteries with a localized orientation that hindered rather than fostered the development of urbanism. If these monasteries were indeed urban in a period when the conditions usually associated with fostering urbanization were not prevalent, then the regional scale of analysis is not adequate for explaining such cases. Other circumstances fostered urban centers in this setting. Effective exploration of those circumstances depends upon recognizing a distinct local scale of analysis oriented on social dynamics distinct from those associated with the regional scale of analysis.

This paper begins with the link between scales of analysis and conceptions about the social processes fundamental to social complexity. It then presents the preliminary analysis of faunal material from one potentially urban monastery, Clonmacnoise (**Figure 1**), suggesting that the monastery possessed urban qualities *circa* AD 700. If this conclusion is affirmed by further research, Clonmacnoise demonstrates the existence of an alternative dark age economics which fosters a type of urbanism distinct from the emporia which have become the paradigm for northwestern European medieval urbanism. The final sections of the paper identify key aspects of this alternative urbanism in Ireland, its implications for medieval European urbanism, and links with recently emerging approaches to social complexity.

Scales of Analysis and the Origin of Dark Age Economics

The regional scale of analysis elaborated in *Dark Age Economics* breaks from the local scale of analysis found in earlier work, particularly that of Henri Pirenne and Georges Duby. Pirenne argues that the decline of Mediterranean contacts in the post-Roman period is the defining circumstance for early medieval northwestern European society (Pirenne 1925, 1939). For Pirenne, the rise of Islam in the 7th century isolated northwestern Europe from external gold supplies, fostering the development of a self-sufficient or localized economy. In *Dark Age Economics,* Hodges revises Pirenne's view of early medieval Europe. In combination with *Mohammed, Charlemagne and the Origins of Europe* (Hodges and Whitehouse 1983), his refutation of the view that northwestern Europe was isolated in the early medieval period is also couched as a reaction to Georges Duby's thesis that intensification of agricultural production was a main economic engine of change in this period (Hodges and Whitehouse 1983:106-108; Hodges 1989:58-59). Like Pirenne's work, Duby's approach is highly localized with internal developments driving change. Hodges (1989:58) writes:

> Henri Pirenne, F.L. Ganshof and George Duby, to name but three eminent historians of this era, have based their socio-economic model on the miscellaneous documentation which would appear to lend some support to the notion of agricultural intensification preceding urban expansion.

In place of the pan-regional connections that dominated earlier periods, for the early medieval period, these scholars see a turn inward toward nearby resources. For Pirenne and Duby, early medieval urbanism is fundamentally a product of internal, local dynamics.

In place of the gradual accumulation of wealth via agricultural intensification, Hodges favors a more sudden growth spurred by elites seeking to expand trade contacts. As part of their power acquisition strategy, elites established emporia to secure access to long-distance trade goods. Drawing from the anthropological approaches to medieval Europe exemplified by Philip Grierson (e.g. 1959) and the work of Fernand Braudel (e.g. 1979), Hodges combines anthropological literature on gift-exchange with excavation data on early medieval trade centers (*emporia*) to refute the localized view of northwestern Europe between AD 600 and 1000. Hodges views the circulation of Arabic silver and other goods through northwestern emporia as essential to the growth of royal power in northwestern Europe. In the quest for prestige items, rulers established trade centers and long-distance trade networks to acquire rare and precious goods that would allow them, via continued gift-exchange, to enhance their own power (Hodges 1982:193-194). These efforts led to the establishment of a precocious market-exchange system centered in emporia. In this manner, Hodges conceptualizes interregional royal gift-exchange as a mechanism which fostered change from reciprocity and redistribution to quasi-market exchange. Urbanization and social complexity were a by-product of that process.

Superficially, the distinction between the approach Hodges develops and that of his predecessors appears to be a matter of selecting one sector of an economy over another; however, the division runs much deeper, into basic social processes. Consider for example the difference between Duby's assessment of Carolingian social organization and the social dynamic Hodges describes. Duby (1981:58-60) writes:

> Couldn't the economic historians, as their contemporaries obviously did, consider the great demesnes the area of lordly rule, centering on the castle or the monastery, as self-sufficient families, as places of redistribution between a paternal force and all the satellite familiar networks. At a higher level, the State manifested a similar structure . . . [It] was like a large family.

Here Duby sees the self-sufficient, communal agricultural unit as the model for all levels of medieval society. Change occurs through the elaboration of that organization.[1] By contrast, Hodges views royal gift-exchange and emporia as a means for escaping that social organization. Long-distance trade was significant for the development of market economics because it occurred outside of the social ties that otherwise organize exchange. Consequently, it provided the thin end of the wedge that brought an individualistic, competitive market into an area. These emporia were *administered markets*, a term Hodges uses to describe the elite-directed, proto-market economy that was a precursor to the competitive market lying at the core of the later medieval market economy. Hodges (1989:60, emphasis in original) writes:

> We can conclude, therefore, that long-distance trade did not lead *directly* to the development of the 10th- and 11th-century commercial revolution. Instead, the trade in luxury goods was being channeled into the hands of the elite who used this to maintain and in some cases enhance their status.

Elite power acquisition provides the stimulus for urbanism.

In advocating this approach to medieval Europe, Hodges participates in a general shift in archaeological perspectives on social complexity. His socioeconomic orientation is one example of what Brumfiel and Earle have called the *political approach* to social complexity. From this perspective, elites organize specialization and exchange in order to "create and maintain social inequalities, strengthen political coalitions and fund new institutions of control" (Brumfiel and Earle 1987:3). Brumfiel and Earle regard the *political approach* as a reaction against earlier work that is excessively focused on cooperative or managerial functions of elites in complex societies. They argue that the driving force behind the emergence of social complexity is individualistic and competitive behavior. Elites act to enhance their own status. The institutions that they fund are by-products of that process. The con-

---

[1] See below for consideration of the contradiction which the phrase "paternal force" introduces into this perspective.

tinuing prevalence of this approach is demonstrated by a recent volume entitled *The Emergence of Towns* (Nilsson and Lilja 1996). Sven Lilja (1996:22), for example, writes:

> In explicit contrast to the "Pirenne-thesis" of the thirties most researchers today are inclined to point out organized action by a king, a tribal chieftain, or an aristocratic overlord....

Similarly, Blomkvist (1996:140, emphasis and capitalization in original) concludes:

> Modern Medieval archaeologists, however, do not seem inclined to follow the thoughts of Pirenne.... Many of them think that the foremost factor behind towns was *power* and *redistribution* rather than trade and craft.

Graham suggests that this orientation on power stems in part from Max Weber's work linking the development of urbanism with the price-fixing market and the development of "a complex of domination" (Graham 1987:3). For each of these perspectives, this ability to subordinate is the fulcrum on which social complexity rises.

One consequence of this perspective is the marginalization of Duby's localized, internal dynamics. To the extent that they have any role in shaping change, they hinder it. While Brumfiel and Earle do not specifically refer to Duby, they classify similar approaches as *adaptationist*, which they characterize as mistakenly assessing the role of elites as integrating increasingly disparate elements of increasingly complex societies. By rejecting the adaptationist approach, Brumfiel and Earle parallel Hodges in his relegation of agriculture to a secondary role in social change. Brumfiel and Earle (1987:6) state in the introduction to their volume that:

> One of the most important conclusions to be drawn from the cases in this book is the lack of importance of subsistence goods specialization for political development.

As with Hodges, agriculture may provide the surplus that funds elite power strategies, but subsistence activity itself does not contribute independently to the development of social complexity. Agriculture, a core of localized economic activity, becomes of marginal significance to the trajectory of social change.

This rejection of subsistence as having a significant role in shaping the development of social complexity is widespread. It underlies, for example, Fernand Braudel's assessment of European capitalism. For Braudel, the complexity of capitalist society requires a three volume explication, and modern society bears the clear stamp of early proto-capitalists who probably made up less than 10% of the society into the 14th century. The remaining 90% of the population leaves virtually no imprint on this work. His most direct address to them is the page-and-a-half consideration entitled "Beneath the level of the market" (Braudel 1979:59-60). Braudel does not consider a subsistence-based economy as any significant influence. This "subsistence" economy with all its social ramifications is merely an absence, what he calls a *noneconomy*: "the lowest

plane of human existence, where each man must himself produce almost all he needs" (Braudel 1979:59). From this perspective, it is expansion beyond that realm which constitutes social change.

This rejection of subsistence agriculture's social significance is more a rejection of the social processes associated with self-sufficient agriculture than with agriculture itself. Hodges has identified urbanism with particular socioeconomic behaviors that are first found in long-distance interaction. Having reached an area through such regional activity, those socioeconomic behaviors then spread through local activity. In short, the development of urbanism is the replacement of local dynamics with regional dynamics. This process is clearly delineated by Johnson and Earle (1987). In this work, the authors describe the socioeconomic strategies associated with the regional scale of analysis and the political approach as comprising the *political economy*. They contrast this political economy with the *subsistence economy*. Johnson and Earle (1987:13) argue that these two economies have "different rationalities and dynamics". Their notion of a *subsistence economy* has much the same organizing principles Duby finds in early medieval Europe and is analogous to Sahlins' (1972) *domestic mode of production* and Braudel's *noneconomy*. Such an economy is organized around the goal that a given economic unit will be self-sufficient. The basic motivating logic is to fulfill needs "at the lowest possible cost that affords security" (Johnson and Earle 1987:12). Their political economy, by contrast, is oriented around maximizing behavior, through which individuals strive to maximize returns on their labor. For Johnson and Earle, the emergence of social complexity is the replacement of the subsistence economy by the political economy. Johnson and Earle (1987:13) write:

> All cultures have at least a rudimentary political economy . . . A true political economy, however, comes into being only at a certain stage of social evolution.

That point is the one at which elites begin to mobilize surplus from the subsistence economy to consolidate their rule. While subsistence clearly has a role in such a perspective, it is essentially a fund manipulated so that surplus is drawn from it. From this perspective, the development of social complexity is, by definition, the proliferation of the social dynamics associated with the regional scale and the marginalization of Johnson and Earle's subsistence economy.

While Hodges uses different terms, his conception of the rise of social complexity in northwestern Europe follows the same pattern. A localized, cooperative, subsistence economy is supplanted by a regional, competitive, manufacturing economy. Hodges refers to what Johnson and Earle call a subsistence economy as a "closed economic environment" (Hodges and Whitehouse 1983:85). Monasteries are the prototype of this closed economy. He concludes from his excavations at the Italian monastery of San Vincenzo al Volturno that this monastery did not engage in significant programs of economic development and agricultural intensification until after AD 900. Prior to that date, wealth acquired by the monastery was directed toward display items designed to stabilize "a fragile political situation" (Hodges 1989:70; 1997). Such closed economies are the antipode of the economy he associates with emporia. Open, regional trade fostered the administered markets typified by emporia. It is from such activity that Hodges sees truly competitive markets forming as individuals gradually disentangle exchange from social ties. Monasteries fail to generate such a pattern because they do not have even the inchoate market mechanism seen in the administered markets of emporia (Hodges 1988:56). For Hodges, they are economies of sufficiency, not maximization. Consequently, they do not advance the development of social complexity.

In *Dark Age Economics*, this view of monasteries merges with an assessment of early medieval Ireland's socioeconomic organization to produce an argument that Ireland fails to generate urbanism early on because the requisite social conditions are not prevalent. As many have done, Hodges recognizes monasteries as an extremely dynamic sector of early medieval Irish society. He begins a chapter on the nature of emporia with a quote out of Cogitosus' *Life of St. Brigit* that is the most commonly used documentary evidence for the existence of urban centers at monasteries in the 7th or 8th century. Of Brigit's monastery (Kildare), Cogitosus (translation by Connolly and Picard 1987:26)[2] writes:

> since numberless people assemble within it and since a city gets its name from the fact that many people congregate there, it is a vast and metropolitan city . . . . [T]ogether with all its outlying suburbs it is the safest city of refuge in the whole land of the Irish for all fugitives.

But, the "closed" economy associated with such monasteries leads Hodges to argue that they cannot be urban. Calling a town "a market-place operating within . . . an interlocking central-place system which is fully commercialized", Hodges states that even though Clonmacnoise and other such monasteries might have had large populations, "clearly these were not towns" (Hodges 1982:47). By contrast, the emporia participated in a more open economy. Furthermore, their success or failure was dependent on the extent to which they participated in a fully commercialized economy. The more they became mired in a closed economy with its social ties that redirected economic investment to social display, the more likely they were to decline.

Hodges offers Ireland as the paradigm of such failure. There, prior to *circa* AD 900, kings did not achieve sufficient independence from the social obligations which restrained their ability to institute emporia and the associated social change:

> The inability to centralize power, to generate sufficient control of scarce resources, meant that the Irish kings remained systematically restrained . . . . Contact with the rest of Europe was too infrequent or spasmodic for the negative feedback to be overcome (Hodges 1982: 195-196).

This circumstance leads him to agree with the description of Ireland as "an abortive civilization" (Hodges 1982:193). According to *Dark Age Economics,* the lack of centralized power

stunted the social evolution of Ireland and inhibited the growth of urban centers there at the time when they begin to appear elsewhere. When cities did eventually develop, Hodges echoes the view that these towns were foreign foundations imposing an alien institution on a moneyless, rural Irish society (e.g. Binchy 1962). Hodges writes, "virtually no evidence of interaction [exists] between the Viking colonies isolated on the coastlines and the great heartland of Ireland".

If monasteries such as Clonmacnoise were indeed urban significantly prior to AD 900, their presence represents an important challenge to the regional scale adopted in *Dark Age Economics* and to prevailing conceptions about social complexity. Both scholars who reject the notion that monasteries were urban in the 8th century and those who advocate their urban status agree that socioeconomic conditions differ significantly between the 8th century and two centuries later when Dublin develops. Long-distance trade goods were considerably rarer in 8th century Ireland than they were in 10th century Ireland. Also, unlike Dublin, Clonmacnoise is not a particularly good location for a long-distance trade port, and the New Graveyard excavations at Clonmacnoise have turned up relatively few long-distance trade goods in this period (Heather King 1998 pers. comm.). Evidence for market exchange, such as balance weights and coin use, and the use of silver as an exchange medium are associated with the post-900 period (Wallace 1987). Sheehan (1998:176) argues that, in the 10th century, silver hoards suggest that monasteries were centers for the spread of a market economy. But, two hundred years earlier, it is difficult to associate them with such a role. Some degree of socioeconomic centralization certainly exists in 8th century Ireland, but the critical question is whether or not the level of social stratification is sufficient to support elite efforts to found urban centers. Elsewhere in Europe that centralization manifests itself archaeologically in the form of dramatic settlement hierarchies and disparities of wealth in grave goods. Parallel evidence is difficult to identify in Ireland (Soderberg in press). Similarly, Wailes (1995) notes a lack of evidence for the level of intense manufacturing seen elsewhere.

Considering such information about 8th century Ireland, it is quite reasonable to conclude with Hodges that Clonmacnoise should not be urban in that period. But, if evidence stubbornly suggests that Clonmacnoise was urban well prior to AD 900, it may be that Hodges' conception of dark age economics and the role of social centralization in advancing social complexity needs reconsideration. Reintegrating a local scale of analysis into the study of urbanism can bring about that reconsideration by establishing that the social processes associated with the local scale have a significant impact on social complexity.

This reintegration does not entail denial of the importance of long-distance trade goods or the strategies associated with the regional scale of analysis. Works by Hodges and others using a heavily regional perspective are the source of profound advances in both European and world-wide archaeology. The problem lies, rather, in the relationship that these studies generally posit between the local and regional scale. Most regionally oriented studies equate the development of social complexity with a shift from local dynamics to regional dynamics. A more effective approach may be to consider social

---

[2] The Latin text of the *Vita Sanctae Brigidae* is available in Migne (1849).

change a product of interaction between regional and local scales, not the replacement of one by the other. Before considering the nature of such an alternative dark age economics and the sort of urban center it would produce, it is essential to consider if any evidence exists to motivate reconsideration of the conclusion that no urban centers existed in Ireland well before AD 900.

Clonmacnoise, Provisioning, and the Origin of Urbanism

Subsequent building activity at potentially urban monasteries greatly impedes understanding the nature of settlement at these sites prior to AD 900. Similarly, relevant textual sources generally date to later periods, and those sources which do concern the early period are elliptical on the details of settlement. While the sources have great potential in many ways, they lack detailed and extended descriptions of settlement organization and activities. Fortunately, one monastic center is increasingly an exception to this pattern. Several decades of excavation at Clonmacnoise are beginning to reveal the origins of settlement there.

Clonmacnoise is located in central Ireland at the intersection of the Shannon river and the *Eiscir Riada*, primary water and land routes across Ireland during the Middle Ages and earlier. Probably founded in the mid 6th century, Clonmacnoise became a leading ecclesiastical center, accumulating powerful patrons, valuable manuscripts, and numerous dependent establishments. Several studies suggest that Clonmacnoise's network of dependent monasteries began to flourish in the 7th century and that over succeeding centuries various groups vied for patronage rights to the monastery (Kehnel 1997; Ó Floinn 1995). Perhaps resulting from the political and ecclesiastical changes in Ireland during the 12th century, the stature of Clonmacnoise began to decline in that period, until in the later Middle Ages it became the center of a parish that was gradually consumed by its more powerful neighbors (Manning 1998:16).

Clonmacnoise now stands as the most thoroughly excavated of the large monastic centers. During the last several decades, numerous excavations have occurred in the central enclosure and the surrounding area. In general, these excavations have confirmed the presence of settlement around the central core of the monastery. One set of excavations within the central precinct has identified a shift from habitation to burial in this central area at approximately AD 700 (King 1997). Underwater archaeology in the Shannon river adjacent to the monastery has identified the remains of a substantial bridge built *circa* AD 800 (Duke 1998; O'Sullivan and Breen 1996). Although the results of these excavations are still under study, they do suggest a level of settlement complexity well before AD 900 that is only obvious in documentary records of the 11th or 12th century.

Ten years ago, Heather King began a series of excavations at Clonmacnoise in an area called the New Graveyard, which is located where urban settlement is thought to have developed: just outside the central enclosure. The final season of excavation ended in 1998. An extremely rare example of a large-scale excavation of such a monastery, King's work in

this area has revealed stratified deposits running from the 4th century BC up through the 12th century AD. The strata of importance to the origin of the settlement around Clonmacnoise are designated *Early Christian Phase One* and date approximately between the late 7th and the mid 8th century AD. This phase consists of layers containing decorated stone and bronze, bone trial pieces, stake holes, burned areas, and artifacts such as nails, bone pins, and iron slag, but no readily discernible structures. While any definitive conclusions must await full study of the massive body of data collected by King, preliminary assessment of one part of the archaeological material—the animal bones—does provide a means of examining urbanization at Clonmacnoise.[3]

Animal bones track the development of urbanism because, fundamentally, cities cannot feed themselves (Zeder 1991). They must be provisioned. While some food is generally produced within the confines of a city, urban population densities require that towns secure food and raw materials from producers who—willingly or unwillingly—export a portion of their herd. Since herders must maintain the ability to reproduce their stock, generally, only a portion of the range of animals found on a producer site is transferred to an urban center. Wapnish and Hesse (1988) propose that sites with different roles in the provisioning process will create animal bone assemblages with distinct age profiles. They identify three idealized economic orientations: self-sufficient, producer, and consumer. Self-sufficient sites should have the full range of mortality expected from a herd. Consumer sites should have a predominance of market-age animals, and producer sites should have a preponderance of animals of reproductive age and those dying very young. Research has confirmed Wapnish and Hesse's basic assumption that provisioning is reflected in animal bone assemblages; however, that research has also demonstrated that the relationship between those giving and those receiving animals is considerably more complex than the three part model described above.

Crabtree (1990) describes four means of identifying provisioning in faunal assemblages, including a contrast in age-at-death patterns found in animal bones assemblages on urban and relatively self-sufficient sites. Each of the four approaches to examining provisioning is relevant to the topic of urbanism in early medieval Ireland; however, due to limitations of space and to the circumstance that age-at-death ratios, or slaughter patterns, have formed the crucial element of past work in faunal analysis of early medieval urbanism in northwestern Europe, this discussion will focus upon how slaughter patterns reflect provisioning.

A slaughter pattern is constructed from skeletal elements which have a known sequence of change throughout an animal's life. Teeth offer the most reliable method of assessing age-patterns. The teeth of different species erupt and wear down in a characteristic pattern. While individual teeth are not

---

[3] This review of the animal bone evidence from Clonmacnoise is a limited survey intended only to show that reasons exist for considering that Clonmacnoise might be urban early on. Since the intention is not to present definitive conclusions, the methodological issues upon which such conclusions rest are not addressed here. For a complete examination of the faunal sample see Soderberg (in prep).

very useful in assessing age, tooth rows can often be assigned to specific age ranges, indicating the age at which the animal died relative to other animals in the sample. Faunal analysts typically group several stages into a larger developmental category. While the various faunal reports discussed here use different grouping strategies, in this paper, all are correlated with the five stage method described by Bourdillon with stage 1 representing "very young" animals, stages 2 and 3 representing juveniles, stage 4 younger adults, and stages 5 and 6 older adults (Bourdillon 1988:181). The graphs presented here show the percentage of identified mandibles which falls into each category.

A pattern for early medieval urban centers in Britain has emerged from numerous studies done over the past two decades.[4] As Wapnish and Hesse suggest, the urban centers have very few extremely young animals and animals of reproductive age. In contrast to Wapnish and Hesse, however, the assemblages are not dominated by market-age animals, those which have lived to their peak weight but not beyond that age. At Hamwic, for example, the age distribution is skewed towards the oldest age category. 46.1% of the cattle are in stage 5/6 (**Figure 2**) (Bourdillon 1988; Bourdillon and Coy 1980). Fishergate and Ipswich have similar patterns (Crabtree 1994; O'Connor 1991). This pattern contrasts with that found at West Stow, a relatively self-sufficient site (Crabtree 1989), and similar sites in Ireland. In the assemblages from these sites, the percentages of elderly cattle are lower (**Figure 3**). While the following quote does not refer to any of the sites mentioned above, Crabtree (1994:47) interprets the predominance of elderly adult cattle in such assemblages as indicating that "the inhabitants were supplied with older cattle which may have been culled due to barrenness, to bad character, or for economic reasons".

McCormick has identified much the same pattern in the animal bone assemblage from excavations in early medieval Dublin (McCormick 1983, 1987). McCormick finds that slaughter patterns for Dublin cattle are overwhelmingly dominated by old individuals (**Figure 4**). Such a pattern suggests that inhabitants are not involved in the production of the animals and are likely to receive cattle from other sites. Since textual sources and data from rural sites elsewhere in Ireland almost uniformly suggest a dairy herding orientation, McCormick argues that Dublin was provisioned with the excess cattle from dairy herds in an unidentified hinterland.

Was Clonmacnoise a provisioned settlement in the 8th century? One might expect the animal bone assemblage from Clonmacnoise to look very different from that of a settlement such as Dublin. Viking Dublin was a coastal settlement founded as a link in a long-distance trade network. Excavation has provided abundant evidence for market exchange and Dublin's role as a center from which a money economy spread to Ireland. In contrast, Clonmacnoise was located in the middle of Ireland at the intersection of several political territories, and it does not appear to have had an intimate connection with long-distance

trade. Also, Clonmacnoise was fundamentally a monastery; Dublin was not. Oddly though, the bone assemblages are quite similar.

The total bone assemblage from the New Graveyard excavation at Clonmacnoise contains between 80,000 and 100,000 fragments, which were hand-collected, washed, and stored after each season. The portion of that material considered here derives from an initial study including approximately one third of the bones. For identifying the origin of provisioning, the most significant phase of the site is *Early Christian Phase One*, which dates to *circa* AD 700. The sample from this period considered here includes approximately 3,000 identified fragments. As with nearly all early medieval Irish sites, cattle are the most abundant animal. They comprise approximately half of the material, 60% by fragment count (NISP), 45% by a count of the minimum number of individuals necessary to account for the bones present in the assemblage (MNI). The preliminary sample for phase one contains 46 mandibles which can be assigned an age estimate based on tooth eruption and wear. **Figure 5** shows the percentage of the sample which falls into each age category.[5] No mandibles from the youngest stage are present. Stage 2 contains 15%, stage 3: 10.9%, stage 4: 19.6%, stage 5/6: 56.5%. The relationship to other Irish sites is most apparent in the oldest age category. It is quite similar to Dublin, which has 55.7% in this category, and is quite distinct from Moynagh Lough which has 27.2%. This pattern provides one key piece of evidence that Clonmacnoise developed a similar provisioning system to Dublin's, but did so several centuries earlier. This sort of economic complexity is otherwise unknown from Ireland in this period; however, it is roughly contemporary with the development of Hamwic into an urban provisioned settlement in the 8th century.

Firm conclusions must await full study of the assemblage and other archeological data from the site; however, the preliminary conclusions presented here are bolstered by Bradley's recent review of textual evidence describing urban settlement at Clonmacnoise (Bradley 1998). He regards those texts as providing evidence for the presence of criteria he has established as the fundamental components of a monastic town:

> It had settlement complexity, houses, workshops and streets, as well as evidence for trade, enclosure, and political importance. (Bradley 1998:50)

In terms of chronology, Bradley notes that documentary evidence is concentrated in the 11th and 12th centuries. For example, the *Annals of the Four Masters* record a raid on Clonmacnoise in AD 1179 in which 105 houses were burnt (Bradley 1998:46). Significantly though, he adds that archaeological data suggest the monastery developed considerably earlier. Although nothing was known of the animal bone

---

[4] See for example Bourdillon (1994), Crabtree (1989, 1994, 1996a, 1996b), Grant (1988), and O'Connor (1991). Some Continental sites have produced broadly similar assemblages to those in Britain, including Haithabu (Reichstein and Teissen 1974) and Dorestad (Prummel 1983).

[5] Interpreting the significance of this pattern is complicated by the fact that the recovered assemblage is not the same as the deposited assemblage or the assemblage of animals that arrived on the site in the Middle Ages. For example, the mandibles of young cattle survive deposition and excavation less well than those of mature cattle. Consequently, mandibles from old cattle can be over represented in recovered assemblages. Various means of identifying such biases exist. Results from tests for these *taphonomic* biases in the Clonmacnoise assemblage suggest that—while some young cattle are missing—very old cattle did in fact predominate.

assemblage at the time of writing, based on other aspects of the archaeology of the site, Bradley (1998:50) concludes:

> The recent excavations, however, suggest that [the date for the origin of the urban settlement] must be stretched backwards in time, perhaps by several centuries.

The bone sample discussed here affirms that assessment.

From a heavily regional perspective, data suggesting that Clonmacnoise is urban in the 8th century are surprising. Given the opposition Hodges and others see between the development of social complexity and the "closed economy" of such monasteries, an urban center should not appear there. Several recent publications adopt this conclusion about the likelihood of urban centers at 8th century Irish monasteries (Graham 1987, 1993; Swift 1998; Valente 1998). In part, these studies cite a lack of definitive evidence for urban features prior to AD 900. On this point, arguments against the presence of urban centers in Ireland *circa* AD 700 are both trenchant and much needed. As was discussed earlier, documentary records are generally equivocal on the structure of settlements and—aside from work at Clonmacnoise—archaeological excavations have generally been small scale.

Beyond this concern with evidence, however, these articles also question the very possibility that monastic urban centers could exist in this period. Max Weber's approach to urbanism, which sees market exchange and centralization as necessary conditions for urbanism, is the starting point for both Valente and Graham. Valente (1998:12) writes:

> ninth-century Irish monasteries cannot be called market centers or towns since they did not function as true trade centers.

Graham's approach is similar to Valente's in that he also emphasizes Weber's "fully commercialized competitive market" (1987:9), but Graham sees that economic organization developing specifically in the context of the emergence of "domination" (1987:3). Both Valente and Swift adopt much the same parameters identified earlier in the discussion of the regional scale of analysis and Brumfiel and Earle's "political approach". From this regional perspective, since neither a market economy nor "domination" is prevalent well before AD 900, the presence of urbanism at Clonmacnoise appears inherently unlikely.

If further research stubbornly continues to identify urban features at Irish monasteries well prior to AD 900, two alternatives exist: either the regional dynamics are prevalent earlier than is currently thought or it is possible for a different set of dynamics to foster urbanism. The remainder of this paper considers how the local scale of analysis earlier identified with Pirenne and Duby provides an explanation for Clonmacnoise's development. This reintegration of the local scale into approaches to early medieval urbanism transforms this monastery from an anomaly into a manifestation of an alternative process by which social complexity develops in medieval Europe. Rather than urbanism emerging purely from elite power acquisition strategies and the replacement of a

"closed" economy with an "open" economy, by recognizing a distinct local scale, urbanism also springs from the elaboration of the "closed" economy and the social dynamics associated with it. As Duby suggests, changes become a product of expanding the boundaries of the self-sufficient, communal agricultural unit, not its replacement. From this perspective, an urban Clonmacnoise is—at least in part—that socioeconomic organization writ large.

Consider provisioning as an illustration of the contrast between approaching urbanism with and without a distinct local scale. At a simple definitional level, provisioning typically refers to the trade in food and raw materials that develops with urbanism. The regional scale of analysis, however, fosters an emphasis on coercive relationships between urban centers and supporting hinterlands. As urban elites gain dominance, they extract surplus in order to fund institutions which, in turn, further enhance their control. This perspective generally prevails in the interpretation of provisioning evidence from emporia such as Dorestad and Hamwic, where the transfer of animals is thought to be royally directed.[6]

This regional dynamic does not encompass the whole range of relationships associated with provisioning. The presence of provisioning in a locality where centralized authority is not robust enough to compel transfer of goods and where market exchange is not the norm implies the existence of more symbiotic relationships between city and hinterland, including cooperation stemming from a perception of common interest or a common identity. This possibility provides a reminder that provisioning is not merely a matter of subsistence specialization which differentiates rural producers from urban consumers. Provisioning both links and divides city and hinterland, simultaneously creating distinct identities and a common identity. In highly coercive settings, the regional scale of analysis is effective for capturing the ways in which the common identity becomes empty ideology deployed so that urban consumers can more effectively exploit producers (e.g. Kolb 1994). In other circumstances, however, the common identity may have a more direct role in shaping the socioeconomic relationships upon which an urban center rests. The local scale of analysis with its orientation on internal exchange is essential for exploring urbanism in such settings and for developing an alternative to the conclusion that urbanism does not exist in such settings.

The Local Scale of Analysis and Monastic Towns in Early Medieval Ireland

Since the 1960s the terms "monastic city" and "monastic town" have identified a category of urban settlement in Ireland distinct from the urban form described in *Dark Age Economics*: trade centers such as Dublin (Swift 1998:105). Arguments for the existence of monastic towns frequently draw from the alternative dark age economics identified with the local scale of analysis. Charles Doherty is the best known advocate of an early and distinct form of urbanism in Ireland (Doherty 1985). Doherty cautions against viewing early medieval towns through the lens of later medieval or modern

---

[6] A notable exception to this trend (Bourdillon 1988) is considered below.

towns. Specifically, he points to the centrality of religion—rather than trade—to many early urban centers. Doherty links this orientation to the concept of "ceremonial centers" developed by Paul Wheatley (1971), who argues that the commercial orientation springing from Weber's model of urbanism does not account for all cases of urbanism. Wheatley views reluctance to consider alternatives to Weber's approach a serious failure of scholarship on urbanism: "A general, as opposed to a Western, theory of urbanism is still some way in the future" (Wheatley 1969:26).

As an alternative, Wheatley proposes the existence of an urban ceremonial center that is the focal point of a non-centralized community and acts as a point of contact for the relatively autonomous components of that community. Although the sometimes metaphysical terms of Wheatley's argument are difficult to interpret, he suggests that "cosmic certainty" develops in these centers. This phrase appears to refer to the process by which a sense of belonging to an extended community is created and maintained both in the city and the hinterland. He presents this common identity as a contrast to the alienation prevailing in Weber's view.

This notion of urbanism has some affinity with the approach to urbanism that Finley adopts.[7] He (1985:125) argues that cities are fundamentally variable:

> Hypothetically, the economic relationship of a city to its countryside . . . can range over a whole spectrum, from complete parasitism at one end to full symbiosis at the other . . . . The question is whether ancient cities were, as Max Weber thought, primarily centers of consumption. Stated differently, how did the cities pay for what they drew from the country?

In Finley's spectrum, Weber's model is effective for parasitic cities but does not have the same utility for other types of city. Finley's notion of a spectrum recognizes a role for regional dynamics such as coercion and alienation, but it also recognizes that these dynamics are not the sole foundation for urban centers. Alternative types of urbanism also depend on commonality between city and hinterland, a fundamental element of the local scale of analysis. In fact, the circumstances fostering Finley's and Wheatley's types of urbanism are strikingly similar to those associated with Johnson and Earle's subsistence economy and Hodges' closed economy. Each stresses the creation of a common base from which socioeconomic activity proceeds and which is not purely an instrument of coercion.[8] The contrast is that, while Hodges and Johnson and Earle consider these dynamics of the local scale of analysis inconsequential in shaping social complexity, for Finley and Wheatley, they are a driving force of change.

Doherty captures the distinctive nature of Irish monastic towns in his description of their position as a city of refuge (*civitas refugii*) in which one could claim asylum. He elaborates on the significance of asylum in the context of increasingly centralized rule: "such islands of asylum prevented the power of the

kings from totally embracing all of their subjects" (Doherty 1985:70). In doing so, Doherty places monasteries in fundamental opposition to the regional strategies that have become associated with developing social complexity. Through Wheatley, Doherty defines a type of urbanism that was not founded on royally directed commerce, the core of Hodges' dark age economics. In fact, these ceremonial centers developed in opposition to increasingly centralized royal authority. They were associated with the development of a decentralized network for which the monastery served as an axis. Doherty views these cities of refuge as bulwarks against the sort of centralized authority that animates heavily regional approaches to urbanism.

The contrast between this type of urbanism and the better recognized forms becomes particularly clear in the distinction Doherty draws between urban centers before and after AD 900. Doherty refers to Irish monasteries prior to AD 900 as "ceremonial centers," stating that they had reached a "high degree of elaboration" by AD 800 (Doherty 1985:60).[9] Of the post-900 period, he (1985:70) writes:

> It is only when . . . 'sacred' towns are brought within secular [i.e. royal] control, when sanctuary is confined to the actual churches themselves, that one can speak of a town in the modern sense.

Consequently, for Doherty, while prior to AD 900 monasteries such as Clonmacnoise are not urban in the manner that Dublin and other emporia are urban, they are urban in the sense that Wheatley uses the term. From this perspective, Graham, Valente, and Swift are correct in questioning the likelihood of the sort of urbanism they discuss being present in Ireland *circa* AD 700. But that point does not address the likelihood of Wheatley's non-Weberian sort of urbanism being present.[10]

While Doherty's centering of his theory on the concept of "refuge" presents problems for identification in the archaeological record, the more important implication of his theory is the basis it provides for understanding what could foster an urban settlement at a monastery in Ireland *circa* AD 700. While he does not suggest that regional dynamics are irrelevant

---

[7] The association between Finley and Wheatley had not occurred to me until I heard Rae Ostman's (2000, this volume) paper on Finley's views.

[8] For a full review of this socioeconomic orientation, see Gudeman (1986) and Gudeman and Rivera (1990).

[9] As Swift (1998) points out, Doherty unequivocally states that monasteries become urban after AD 900. Swift adds that Doherty also states that these monasteries are not urban prior to AD 900. This second conclusion may not be warranted. Since the fundamental point of Wheatley's work is that "ceremonial centers" *are urban*, it does not seem reasonable to conclude that Doherty considers the pre-900 period as simply non-urban. Doherty is distinguishing between types of urbanism more than identifying presence or absence.

[10] Others have called for a similarly localized view of early medieval Ireland. For example, Griffiths (1994) advocates increased attention to localized economic activity in his assessment of the Irish Sea littoral. He suggests that internal or short-distance trade is a far more significant factor in shaping settlement in this area than the long-distance trade often described as the prime mover of change (e.g. Thomas 1959, 1990). Griffiths finds regional approaches of limited use for understanding this area. In their stead, he advocates a turn to mundane items to which most of the population would have had access and which have localized distributions. Griffiths' approach meshes nicely with Doherty's approach to Irish urbanism. Greater attention to local interaction also characterizes the work on post-900 urban centers that has been done since the publication of *Dark Age Economics*. For example, McCormick's work on provisioning in Dublin identifies the importance of stable exchange relationships between Dublin and its hinterlands. See also Wallace (1987) and Bradley (1988).

to monastic towns, Doherty defines an additional dynamic as essential. His "ceremonial center" is remarkably similar to the organization Duby places at the center of his approach to the early medieval period. In both texts and iconography, monasteries are conceptualized as *familia*, households. The animal bone assemblages from Dublin, Hamwic, and other trade centers show evidence of market exchange, such as commodity production in red deer antler combs. Such evidence appears in the bone assemblage from the New Graveyard at Clonmacnoise only in the final phase dating to *circa* AD 1100 (Soderberg 2000). By contrast, changes in internal agricultural production, a key factor in change for Duby, are evident in the provisioning evidence from *circa* AD 700. Such a pattern is only puzzling if one requires, with Hodges, that a town is "a market-place operating within . . . an interlocking central-place system which is fully commercialized". If elaborations in what Johnson and Earle call the subsistence economy have a significant role in fostering social complexity, instead of being an oddity produced by an "abortive" peripheral civilization (Hodges 1982), Clonmacnoise becomes a settlement thriving for half of a millennium that demonstrates the importance of social dynamics obscured by heavily regional approaches.[11]

Clonmacnoise and Northwestern European Urbanism

The reconsideration of dark age economics offered here also raises questions about urbanism in areas where the regional scale of analysis generally provides a robust explanation for why towns develop. Heavily regional approaches conceptualize change as spreading from primary to secondary areas, in much the same way that regional dynamics spread from elites to subordinates. Recognizing a distinct local scale allows for the possibility that influence is multi-directional. If regional dynamics do not simply spread from center to periphery and from high to low, it is not necessary to identify the replication of the same conditions from area to area. Without a distinct local scale, variation in the process of change from place to place becomes epiphenomenal, copying-error essentially. With a distinct local scale, a region-wide process can still exist, but variation from place to place is a guide to the nature of the region-wide process.[12]

Consequently, the urbanism found at Clonmacnoise is not just a reflection of urbanism at Hamwic. Hamwic is also a reflection of Clonmacnoise. Most considerations of Hamwic, for example, see this center in the context of developing royal authority. This perspective undoubtedly offers considerable insight about why Hamwic emerged as it did. But an urban Clonmacnoise raises the possibility that other processes were also at work there as well as in Ireland.

A few researchers have already raised doubts about the suf-

ficiency of the regional argument for the development of British urban centers. Bourdillon's study of the faunal material from Hamwic, for example, suggests that the Anglo-Saxon town is well, if monotonously, provisioned (Bourdillon 1988, 1994). But, she notes that, unlike Dorestad, Hamwic does not have farmsteads located on the outskirts of the settlement. For Dorestad, van Es (1990) argues that these outlying farms are established to provide the town with food. Bourdillon suggests that the lack of such farms at Hamwic may indicate a less centrally organized supply system for Hamwic. In this context, she emphasizes Hamwic's role as a production center for mundane items that are unlikely to be exported as prestige goods, such as cloth, pins, needles, and combs. The absence of supply farms at Hamwic fits well with Bourdillon's interpretation. Their absence makes the town dependent on a more dispersed hinterland that is consequently more difficult to administer via highly centralized control. While she does not carry her argument to the point of calling for a general revision of how such settlements develop, her study does raise questions about explaining Hamwic as a product only of centralized authority. Rather than being the product of replacing a local dynamic with a regional dynamic, Clonmacnoise and studies such as Bourdillon's suggest that the urbanization of northwestern Europe results from mediation between the order articulated by Hodges and the order articulated by Duby. Differences from region to region stem from differences in mediation.

Clonmacnoise and the Nature of Social Complexity

Viewing urbanism and other elements of social complexity from the perspective of both local and regional scales of analysis has advantages, but it also must confront significant problems. One particularly significant problem is that, for the most part, the local scale of analysis as originally constituted ignored power and coercion. Earlier, Georges Duby (1981:58-60) was quoted as a representative of views about the distinct nature of the local social dynamic:

> Couldn't the economic historians, as their contemporaries obviously did, consider the great demesnes the area of lordly rule, centering on the castle or the monastery, as self-sufficient families, as places of redistribution between *a paternal force* and all the satellite familiar networks. At a higher level, the State manifested a similar structure . . . . [It] was like a large family. (Duby 1981:58-60, emphasis added)

Here, modeling large scale social institutions as households, Duby isolates sufficiency and cooperation as the core of a localized social dynamic. Significantly though, the phrase "paternal force" creeps into Duby's description and reveals a contradiction in such conceptions of internal exchange. His cooperative association includes, and may be directed by, paternal force.

The exploration of this contradiction is a primary motivation for much impressive research. For example, numerous studies in household archaeology have critiqued the supposedly co-

---

[11] Significantly, Clonmacnoise declines precipitously as both a settlement and a religious center in the wake of 12th century reforms to the Irish Church which established a more centralized ecclesiastic organization and when an interlocking central-place system becomes well established in some areas of Ireland.

[12] See Crumley (1995) for a discussion of how to consider regional influences without resorting to a core/periphery model. Morrison's account of monasticism in the Western Deccan region of India provides a similar model for developing an approach to scales of analysis that retains a distinct local scale without losing sight of the regional scale (Morrison 1995).

operative orientation of exchange within a household.[13] In general, consideration of the prevalence of "paternal force" in households has led to the insight that the social dynamics associated with the regional scale of analysis are also operant inside the household. Essentially, these studies have brought the regional scale of analysis across the threshold of the house. Asymmetries of age, class, and gender are now seen as equally prevalent inside a household as outside. For example, Brumfiel (1994) argues that state development generally necessitates changes in household structure because production is household-based in smaller-scale societies and households tend to be kin-based. For other institutions to gain access to resources, a redefinition of household and kinship must occur. In this manner, while such studies often emphasize local variation in household structure, the insight they offer derives from the extension of the social perspective associated with a regional scale of analysis into the local scale. This perspective has raised the possibility that the same dynamics prevail at all scales of analysis: the possibility that no distinct local scale of analysis exists.

An urban Clonmacnoise raises a different possibility. Having extended the regional into the local, it may now be necessary to explore the complementary extension: the local into the regional. Wheatley (1971:302-305) provides a beginning for this extension. His ceremonial centers stem from the interaction of autonomous groups at religious sites. As the interaction develops, these sites provide a basis upon which relatively autonomous groups join together without creating a centralized society. Unfortunately, having expended considerable effort to identify the distinction between ceremonial centers and the more familiar commercial centers of late medieval Europe, Wheatley collapses the distinction by suggesting that his alternative form of urban center is co-opted by royal authority that controls subsequent development to suit its own purposes. Doherty follows Wheatley here by suggesting that, after AD 900, urban centers are no longer ceremonial centers. In both cases, the ceremonial center is simply superannuated. This conclusion to the development of ceremonial centers aligns their trajectory with the trajectory for urbanism discussed by Hodges. This turn in Wheatley's work may explain the odd contradiction found in descriptions of Wheatley's views. They often suggest that religion or ceremony are both essential to urban development and extraneous to its actual form (e.g. Fagan 1995:351).

Emerging perspectives on social complexity may help to restore the distinction between local and regional scales without repeating the mistakes of earlier approaches to the local scale. During the course of the last decade, a growing number of works have questioned the validity of exclusive reliance on centralized power to explain change. Randal McGuire characterizes these new approaches as recognizing the "heterogeneity of power" (Paynter and McGuire 1991). They advocate consideration of a broader range of strategies as essential to the emergence of social complexity. For example, McGuire argues that, while it is valid to study social complexity from a "top down" perspective, often this approach fails by "[confusing]

this perspective with the totality of social life" (Paynter and McGuire 1991:10). Stein (1998:7) similarly concludes that a more effective approach "to power relations in complex societies retains the conflict-based model of social organization, but questions the idea of fixed social hierarchy as the crucial defining element in complex societies". In short, these works argue that elite power acquisition strategies are not sufficient to explain social complexity.

Many of those who recognize fundamental heterogeneity in social complexity characterize the different types as running along a spectrum that has coercion as one pole and cooperation as the other (e.g. Blanton et al. 1996; Feinman 1995; McGuire and Saitta 1998; Renfrew 1972). McGuire and Saitta (1998), for example, argue that urban centers in the southwestern United States represent a communal form of social complexity that stems from a relatively decentralized society, but one which is also stratified. The crucial distinction between this approach and their predecessors' work is that McGuire and Saitta avoid conceptualizing change as a shift from one pole to the other, from a subsistence economy to a political economy. Their approach is dialectical, with any period or locality characterized in terms of interaction between two opposed orientations. Consequently, they are able to discern a fundamentally different type of social complexity from the type associated with the development of hegemonic elites without losing sight of the role coercive strategies have in all cases. They find the essence of their approach in the words of an ethnographer: "Though they have petty captains, they obey them badly and in very few things" (McGuire and Saitta 1998:283). The urbanization of Clonmacnoise appears to follow a similar course.

Conclusion

In Adomnán's 8th century *Life of Columba*, Columba describes that his gift of prophesy collapses the world so that he can see it all at once (Anderson and Anderson 1961). Events from across Europe are part of the world he sees, but they neither obscure nor control the local events that make up the bulk of the narrative. Adomnán is located on the far rim of Europe, but he does not consider himself on the periphery. This perspective offers a challenge to reconsider the relationship between the local and the regional. The origin of the first towns in Ireland present a similar challenge. Debate on this subject has long been divided between those advocating a local perspective and those advocating a regional perspective. As data accumulate suggesting that urbanized monasteries such as Clonmacnoise predate the more familiar type of urban centers of the later period, it becomes increasingly apparent that examining this phenomenon successfully requires a local scale of analysis to complement the regional scale from which northwestern European urbanism is generally viewed. In this manner, Clonmacnoise points the way toward a means of approaching the perspective valorized by Adomnán some 1300 years ago. This mediation between the local and the regional is the essence of dark age economics.

Acknowledgements

I would like to thank Heather King and Dr. Finbar McCormick

---

[13] For a survey of household archaeology, see Hendon (1996) and McGuire (1992:158-161).

for their generosity in granting me access to the Clonmacnoise faunal assemblage and for their extensive support while I analysed the assemblage. I would also like to thank Dr. Peter S. Wells and Dr. Martha Tappen for their advice in designing this research. Financial support was provided by Dúchas, The Heritage Service; the Graduate School of the University of Minnesota; and the Department of Anthropology at the University of Minnesota.

Biographical Sketch

John Soderberg received his Ph.D in the Department of Anthropology at the University of Minnesota. The title of his dissertation is *Religion, Cattle, and Complexity: Urban Development and Decline at an Early Medieval Irish Monastery*. His other ongoing research projects include developing a methodology for using digital images to quantitatively analyze cut mark morphology on archaeological bone. He received an M.A. from the Irish Studies Program at Boston College and a B.A. from Middlebury College.

References Cited

Anderson, A.O. and M.O. Anderson (eds) 1961 *Adomnán's Life of Columba* T. Nelson (London).

Binchy, D.A. 1962. 'The passing of the old order' in B.Ó. Cuív (ed) *The Impact of the Scandinavian Invasions on the Celtic-speaking Peoples, c. 800-1100 AD*, Proceedings of the [First] International Congress of Celtic Studies (Dublin):119-132.

Blanton, R., G. Feinman, S. Kowalewski, and P. Peregrine 1996 'Agency, ideology, and power in archaeological theory: I. a dual-processual theory for the evolution of Mesoamerican civilization' *Current Anthropology* 37:1-86.

Blomkvist, N. 1996 'Yet another Viking archetype – the medieval urbanist' in L. Nilsson and S. Lilja (eds) *The Emergence of Towns: Archaeology and Early Urbanization in Non-Roman, North-west Europe*; Studier I Stads-Och Kommunhistoria, 14 Stads-och kommunhistoriska institutet (Stockholm):138-146.

Bourdillon, J. 1988 'Countryside and town: the animal resources of Saxon Southampton' in D. Hooke (ed) *Anglo-Saxon Settlements* Basil Blackwell (New York): 177-195.

Bourdillon, J. 1994 'The animal provisioning of Saxon Southampton' in J. Rackham (ed) *Environment and Economy in Anglo-Saxon England* Council for British Archaeology Research Report 89 (York, UK):120-125.

Bourdillon, J. and J. Coy 1980 'The animal bones' in P. Holdsworth (ed) *Excavations at Melbourne Street, Southampton, 1971-76* Council for British Archaeology Research Report 33 (London):79-121.

Bradley, J. 1988 'The interpretation of Scandinavian settlement in Ireland' in J. Bradley (ed) *Settlement and Society in Medieval Ireland* Boethius Press (Kilkenny):49-78.

Bradley, J. 1998 'The monastic town of Clonmacnoise' in H. King (ed) *Clonmacnoise Studies*, Vol. 1, Dúchas (Dublin):42-56.

Braudel, F. 1979 *The Wheels of Commerce, Vol. II: Civiliza-tion and Capitalism 15th-18th Century* Harper and Row (New York).

Brumfiel, E. (ed) 1994 *The Economic Anthropology of the State*. Monographs in Economic Anthropology, University Press of America (New York).

Brumfiel, E. and T. Earle 1987 'Specialization, exchange, and complex societies: an introduction' in E. Brumfiel and T. Earle (eds) *Specialization, Exchange, and Complex Societies* Cambridge University Press (New York):1-9.

Connolly, S. and J.-M. Picard 1987 'Cogitosus: Life of Saint Brigit' *Journal of the Royal Society of Antiquaries of Ireland* 117:11-27.

Crabtree, P. 1989 *West Stow, Suffolk: Early Anglo-Saxon Animal Husbandry* East Anglian Archaeology Report No. 47, Suffolk County Planning Department (Ipswich, UK).

Crabtree, P. 1990 'Zooarchaeology and complex societies: some uses of faunal analysis for the study of trade, social status, and ethnicity' *Archaeological Method and Theory* 2:155-205.

Crabtree, P. 1994 'Animal exploitation in East Anglia' in J. Rackham (ed) *Environment and Economy in Anglo-Saxon England* Council for British Archaeology Research Report 89 (York, UK):40-54.

Crabtree, P. 1996a 'Production and consumption in an early complex society: animal use in Middle Saxon East Anglia' *World Archaeology* 28:58-75.

Crabtree, P. 1996b 'The wool trade and the rise of urbanism in Middle Saxon England' in B. Wailes (ed) *Craft Specialization and Social Evolution: In Memory of V. Gordon Childe* University of Pennsylvania Museum of Archaeology and Anthropology (Philadelphia):99-106.

Crumley, C. L. 1995 'Heterarchy and the analysis of complex societies' in R.M. Ehrenreich, C.L. Crumley, and J.E. Levy (eds) *Heterarchy and the Analysis of Complex Societies* Archaeological Papers of the American Anthropological Association No. 6 (Arlington, VA):1-6.

Doherty, C. 1985 'The monastic town in early medieval Ireland' in H.B. Clarke and A. Simms (eds) *The Comparative History of Urban Origins in Non-Roman Europe* British Archaeological Reports, International Series 255(i) (Oxford):45-75.

Duby, G. 1981 'Symposium: economic anthropology and history: the work of Karl Polanyi' *Research in Economic Anthropology* 4:58-60.

Duke, S. 1998 'Irish bridge sheds light on Dark Ages' *Science* 279:480.

Fagan, B.M. 1995 *People of the Earth: An Introduction to World Prehistory*, 8th ed. Harper Collins (New York).

Feinman, G.M. 1995 'The emergence of inequality: a focus on strategies and processes' in T.D. Price and G.M. Feinman (eds) *Foundations of Social Inequality* Plenum (New York): 255-279.

Finley, M. 1985 [1973] *The Ancient Economy*, 2nd ed. University of California Press (Berkeley, CA).

Graham, B.J. 1987 'Urban genesis in early medieval Ireland' *Journal of Historical Geography* 13:3-16.

Graham, B.J. 1993 'Early medieval Ireland: settlement as an indicator of economic and social transformation, c. 500-1100' in B.J. Graham and L.J. Proudfoot (eds) *An Historical Geography of Ireland* Academic Press (New York):19-57.

Grant, A. 1988 'Food, status, and religion in the Middle Ages: an archeozoological perspective' in L. Bodson (ed) *L'animal dans L'alimentation Humaine: Les Criteres De Choix*, Anthropozoologia, Second Special Number (London):139-146.

Grierson, P. 1959 'Commerce in the Dark Ages: a critique of the evidence' *Transactions of the Royal Historical Society* 9:123-140.

Griffiths, D. 1994 'Trade and production centre in the Post-Roman north: the Irish sea perspective' in P.O. Nielson, K. Randsborg, and H. Thrane (eds) *The Archaeology of Gudme and Lundeborg* Akademisk Forlag Universitetsforlaget i Kobenhavn (Kobenhavn):184-188.

Gudeman, S. 1986 *Economics as Culture: Models and Metaphors of Livelihood* Routledge and Keegan Paul (London).

Gudeman, S. and A. Rivera 1990 *Conversations in Columbia: The Domestic Economy in Life and Text* Cambridge University Press (New York).

Hendon, J. 1996 'Archaeological approaches to the organization of domestic labor: household practice and domestic relations' *Annual Review of Anthropology* 25:45-61.

Hodges, R. 1982 *Dark Age Economics: The Origins of Towns and Trade, AD 600-1000* Duckworth (London).

Hodges, R. 1988 *Primitive and Peasant Markets* B. Blackwell (New York).

Hodges, R. 1989 'Emporia, monasteries and the economic foundation of medieval Europe' in C. Redman (ed) *Medieval Archaeology* SUNY Binghamton (Binghamton, NY):57-72.

Hodges, R. 1997 *Light in the Dark Ages: The Rise and Fall of San Vincenzo al Volturno* Duckworth (London).

Hodges, R. and D. Whitehouse 1983 *Mohammed, Charlemagne and the Origins of Europe* Cornell University Press (Ithaca, NY).

Johnson, A.W. and T. Earle 1987 *The Evolution of Human Society: From Foraging Group to Agrarian State* Stanford University Press (Stanford, CA).

Johnson, M. 1999 'Historical, archaeology, capitalism' in M. Leone and P. Potter (eds) *Historical Archaeologies of Capitalism* Kluwer/Plenum (New York):219-232.

Kehnel, A. 1997 *Clonmacnoise – The Church and Lands of St Ciaran: Change and Continuity in an Irish Monastic Foundation (6th to 16th century).* Vol. 8. Vita Regularis: Ordungen und Deutungen religiosen Lebens im Mittelalter Lit Verlag (Munster).

King, H. 1997 'Burials and high crosses at Clonmacnoise (Ireland)' in G. De Boe and F. Verhaeghe (eds) *Death and Burial in Medieval Europe, Papers of the "Medieval Europe Brugge 1997" Conference, Vol 2* (Brugge): 127-131.

Kolb, M. 1994 'Monumentality and the rise of religious authority in Precontact Hawai'i' *Current Anthropology* 34:521-547.

Lilja, S. 1996 'A "proto-urban" stage – some tentative reflections on the historical emergence of urbanism' in L. Nilsson and S. Lilja (eds) *The Emergence of Towns: Archaeology and Early Urbanization in Non-Roman, North-west Europe*; Studier I Stads-Och Kommunhistoria, 14 Stads-och kommunhistoriska institutet (Stockholm):15-28.

Manning, C. 1998 *Clonmacnoise*, 2nd ed. Stationary Office (Dublin).

McCormick, F. 1983 'Dairying and beef production in early Christian Ireland: the faunal evidence' in T. Reeves-Smith and F. Hamond (eds) *Landscape Archaeology in Ireland*, British Archaeological Reports, British Series 116 (Oxford):253-267.

McCormick, F. 1987 Stockrearing in Early Christian Ireland. Unpublished PhD dissertation, Queen's University (Belfast).

McCormick, F. and E. Murray (in press) *The Animal Bones from Deerpark Farms*.

McGuire, R. 1992 *A Marxist Archaeology* Academic Press (New York).

McGuire, R. and D. Saitta 1998 'Although they have petty captains, they obey them badly: the dialectics of prehistoric western Pueblo social organization' in D. Whitley (ed) *Reader in Archaeological Theory* Routledge (New York):275-298.

Migne, J.P. 1849 'Sanctae Brigidae Virginis Vita A Cogitoso Adornata' in *Patrologiae Cursus Completus*, Vol. 72 (Paris):775-790.

Morrison, K. 1995 'Trade, urbanism, and agricultural expansion: Buddhist monastic institutions and the state in the Early Historic western Deccan' *World Archaeology* 27: 203-221.

Nilsson, L. and S. Lilja 1996 *The Emergence of Towns: Archaeology and Early Urbanization in Non-Roman, North-west Europe*; Studier I Stads-Och Kommunhistoria, 14 Stads-och kommunhistoriska institute (Stockholm).

O'Connor, T.P. 1991 *Bones from 46-54 Fishergate, Vol. 15: The Archaeology of York* Council for British Archaeology (London).

Ó Floinn, R. 1995 'Clonmacnoise: art and patronage in the early medieval period' in C. Bourke (ed) *From the Isles of the North: Early Medieval Art in Ireland and Britain* HMSO (Belfast):251-261.

O'Sullivan, A. and C. Breen 1996 'An early Christian wooden bridge on the River Shannon at Clonmacnoise, Co.Offaly' *Newswarp: The Newsletter of the Wetland Archaeology Research Project* 20:23-25.

Ostman, R. 2000 'Volterrae, Volterra: change and continuity in the economy of an Etruscan, Roman, and Late Antique Center', paper presented at the Society for American Archaeology meetings, Philadelphia, PA.

Paynter, R. and R.H. McGuire 1991 'The archaeology of inequality: material culture, domination, and resistance' in R.H. McGuire and R. Paynter (eds) *The Archaeology of Inequality* Blackwell (London):1-27.

Pirenne, H. 1925 *Medieval Cities: Their Origin and the Revival of Trade* Princeton University Press (Princeton, NJ).

Pirenne, H. 1939 *Mohammed and Charlemagne* W.W. Norton (London).

Prummel, W. 1983 *Excavations at Dorestad 2: Early Medieval Dorestad, An Archaeozoological Study* ROB (Amersfoort).

Reichstein, H. and M. Teissen 1974 'Ergebnisse neuerer Untersuchungen an Haustierknocken aus Haitabu (Ausgrabung 1963-1964)' in K. Schietzel (ed) *Berichte über die Ausgrabungen aus Haithabu* Vol. 7, Wachholz (Neumünster):9-101.

Renfrew, C. 1972 *The Emergence of Civilization: The Cy-*

clades and the Aegean in the Third Millennium B.C. Methuen (London).

Sahlins, M. 1972 *Stone Age Economics* Aldine (New York).

Sheehan, J. 1998 'Early Viking Age silver hoards from Ireland and their Scandinavian elements' in H.B. Clarke, M. Ní Mhaonaigh, and R. Ó Floinn (eds) *Ireland and Scandinavia in the Early Viking Age* Four Courts Press (Dublin): 166-202.

Soderberg, J. 2000 'Combs for a new millennium: industrial production in central Ireland during the Viking period', paper presented at the International Congress on Medieval Studies, Kalamazoo, MI.

Soderberg, J. (in press) 'Clientage and social hierarchy in early medieval Ireland: an archaeological perspective' *Proceedings of the Harvard Celtic Colloquium* 19.

Soderberg, J. (in prep.) 'The animal bones from the earliest monastic phase of the New Graveyard excavations at Clonmacnoise (Co. Offaly, Ireland)' in J. Boyle (ed) *Settlement in Medieval Ireland*.

Stein, G. 1998 'Heterogeneity, power, and political economy: some current research issues in the archaeology of Old World complex societies' *Journal of Archaeological Research* 6:1-44.

Swift, C. 1998 'Forts and fields: a study of "Monastic towns" in seventh and eighth century Ireland' *The Journal of Irish Archaeology* 9:105-125.

Thomas, C. 1959 'Imported pottery in Dark Age western Britain' *Medieval Archaeology* 3:89-111.

Thomas, C. 1990 '*Gallici nautae et Galliarum provinciis* – a sixth/seventh century trade with Gaul reconsidered' *Medieval Archaeology* 34:1-26.

Valente, M. 1998 'Reassessing the Irish "monastic town"' *Irish Historical Studies* 31:1-18.

van Es, W.A. 1990 'Dorestad centered' in J. C. Bestemann, J. M. Bos, and H. A. Heidinga (eds) *Medieval Archaeology in the Netherlands* Van Gorcum (Assen/Maastricht):151-182.

Wailes, B. 1995 'A case study of heterarchy in complex societies: early medieval Ireland and its archaeological implications' in R.M. Ehrenreich, C.L. Crumley, and J.E. Levy (eds) *Heterarchy and the Analysis of Complex Societies* Archaeological Papers of the American Anthropological Association No. 6 (Arlington, VA):55-71.

Wallace, P. 1987 'The economy and commerce of Viking Age Dublin' in K. Düwel (ed) *Abhandlung der Akademie der Wissenschaften in Göttingen: Untersuchen zu Hendel und Verkher der vor und frühgeschichtelichen Zeit in Mittel und Nordeuropa*, Vol. IV, ser. 3, #156 (Göttingen):200-245.

Wapnish, P. and B. Hesse 1988 'Urbanization and the organization of animal production at Tell Jemmeh in the Middle Bronze Age Levant' *Journal of Near Eastern Studies* 47:81-94.

Wheatley, P. 1969 *City as Symbol* H.K. Lewis and Co. Ltd (London).

Wheatley, P. 1971 *The Pivot of the Four Quarters* Aldine (Chicago).

Zeder, M. 1991 *Feeding Cities: Specialized Animal Economy in the Ancient Near East* Smithsonian Institution Press (Washington, DC).

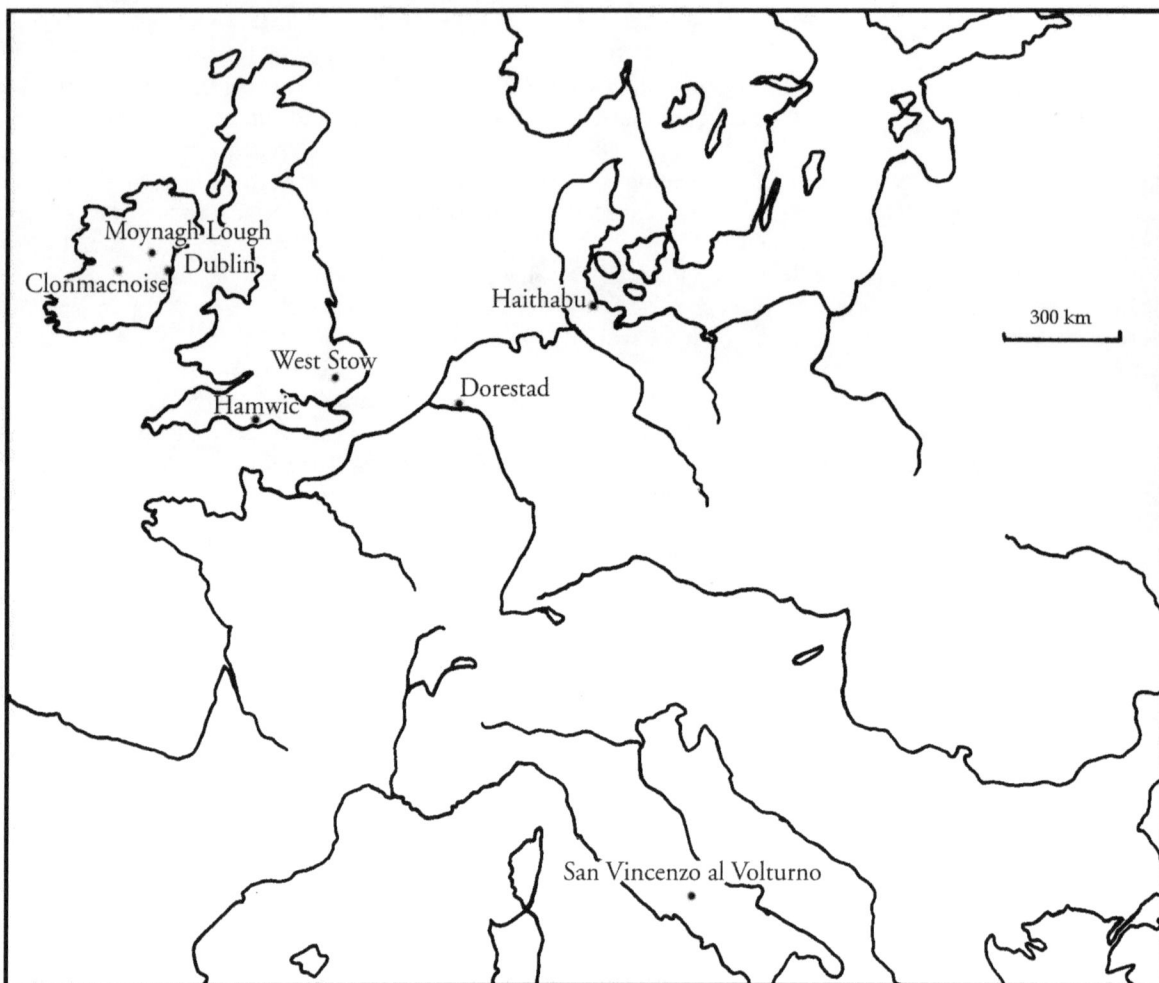

Figure 1: Map of Europe showing sites mentioned in the text.

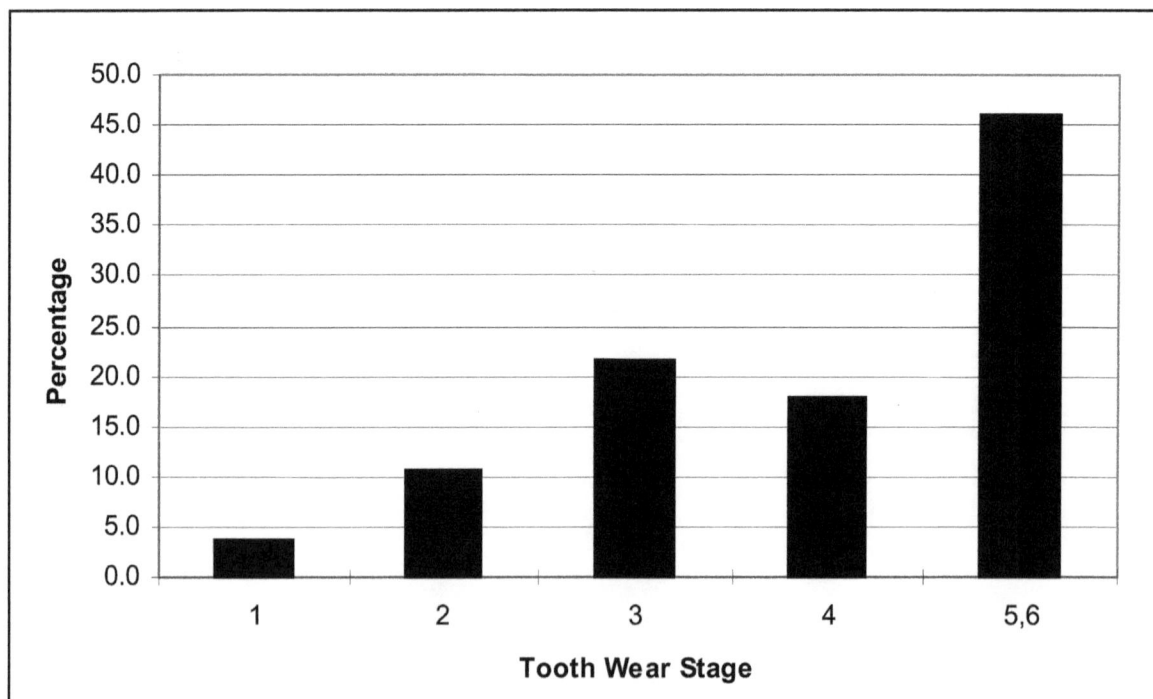

Figure 2: Cattle slaughter pattern for Hamwic, after Bourdillon (1988).

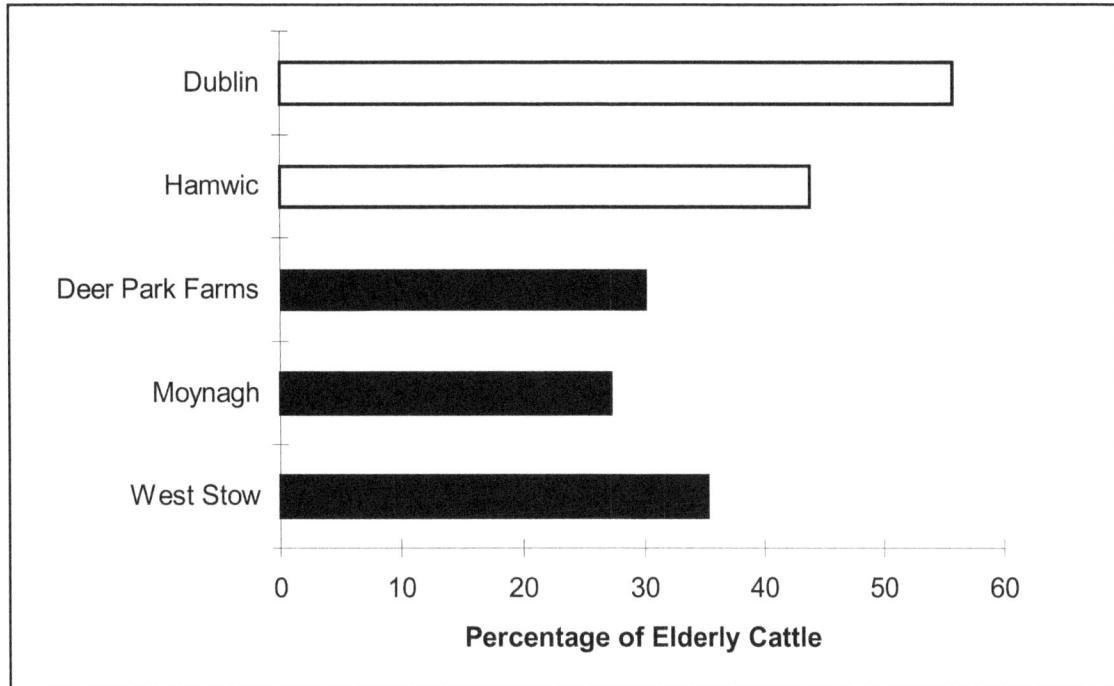

Figure 3: Percentage of cattle in oldest age category (stage 5, 6) for urban, provisioned sites (Dublin and Hamwic) and rural, relatively self-sufficient sites (Deer Park Farms, Moynagh Lough, and West Stow), after McCormick (1987), Bourdillon (1988), McCormick and Murray (in press), and Crabtree (1989).

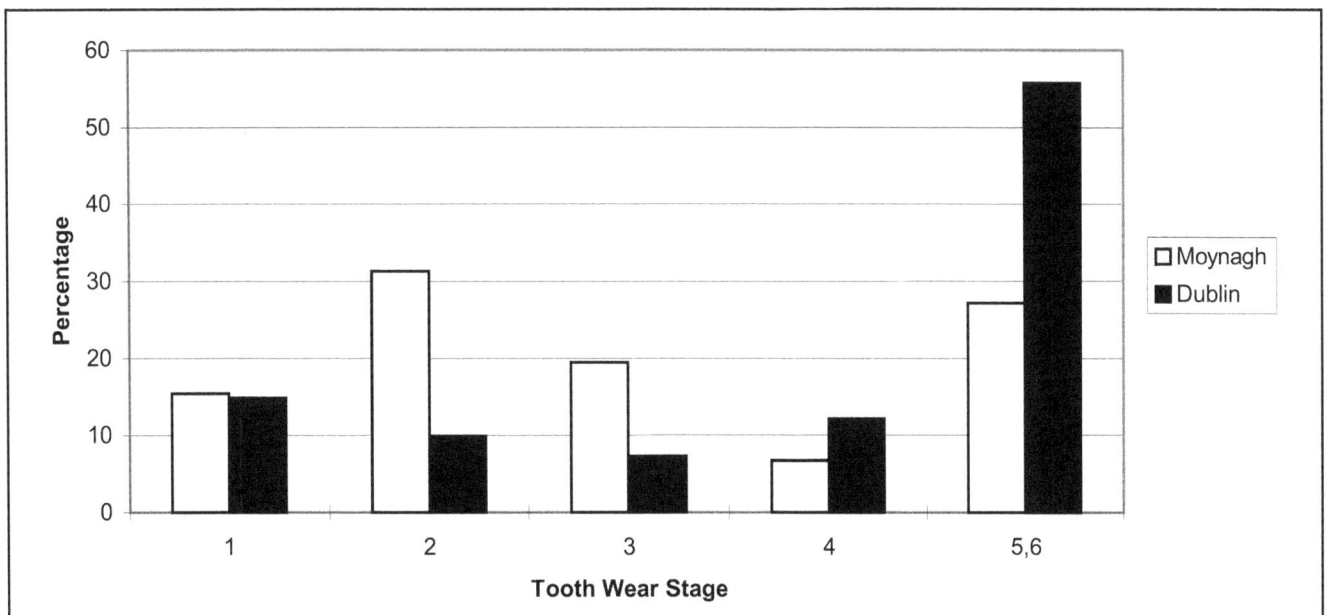

Figure 4: Cattle slaughter pattern for early medieval phases of Moynagh Lough and Dublin, after McCormick (1987).

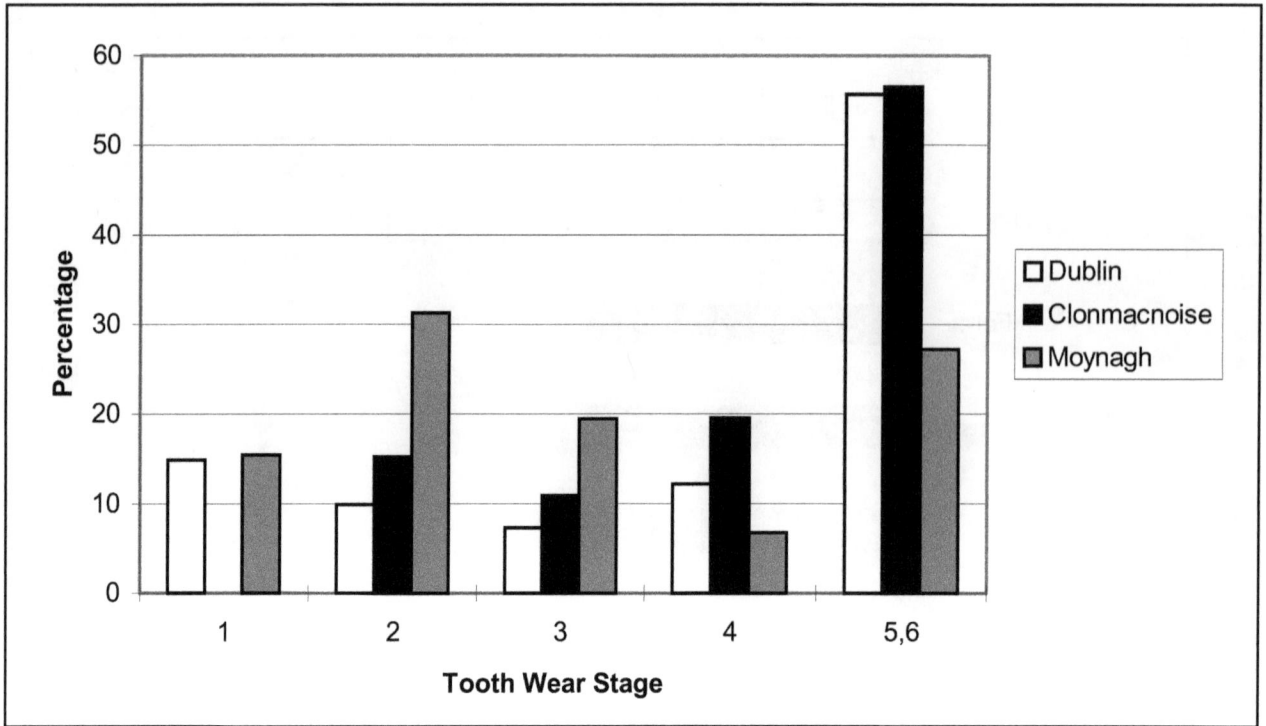

Figure 5: Cattle slaughter pattern for Dublin, Clonmacnoise, and Moynagh Lough, after McCormick (1987).

Patterns in Time and the Tempo of Change:
A North Atlantic Perspective on the Evolution of Complex Societies

Kevin P. Smith

Abstract

Between AD 1175 and 1250 medieval Iceland transformed itself from a network of decentralized simple chiefdoms into a unified proto-state. Uniquely, a vast corpus of vernacular writing—much written by the chieftains themselves—describes actors' ideologies, histories, motivations, and understandings of the processes involved. Archaeological data provide alternative perspectives, highlighting processes that extend over temporal scales beyond actors' abilities to observe or manage. How robust can our explanatory frameworks be if the changes we seek to explain occur too rapidly to be monitored by most archaeological methods? Do archaeological perspectives provide valuable or illusory insights on the processes involved?

Issues of Scale: Actors, Processes, Sources, and Change in Early Medieval Iceland

In recent years, many archaeologists studying political change in complex societies have shifted course from a concern with processes operating on whole social groups or societies to perspectives that emphasize the motivations and dynamic interactions of the people who participated in these systems over long periods of time. The context of debate has expanded from one that viewed the individual as somewhat irrelevant to one that includes individuals as actors with motivating power who constitute important, if hard to recognize, creators of the archaeological record. I do not intend to review the various sides of this debate nor to describe the contributions of those who have addressed it so well (e.g. Bourdieu 1977; Brumfiel 1992; Brumfiel and Fox 1994; Dobres and Robb 2000; Giddens 1979; Pauketat 1994, 2000). Rather, in keeping with the theme of this volume, my concern is with the very different temporal, spatial, social, and material-analytical scales these different approaches to perceiving the past require us to monitor and understand. To explore these issues, I focus on a relatively unique, important, and under-studied case of complex society transformations that took place in Iceland during the 12th-13th centuries AD. My goal in introducing this material is to examine how different the processes involved in the transformations would look when viewed from the perspective of the analyst confronting archaeological data and from the very differently scaled vantage points of actors who participated in the system and observed its operation.

The archaeological and documentary records of early medieval Iceland (*circa* AD 1000-1264) should be important to anyone studying complex societies as this is one of the only cases, world-wide, in which chiefdom consolidation and state formation were described in written form, nearly contemporaneously, by participants directly involved in the processes involved. As in most chiefly societies, dynastic history and "singing the praise" of ruling elites were important forms of entertainment and legitimation in Icelandic chieftains' households. Both orality (the poetic construction of history) and literacy became hallmarks of elite culture, serving as potent symbols of rank and as vehicles for transmitting the esoteric knowledge maintained, used, and created by Norse chieftains and their peers (e.g. Helms 1979). One result of this linkage between literacy and power was the creation of a suite of texts that describe in detail the internal operation and evolution of Icelandic chiefdoms, as interpreted and recorded by the actors involved, over a span of more than 150 years.

The available texts include law codes, annals, poetry, histories, and sagas—extensive literary compositions retelling the accepted histories of regions, families, and individuals. The best-known among the latter are the *Family Sagas*, literary-historical works set several centuries before the dates of their composition (Clover and Lindow 1985; Kristjánsson 1997). However, the genre also includes the so-called *Contemporary Sagas*—less familiar, sweeping narratives which describe events that took place within the lifetimes of their authors or within the memories of those living at the time of their composition (McGrew 1970; McGrew and Thomas 1974; Thorsson 1988). These latter sagas describe processes of change in Iceland *circa* AD 1120-1280. The authors of many of these works are known, as are their sources. For example, Sturla Þórðarson (1214-1284), the most prolific author, was a paramount chieftain who lived in western Iceland. Through his contacts and alliances, he had access to the perspectives of all his peers and rivals. He and his family members were directly involved in the processes of centralization and state formation that he described. His father and uncles consolidated complex chiefdoms in western and northern Iceland. Sturla Þórðarson himself ruled one of them and his cousin unified Iceland in the 1240s, creating the first Icelandic proto-state. Yet, Sturla Þórðarson's family were among those who lost the most in 1264 when Iceland was annexed by the Norwegian state. The narratives he, and other similar authors, created were, therefore, informed by personal knowledge and same-generation sources, yet were constrained from unbridled partisan advocacy by their creation for audiences that included other actors with first-hand knowledge of the same events. While these sources are certainly not fully objective, they are nonetheless remarkable for their detail, the comparability of events recorded in different accounts, and their even-handedness in recounting processes of triumph and defeat. As indigenous sources of information on the internal operation and dynamic processes of change in chiefdoms, they are unparalleled.

Early Medieval Iceland: Background

Describing a complex historical reality at its broadest temporal and social scales, the story told by the medieval Icelandic authors is this: Iceland was discovered by Norwegian Vikings in the late 9th century AD and was settled primarily by elite refugees and their supporters fleeing the process of state formation in Norway. In Iceland they created a society led by chieftains and organized by a commonly accepted set of laws that established ground-rules for regulating conflict among chieftains and their supporters. These ground-rules seem to have been intended explicitly to prevent any one chieftain or faction from establishing hegemony over the others—in other words, to protect the status quo of autonomous chiefly authority that had been violated by the creation of a state in Norway.

Icelandic chieftains (goðar) were recruited by birth from a relatively closed social class that viewed itself as distinct from the non-elite, to whom they were, however, related through more distant levels of kinship. They inherited titles to offices (goðorð) that existed independently of the individuals holding them. They lived in much larger houses, ate better food, drank more beer and wine, and carried more expensive weapons than the non-elite. They mobilized supporters for offensive and defensive action, held feasts, and had the right to interpret law and execute justice through lethal means. They distributed prestige goods to their peers and supporters to maintain alliances and support networks. Most of these prestige goods were obtained through trade with Europe and were secured for elite use through laws that gave chieftains the rights to purchase first from foreign merchants and to set prices on those merchants' remaining goods (Gelsinger 1981). Chieftains and their kinsmen traveled overseas to learn and gain status in the courts of European kings, to reinforce their authority through knowledge of distant places and ways, and to symbolize it by the gifts and styles they carried back from abroad (Bagge 1991). Through literacy and poetry they transmitted esoteric lore, including the law codes that defined and supported their rights.

In AD 930, a coalition of these chieftains established an annual, national-level assembly—the Alþing—where major disputes were settled and the laws were reviewed, as well as a series of regional assemblies for resolving minor disputes at the local level. By AD 965, thirty-nine decentralized chieftaincies were recognized in thirteen districts distributed around the country (**Figure 1**). Chieftaincies were defined by law as constituting authority over men (mannaforráð), rather than rule over territories.[1] Accordingly, each independent

householder had to declare his alliance with one of the chieftains, but not necessarily the one living nearest to him. Householders could theoretically change their allegiance, by public declaration at an assembly, to other chieftains if they felt that their interests were not being met, that their chieftains were becoming too avaricious, or that they could not expect potent support on their behalf. The creation of assemblies for resolving disputes, the establishment of chieftaincy as a decentralized, non-regional power structure, and the provisions for shifting alliances were all clearly intended to prevent any one chieftain from consolidating power, while supporting the legitimacy of the chieftains' rule.

Yet, despite the existence of leveling mechanisms to prevent the consolidation of authority into fewer hands, most of Iceland's districts were being transformed by the late 12th century into territorially bounded polities ruled by chieftains who had subordinated or eliminated their rivals (Sigurðsson 1989, 1999). By AD 1220 power in Iceland was held by six kindreds engaged in nearly constant civil war. Their leaders controlled complex chiefdoms that had absorbed formerly independent chieftaincies as subordinates, and in 1246, one of them, Þórður kakali Sighvatsson, unified all of Iceland. He then established a court modeled on European royal examples, appointed regional governors, and raised an armed bodyguard from the non-elite to enforce his interests, punish his enemies, and ensure tax collection. Leaders among the non-elite, who had held consensual authority among their peers in earlier centuries, were promoted to higher positions of authority within this system, while Þórður assumed sole authority to judge disputes, approve local judges, and enforce judgements—thereby subordinating the authority of the Alþing and establishing an official executive power for the first time in Iceland's history. Before this time, disputes could be judged according to the law but the responsibility to enforce judgements or take action against offenses was the duty of the aggrieved party, generally with the support of his chieftain, and was accomplished through blood-feud (Miller 1990).

Þórður kakali's polity endured while he occupied its highest seat, but fell apart when he traveled to Norway and never returned. His potential heirs and enemies fought over its parts, briefly reconsolidating elements of his realm, until the entire island came under the control of the Norwegian state in 1264. What is important, however, is that once Þórður established the mechanisms, structures, and lexicons of state control in Iceland, they endured among the elite. Each of his potential successors tried to re-establish his realm, or a realm modeled on it, rather than returning to earlier power structures. Iceland's non-elites, in contrast, resisted this process and sought to re-establish a model of less-centralized governance with greater local self-control. The incorporation of Iceland into the Norwegian state followed the rejection of Icelandic elites' claims to succession by non-elites in two northern districts during the 1250s—those same districts

---

[1] The terms chiefdom, chieftaincy, and chieftain are not used synonymously in this paper. Chiefdom is used to reference the anthropological construct first articulated by Oberg (1955), and since expanded and modified by many others (among them Carneiro 1981; Earle 1997; Service 1971; Wright 1984) to describe pre-state polities integrating many local communities under one hereditary ruler's authority. The term chiefdom carries, from its inception, assumptions that I question in the body of this paper about the territorial integrity of the polity under the chieftain's control. Chieftaincy therefore represents an alternative, yet linked, perspective referring not only to the office (in Icelandic goðorð) held by a chieftain but also to a politically corporate, supra-regional polity comprised of individuals allied, in a non-territorial way, to the chieftain. As an alternate form of regional polity linked to the chiefdom concept, the chieftaincy differs subtly in its non-territorial yet still supra-local implications for power-holding and political incorporation. The term chieftain (in Icelandic goði, pl. goðar) identifies the holder of such an office, whether his/her power base is organized as a territorial polity (a chiefdom in the "standard" sense) or non-territorially, yet regionally, into an alliance network built around the leader (a chieftaincy in this paper's sense). In Iceland, chiefdoms and chieftaincies appear to have co-existed at times before AD 1150, employing the same lexicon and legitimating charters for power-holding. After that time processes of regional

centralization resulted in the creation of regional polities (chiefdoms and complex chiefdoms) of ever-increasing size. Ultimately, I suspect that many, or most, chiefdoms known archaeologically went through phases of territorial integration matching the traditional view of chiefdoms and through periods of personal or non-territorial integration (chieftaincies) as a process parallel to, or linked with, the "cycling" described by Wright (1984) and elaborated by Anderson (1994).

were among the first to pledge tribute to the king of Norway in return for his promises of internal peace.

Conceptualizing Change: Actors' Motivations vs. Archaeologists' Expectations

In neo-evolutionary terms, Icelandic society transformed itself between AD 1175 and 1220 from a confederation of simple chiefdoms—with one or two levels of decision-making hierarchy above the household level—to a competitive network of complex chiefdoms. From that, it developed indigenously into a state with four levels of decision-making hierarchy and the elements of a bureaucracy. The transformation from simple to complex chiefdoms took less than two generations; the evolution from complex chiefdoms to a unified state took less than one – in fact, Þórður kakali's unification and transformation of the system took less time than it takes to earn an undergraduate degree. The entire process occupied a temporal span half the duration of a common archaeological phase and less than the typical 1-sigma error of a standard radiocarbon date. It is unlikely that as archaeologists we could monitor the actual processes involved in the rise of complex chiefdoms or the state with changes occurring at this speed, yet there is nothing to suggest that Iceland's trajectory was unusual. The emergence of the Mississippian polity of Cahokia, for example, appears to have taken place within one political generation (Pauketat 1994) and is matched by similarly rapid trajectories in other parts of the Mississippi valley (Brain 1989; Knight 1997; Knight and Steponaitis 1998; Steponaitis 1998; Pauketat 2000). Similarly, where tight chronological control over the processes can be obtained, the rise and dynamic cycling of primary states in Mesoamerica (Flannery and Marcus 1983; Joyce 2000; Kowaleski 1990; Marcus 1998; Schele 1990), Egypt (Kemp 1989; Lehner 2000), and elsewhere (Spencer 1990) appears to have been similarly rapid. What *is* unusual about the Icelandic case of state formation is that the available documentation allows us to understand the internal dynamics at very much finer social and chronological scales than are available in other parts of the world where states arose.

Although many different theories have been proposed to account for developmental processes in complex societies, including the rise of states, conflict theories (e.g. Carneiro 1970, 1977, 1981) loom large and would seem to be appropriate in considering the Icelandic case. Conflict was obviously a central concern of the Icelandic elite. The processes of centralization and political consolidation were to a large degree promoted and sustained by the twin powers of the sword (conflict) and the feast (alliance). In some cases, the sword enforced what the feast could not, while at other times the feast consolidated and rectified what the sword had accomplished. The literature of medieval Iceland is a literature of conflict, written by elites for elites, and about elite concerns. At times the theme is conflict as a form of resolution, at other times the theme is the resolution of unchecked aggression; but conflict forms the core of the narratives whether sagas or law codes are considered (Byock 1982; Miller 1990). What motivated conflict, how it was prosecuted, how it developed, and what it achieved can be examined in detail in these sources, since this was what interested the sagas' authors most. Although the Icelandic data allow other theoretical perspectives to be examined in equal detail,

I turn to this subject now in order to reflect on the motives, scale, and consequences of conflict in this case of state formation.

Negotiating in a World of Hurt: Conflict as Process in Medieval Iceland

The remarkable detail contained in the *Contemporary Sagas* frequently allows the growth and development of episodes of conflict among chieftains across the island to be examined at temporal scales of a year or less and at social scales fine enough to identify most of the major actors and their motivations. **Figure 2** is a graphic representation of one such escalating conflict between two chiefly lines in western Iceland. Each horizontal line represents one of the 36 original Icelandic chieftaincies (see **Figure 1**). Black circles and squares indicate aggressors in each incident of dispute; white circles or squares indicate the group attacked. Circles imply lethal conflicts, while squares designate episodes of legal dispute or non-lethal combat. Vertical lines link parties directly involved in the aggression – who actually attacked whom – while diamonds identify chiefly allies who came to each party's defense. I want to draw attention to two characteristics of the temporal and social structure of aggression: *feud chains* and *alliance cascades*.

The concept of a *feud chain*, coined by Jesse Byock (1982), reflects the social fact that scores are rarely evened in interpersonal conflict and that one event, lethal or legal, often leads to another. Such feud chains are seen in the enduring and cumulative nature of the conflicts represented in **Figure 2**. The incidents here include clashes between chieftains as well as hostile interactions among their non-elite supporters into which elites were drawn by their obligations to provide support for their followers. This is an important point that I will return to shortly. In feud chains, small incidents built up cumulatively. Some were settled by legal means (primarily the exchange of valuables) and others were resolved by lethal combat; yet the score was never really evened. Defeats in legal disputes eroded chieftains' reputations for being able to defend their followers and required honor to be avenged, while wounds and deaths called out for revenge. Although the number of people involved in each incident could be small—fewer than 10 people on a side in most of these events—their significance loomed larger as incidents accumulated.

One of the cumulative effects of feud chains was the unleashing of *alliance cascades*. When local disputes between chieftains and their factions intensified, allies secured over the years by friendship, gifts of prestige goods, and marriages were called upon for support. As each chieftain tried to gain advantage or build enough support to subordinate or annihilate his rivals, the number of allies called into the fray increased. When allies lost men or accumulated wounds, enmity deepened and spread over wider areas of the country, turning what was once a local dispute into a regional conflict or wider tension zone. The feud chain seen in **Figure 2** starts with a case of petty theft involving two chieftains' followers and ends 38 years later with the involvement of chieftains drawn from all parts of the island, the absorption of one chieftaincy by another, and the formation of the core of a regional complex chiefdom that endured long after this dispute. As complex as this sequence looks, it pales when compared to the wider-scale picture of concurrent conflicts among chieftains and their supporters described in *Sturlunga Saga* (McGrew 1970; McGrew and Thomas 1974; Thorsson 1988) during the late-12th through early-13th centuries (**Figure 3**). Allies called upon for support expected support in return. Consequently, alliance cascades had the potential to create polarized factions or competing confederacies of chieftains, which drew the noose tighter each time they were mobilized and eventually threatened to turn every local conflict into a regional conflagration. A concrete example from western Iceland may, perhaps, provide a better sense of the mechanisms involved in these processes, the scales at which they operated, and their consequences at both the local and the regional levels.

Wood, Wounds, and Death: Actors' Perspectives on Social Change

In AD 1195, two farmers in western Iceland (Þórð the Red and Hámund Gilsson) argued about who was cutting more brushwood from a hillside they owned in common. It led to no violence, but soured feelings between the neighbors. Some time later, a young man took a walk with a young woman. Her father objected and ran after them. The young man, possibly unaware that her father was behind, threw his axe over his shoulder and gouged her father's eye out. The young man was a friend of Þórð the Red, and the father was Hámund's kinsman. Bitterness grew when the young man's family refused to compensate the girl's father for his lost eye. Some months passed and one day the young man and two of his friends (one of them being Þórð the Red's son) rode down the valley to visit a ship berthed nearby. As they passed Hámund's farm, Hámund, one of his workmen, and the wounded father attacked them. In the ensuing fight, Hámund, Þórð the Red's son, and two others were badly wounded.

As this feud chain grew, both sides knew that more violence was certain and sought support from their chieftains. Hámund called on Þórð Sturluson—a member of a powerful western Icelandic chiefly family—to give him aid. Þórð Sturluson sent his brother with a contingent of men to stay at Hámund's home all winter. No further violence occurred that season. However, Þórð the Red was a supporter (*þingmaður*) of a different chieftain, Kolbein the Young, one of Iceland's most powerful paramounts, whose power base was in northern Iceland. In the summer, both chiefly factions gathered allies and took their cases to the Alþing, hoping to use non-lethal means to end the dispute. Þórð Sturluson exploited his kinship ties to build a coalition of six paramounts and chieftains from northern, southern, and western Iceland. While Hámund sought support from Þórð Sturluson to obtain compensation for the wounds he and his friends had suffered, Þórð Sturluson hoped to use this case to counteract Kolbein the Young's growing support network in western Iceland. Kolbein, for his part, called in support from his own allies, all paramount chieftains from northern and southern Iceland, in order to defend his *þingmaður* and extend his sphere of influence.

As this classic case of an alliance cascade developing from a feud chain expanded, each side strategically called in favors

from the enemies of the other coalition's allies. As a result, each coalition member's obligations to provide lethal support was balanced against the fear of acting rashly, knowing that reprisals would ensue in their own districts for wounds given in this dispute. Ultimately, the chieftains played political chess so well that the legal cases deadlocked at the Alþing. Both sides had balanced threats against obligations so skillfully that no one was able to gain supremacy and no one was going to get satisfaction. Rather than the affair being settled at the assembly, Þórð the Red's frustration grew until he attacked Hámund's chieftain, Þórð Sturluson, with an axe. Fighting ensued between the factions at the assembly. Four men were killed and many were wounded. Two of the dead came from each faction, but three of them were actually supporters of chieftains from distant districts who had come in as allies of the principals and who had not in any way been implicated in the original feud (Thorsson 1988:184-185).

While the local dispute was eventually resolved and compensation was obtained for the four deaths, enmity between the coalitions grew. What started as a small-scale, local conflict became, through the process of alliance cascading, a tactical struggle between members of two regionally organized strategic blocks that were growing and becoming stronger through repeated examples of such small-scale feuds. These, in turn, started when non-elite householders needed the support of elite backers to prosecute their local disputes. They became extended when the chieftains used these local disputes to demonstrate their abilities to defend their supporters and to advance their own competitive agendas against their rivals. Finally they expanded across the island as the allies of allies and enemies of enemies were drawn into what began as local affairs through the cascading obligations imposed by alliances.

What were the outcomes of this conflict? Men certainly died and goods definitely changed hands in compensation, troops were mustered and tensions escalated both within factions and across regions—but at the end of the contest no chiefdom expanded at the expense of another, no one gained greater access to high-value resources, and no one controlled a greater share of the system's prestige goods. Contrary to many archaeological models, the goals of the conflict were never to capture resources and its cause was neither environmental nor social circumscription. This conflict, like most others described in medieval Icelandic sources, had its roots in interpersonal problems that are common in isolated rural settings: accusations of theft, seduction, loss of family honor, minor boundary disputes, and unintended accidents, mixed with personality conflicts, family hatreds, obstinacy, and a willingness to use violence to redress old affronts. For the non-elites, the affair met their goals: vengeance was obtained, rights were upheld, and justice was served. The chieftains involved, in turn, maintained their status and gained authority among their followers by providing potent support and fulfilling the obligations that were the flip side of commoners' agreements to support them.

I use the term agreement intentionally because the non-elite were always far more numerous than the chieftains and their families. Lacking overwhelmingly better armaments, it was always possible, at least in theory, to overthrow or ignore elite claims to rule. However, through their wealth, accepted authority, distant kinship connections, and wider networks of support, Icelandic elites clearly had something concrete to offer—the ability to gather enough force to uphold their followers' rights against their neighbors and to maintain the peace when peace could not be regained at the local level. This was a concrete and indisputably valuable reason for accepting and supporting the asymmetries of the system and ultimately formed the basis for sustained elite power in Iceland (and perhaps elsewhere)—not knowledge of distant places, esoteric rituals about the unfathomable, control of exotic goods, or similar symbols of elite rule. Most of these latter social phenomena *were* also present in Iceland, and served as inter-elite currencies to establish and maintain alliances or to strengthen elites' claims for legitimate succession to office, but they appear to have been mechanisms for *maintaining* power rather than causative factors for the acceptance of sustained power differentials or for transformative changes in the socio-political system.

Ultimately, this minor case—one of hundreds described in the *Contemporary Sagas*—started with a non-lethal dispute among neighbors over brushwood, developed into a lethal local feud, and led, after it expanded to draw in people from all parts of Iceland, to a marriage between two elite kindreds on one side of the dispute and the formation of tightly knit coalitions among distant chiefly houses on both sides. Such coalitions, forged through mutual needs for support and bound ever more strongly together by accumulating shared resentments, guided the trajectories along which conflict and regional political consolidation took place over the next 50 years. As chieftaincies declined in number and more offices were controlled directly or indirectly by a small number of emerging paramounts, intermarriage among their houses tended to bring alliance cascades into play faster, over wider regions of the island, and with higher stakes. As disputes among these paramounts strengthened in intensity and bitterness, more often than ever before the only possible resolution for breaking the chains of feud and averting the cascading effects that turned local disputes into regional conflicts was to attack one's rival directly with the intent to kill or to drive him from the country. In so doing, a sphere of influence or a polity was left without a leader.

Yet, despite the expectations we might have that such situations would provide opportunities for the victorious polity to expand, chieftains more often retreated without annexing these vacant areas or held them very briefly. It is clear that one reason for this instability and inability to expand polities was that the victorious chieftains' titles, genealogies, and past alliances provided them with no accepted basis for receiving the support of local non-elites. Further, the territories in question were often too distant to be controlled easily or directly from their estates. Not infrequently, the void would be filled by a kinsman of the recently deposed leader and the cycle of rising tension, feuding, and alliance formation would start again.

In 1242, Þórður kakali Sighvatsson set out explicitly to break this cycle, to avenge his father and brothers who were victims of its violence, and to reclaim the chieftaincy that was his birthright. In a sweeping set of campaigns spanning just four years he gathered the supporters of his deceased family members as well as disaffected subordinate elites and attacked one after another of the rival centers of chiefly power, driving out their leaders, killing their supporters, and bringing their territories under his control. He then began to remake the society's ruling apparatus in the image of a Scandinavian royal court, establishing the first Icelandic proto-state.

Modeling Change: Data, Processes, and Issues of Scale

The Icelandic documentary data suggest that the process and progress of state formation and chiefdom consolidation proceeded at *temporal* scales faster than those we can normally monitor through archaeological means. It also suggests that the factors motivating social change and considered important to the actors were very different from those that are central to most of the explanatory models we employ. Many of these processes also took place at *social* scales too fine-grained or too broadly spread for us to see easily. In fact, how much of this would we see archaeologically? How accurate would organizational models be that we might deduce from analyses of this society's archaeological record? What would we be likely to suggest were important variables generating social change? Would they coincide with the factors that actually motivated Icelandic actors' behavior? Archaeology in Iceland is still relatively young and this period has been relatively neglected, but by combining archaeological and historical data we can get a good sense of regional settlement patterning, comparable to regional surveys and suitable for modeling. Other data in the archaeological record suggest long-term patterns worthy of consideration, but would they have been perceived as significant by the actors whose lives were far shorter than the duration of these trends?

The economic basis of medieval Icelandic households was a combination of northern European pastoralism coupled with fishing and wild resource acquisition (Amorosi 1992; McGovern 1990; McGovern et al. 2001; Smith 1995; Zutter 1992). Excavations, surveys, and historical research concur that the structure of settlement in medieval Iceland consisted of dispersed, unfortified farmsteads with enclosed hay-fields and outbuildings, similar to the present-day settlement pattern in rural Iceland (Smith and Parsons 1989; Vésteinsson 1998). These farmsteads, privately owned as alienable property (e.g. Earle 2000) and normally separated by half a kilometer or more, were occupied by single or joint households, often with a few servants (Miller 1990). Archaeological data suggest that median household size doubled from the time Iceland was settled to the 13th century (Smith nd). A bi- or tri-partite division of household sizes in the 12th-13th century data can reasonably be associated with the residences of common farmers, estates of local non-elite leaders, and elite compounds.

No villages, towns, cities, or other nucleated population centers existed in Iceland until the 18th century. With one undated exception, regional refuges or hillforts are absent. Neither elite nor non-elite residential complexes were located in clearly defensible locations. Documentary sources indicate that some elite residential compounds were temporarily fortified with turf walls, 3-4 meters tall. These were erected in times of hostility and were removed when the conflict ended. In the 13th century, some of these fortifications stood for decades, yet other elite sites were apparently never fortified.

Churches or chapels of varying sizes were found in chieftains' residential complexes, on the estates of many local non-elite leaders, and even on some small farms.

The distribution of residential sites in the Borgarfjörður district of western Iceland, *circa* AD 1180, is shown in **Figure 4**. This reconstruction is based on a combination of medieval sources and archaeological research.[2] Although many more non-elite farms were likely to have been occupied at this time than are shown in this view, **Figure 4** provides an accurate view of the distribution of elite sites and most of the larger non-elite sites across Borgarfjörður 20-30 years before the regional consolidation of chiefly authority.

In **Figure 5** the information presented in **Figure 4** has been recast to examine patterns of regional political control that we might reasonably infer for this region employing simple models based on central place theory that have been used to analyze settlement pattern data in complex societies from many parts of the world (e.g. Arnold 1997; Peebles and Kus 1977; Renfrew 1974, 1975; Renfrew and Level 1979; Scull 1999), including Viking Age Scandinavia (Thurston 1996). Thiessen polygons (Hodder and Orton 1976) were drawn around this region's seven contemporary elite residential complexes to predict polities from political centers. This exercise suggests a relatively even spacing among chiefly centers, comparably sized territories, and roughly similar numbers of non-elite farmsteads in each one. Each chiefly center is located approximately one day's journey on foot or with pack horses from the next, as would be predicted in models that integrate economic processes with settlement structure in chiefdoms (Peebles and Kus 1977). Each predicted territory incorporates some areas of habitable lowland pasture, upland grazing ranges, river segments, and freshwater lakes. Each territory's settlement pattern includes sites of three sizes, the two largest of which contain sacred structures, suggesting a one- or two-tier control hierarchy above the level of the household (Wright 1984). From these patterns, it might well be concluded that the region contained a network of competing simple chiefdoms or perhaps emergent complex chiefdoms. Among these, one territory (A) contains all three of the assembly sites known to have existed in the district, as well as its main harbor, to which foreign merchants came each summer carrying prestige and domestic goods. A second territory (B) controls access to this harbor from the sea and commands three subsidiary landing sites. We might well predict that one of these two polities would emerge as a paramountcy through its control over access to exotic goods, its incorporation of the most extensive areas of lowland pasture, its access to the diverse resources of the coastal/ terrestrial interface, its incorporation of the district's initial elite settlement (in B), or the presence in its territory of assembly sites, which were symbolically, ritually, and politically-charged locations within the landscape.

Unfortunately, this reconstruction bears little, if any, resemblance to the documented organization of the regional system in the late 12th century. As **Figure 6** shows, the district was split by one of the four boundaries that separated Iceland into four Quarters. Until *circa* 1150, chieftains and their followers living northwest of this boundary met each spring at an assembly site located on the northern edge of the district's lowlands, while chieftains and their supporters living south of this boundary met each year near Reykjavík, far to the south. The assembly site for the two chieftains residing at the westernmost edge of the district was located in Breiðafjörður, the next fjord system to the north. Theoretically, the Quarter system both freed and constrained alliances between elites and non-elites. Householders were required to ally themselves with one of the 9-12 chieftains living in their Quarter but were not required to ally themselves with the chieftain living nearest to them: chieftaincy gave authority over men, not control over territories. However, as the dispute over brushwood showed, by the late 12th century some farmers established alliances with chieftains from more distant regions, beyond their Quarters. Þórð the Red [1], for example, was a þingmaður of Kolbein the Young, from Iceland's North Quarter. Hámund's [2] chieftain, Þórð Sturluson, lived in the West Quarter. Both Hámund and Þórð the Red lived in the South Quarter. Neither Hámund nor Þórð the Red were allied to the chieftain in whose Thiessen polygon-defined territory their homes were located, because political leadership itself was not territorially defined. In this case, where regional patterns of alliance and power are extremely well-documented, it is clear that modeling tools such as Thiessen polygons could easily lead us to reach spurious conclusions concerning both the economic and political foundations of elite control and also non-elite community organization.

The distribution of substantial non-elite farms with attached churches might, for example, suggest a subordinate level of administrative control within each modeled chiefly territory. However, *circa* 1180, the distribution of such farms actually reflects the division of the countryside into local communities (*hreppar*) of non-elite farmers established for mutual support and the coordination of seasonal activities. These communities' leaders were elected by their non-elite peers and frequently met at the church-farms. Although chieftains may have exerted considerable control over the *hreppar* in which their estates were located (Sigurðsson 1999), the *hreppur* system was, in theory at least, independent of elite control prior to the period of regional consolidation (Stein-Wilkshuis 1982). As a lower-level, egalitarian political structure existing side-by-side with the hierarchical networks connecting farmers to chieftains, the *hreppur* system demonstrates the simultaneous operation of heterarchical and hierarchical principles within this society, as has been documented in many other prehistoric chiefdoms and states (e.g. Earle 1977, 1978; Ehrenreich et al. 1995; Joyce and Hendon 2000; Mehrer 2000). However, it is unlikely that the specific interlocking dimensions of either structuring principle could be accurately identified in this setting without the documentary clues. The assumption that hierarchy means territorial control (implicit in our use of terms like "centers" and the application of modeling tools such as Thiessen polygons to our data) would, in this case, reduce the actual complexity of this society—with its non-territorial hierarchies and territori-

---

[2] Data used to generate Figure 4 include the names of all farms recorded in medieval documents for this region, combined with information gathered from archaeological research conducted within the mapped area (for this, see especially Ólafsson 1996). Although no area as large as this—the figure covers an area of roughly 6,500 km² —has yet been surveyed in Iceland, the general patterning of sites in the densest areas shown in Figure 4 is comparable to settlement densities and patterning reconstructed from post-medieval censuses and archaeological surveys throughout the country (e.g. Gestsson and Briem 1954; Lárusson 1967; Ólafsson 1996; Rafnsson 1990; Sveinbjarnardóttir 1992; Vésteinsson 1998).

ally defined non-elite communities—to a map that is admittedly satisfying but nonetheless grossly inaccurate in representing the society's organization and dynamic structure.

Figure 7 shows the same district 60 years later, around 1240, after regional political consolidation had taken place. All of the elite residential complexes present in 1180 were still occupied and the time elapsed between **Figures 6 and 7** is less than the use-histories of known elite structures in Iceland. It is therefore likely that these sites would have maintained largely the same form and layout in 1240 as they had 1180, even though the political status of their occupants had changed and they were no longer the residential bases of independent chieftains. However, given that these sites would still look, archaeologically, like chiefly centers, the resulting regional pattern of very large paramount chieftains' compounds, somewhat smaller elite estates, intermediate-sized church-farms, and smaller, non-elite farmsteads would probably suggest that the region was divided between two complex chiefdoms, each with at least three levels of administrative control above the household. The complex chiefdom centered on Reykholt would appear, in this reconstruction, to have had within its territory a population of perhaps 8,000-11,000 people distributed among one paramount's compound, five subordinate elite centers, at least 16 church-farms, and a much larger number of non-elite farms. The territories defined by the Thiessen polygon boundary drawn between the centers of the region's two apparent complex chiefdoms include harbors, assembly sites (one for the western polity is located just north of the boundary of **Figure 7**), and extensive areas of both lowland and upland zones. From this information, it might be suggested that control over basic agricultural resources, assembly sites, and trade were essential to the emergence of Icelandic complex societies. While this is likely, to some degree, it is worth noting that the centers which actually did gain regional power by 1240 (**Figure 5**, C and G) were not those (**Figure 5**, A and B) that had the district's harbors, assembly sites, and most-extensive grazing lands within their Thiessen polygon-defined territories, *circa* 1180. This suggests that factors other than exchange, proximity to symbolically charged political sites, or agricultural potential actually guided the processes by which chieftains gained and maintained political power, which accords with the Icelandic actors' perspectives, described above.

Overall, the reconstructed regional pattern in **Figure 7** is intuitively satisfying. Again, however, the contrast with the historically recorded system is critically important (**Figure 8**). Rather than being secondary elite centers, each of the former chieftains' estates within Reykholt's territory had actually been subsumed within its home territory and had been demoted to the status of local non-elite church-farms after the chieftain residing at Reykholt, Snorri Sturluson (AD 1179-1241), consolidated power in the district, *circa* 1203-10. Snorri appears to have held all of these titles himself or managed them on behalf of those who had previously held them through hereditary right (Ingvarsson 1987). The earlier division of the district between two Quarters was abolished and the assembly site for the West Quarter, which had been moved to the center of the district around 1150, became the regional assembly site for Snorri's polity (Jóhannesson 1974:77). Reykholt itself owned many outlying farms directly, managing them as components of its estate, but few of

the church farms in this district were directly controlled by Reykholt and much of the revenue they collected as tithes may have escaped its control.

However, while this map of Borgarfjörður (**Figure 8**) suggests only one level of elite control over the district's many households, it only tells part of the story. Reykholt in 1240 *was* the center of a complex chiefdom, but it was one that extended over a much wider region, in which Borgarfjörður was just a part (**Figure 9**). In addition to the six titles he held in Borgarfjörður, Snorri Sturluson controlled the titles to at least seven other chieftaincies in northern, western, and southern Iceland. Other chieftains, themselves holders of regional power and generally more than one chieftaincy, served him as subordinate allies, although they remained theoretically independent. In less than a generation, Reykholt's paramount had gained hegemony over most of western Iceland, an area occupied by perhaps 30,000 people, not just the district surrounding his residential complex. A few years later, Reykholt's domain was incorporated into a still larger paramountcy and ten years after that the site had become the seat of a local governor in a newly unified Icelandic state. Although the site remained an elite residence throughout this process, the positions of its occupants in regional and island-wide political hierarchies had changed faster than the typical construction histories responsible for producing two of the most reliably measurable and most frequently employed archaeological correlates of hierarchical relationships—site and residence sizes.

Would Snorri's vast complex chiefdom, or these processes of change, be archaeologically visible as such? The continued occupation of standing elite structures at each of the five subordinate chiefly centers within his own home district might encourage archaeologists to suggest models of shared power, competition among equals, or peer-polity interaction (*sensu* Renfrew and Cherry 1986) within the Borgarfjörður district. The presence of comparable site hierarchies in each of the territories he controlled would make it hard to recognize them archaeologically as parts of his domain. Archaeological reconstructions incapable of monitoring processes that played out over such vast regions and at temporal scales more rapid and more fine-grained than either architectural changes within sites or the resolution of standard dating tools might well see no differences in regional settlement patterns during the 60 year period covered by **Figures 6-9**.

The Shape of Time: Archaeological Realities and Cultural Dynamics

I have asked throughout this exercise whether we, as archaeologists, could recognize, through settlement pattern analyses, the correlates of social changes that took place over large areas and at temporal scales measuring 60 years or less. What if we had an archaeological record built of typical phases 75-100 years, or longer, in duration? What would we see if our survey domains took in only one valley system, or just part of one? Would we see any of this complexity or interpret it accurately?

In medieval Iceland, given the long use-lives of the buildings involved and the shorter temporal scales at which political processes spun themselves out, we would probably miss most of what we seek to understand. If temporary turf defensive walls could not be located or had been removed when dangerous conditions disappeared, we would probably only perceive a pattern of larger and smaller undefended farmsteads, varying in scale through a continuum, with some at each level having ritual facilities (churches and chapels). We might well suggest this was a minimally ranked society with just one level of control (farms with churches) above the household. Differences in the sizes of these farms might well be used to infer differences in wealth, but perhaps not evidence for differential political control. *If* the fortifications were apparent and *if* each elite household was fortified, we could perhaps identify a two-tier hierarchy with political dimensions, as well as wealth-based ranking, but we would probably not be able to monitor the changes that transformed the regional system since the structures elites built were likely to endure through more than one phase, even if the elite status of the site's occupants did not.

Would we correctly understand the role of conflict in this society? With no regional mustering places, no central fortresses, isolated farmsteads set in non-defensible locations, historic sources that indicate no campaigns of regional destruction, and only temporary walls of turf thrown up around household compounds too small to shelter regional populations, it would be hard to conclude that conflict was an active force leading to regional consolidation, as the documentary sources imply. The image of a relatively peaceful, barely hierarchical society that we would be likely to derive from the archaeological record would clearly be at odds with our expectations for a system of complex chiefdoms developing into a state, especially one in which conflict was an important causal element of that process. Yet, that is what the indigenous sources tell us happened.

If it would be so easy to misinterpret Iceland's archaeological record, can we be so sure that we are really seeing what we hope to be understanding in other archaeological cases where no written records exist to help us refine our expectations? Is it possible that some of our models, designed to monitor structure and change on temporal and social scales so different from those in which actors operated (even when our models are actor-centered), could lead us away from understanding the patterning of the past? What long-term patterns *do* we see in the archaeological record of Sturlung Age Iceland? Data drawn from excavations and surveys undertaken across the country suggest a slow and incremental growth in household size and also an increasing range of household sizes (Smith nd). Surveys indicate more farms were built than abandoned in the upland zones, implying an increasing population and dynamically fluctuating settlement areas. We see a shift in herding strategies towards a greater emphasis on sheep and less concern with cattle (Amorosi 1991). We see increases through time in the frequency of imported luxury and domestic goods in household assemblages, with some fluctuations in access to foreign goods around the time of chiefdom consolidation. There are suggestions that more permanent and complex structures were built in at least one harbor after 1150 (Hermanns-Auðardóttir 1986, 1999). We see a slow deterioration in regional climatic conditions, but not yet the onset of the Little Ice Age (Ogilvie 1991), plus indicators of increased erosion and environ-

mental degradation due to human activities (Dugmore and Buckland 1991).

Each of these patterned sets of relationships resonates well with arguments that archaeologists have used to explain trajectories of evolutionary change in complex societies. They include the carrots of expanding labor forces and increased access to exotic goods, as well as the sticks of climatic change, ecological degradation, and population increases in circumscribed areas. However, what is interesting to note is that none of these factors were identified by the Icelandic actors/authors as having had any direct, perceived, or important roles as causes for conflict, political consolidation, or systemic change. When historically reported years of good and bad harvests, famines, or other stresses are plotted against the annual record of conflict and consolidation from Iceland, it is clear that conflict happened in both good years and bad. There is not a single episode in the *Contemporary Sagas* where a chieftain or his followers set off intentionally to defeat a rival and annex his land in order to offset local resource shortages. Similarly, chieftains had the right to make first purchases and to set prices at markets in their districts, and clearly they used those advantages to supply themselves with prestige goods (Gelsinger 1981). Yet there are no instances in which the expressed goal of a raid or campaign was to establish exclusive control over a harbor. On the other hand, there *are* examples in which chieftains' efforts to exert such control led foreign merchants to pack up and sail away to other districts with less arrogant leaders.

The one-way street we often paint in theoretical models seems more often to have run two ways when viewed from an actor-scaled, rather than a system-level, perspective. Chieftains, even those who could claim hegemony over 30,000 people and nearly one-quarter of the country, were constrained by the reality that actors at almost every level of the system had different goals than theirs. Snorri himself was assassinated by a coalition of his former sons-in-law who had many axes to grind—and did; while around 1255 non-elite farmers in northern Iceland walked away from chieftains and rejected chieftaincy altogether. The system itself, a network of competing and allied interests, worked at very different scales depending on from whose perspective it was seen, yet activities undertaken at each level of scale had the ability to impact every other scaled subsystem according to their intersecting logic. This implies, as Flannery (1999) suggests, that neither actor-based nor processual/systemic models are likely to have sufficient explanatory power alone to illuminate complex processes of social change in the past, but are more profitably seen as complementary approaches to building complex explanations.

Seen from the actors' perspective, processes of political change in medieval Iceland seem to confirm the American politician Tip O'Neill's famous dictum that all politics are ultimately local. The nexus of interactions and mutual obligations between chieftains and their far more numerous non-elite supporters—that is, what chieftains actually *did*—was more important for perpetuating the system and motivating social change than what they ate, exchanged, built, or had accompanying them in death. The daily logic of the system, characterized by the intersecting and often contradictory short-term goals of interacting and variously obligated actors, was a more potent vehicle for change than trans-generational, incremental "systemic" adaptations or slowly developing trends in phenomena external to the system of social interaction itself, even if those trends and adaptations helped to set the stage on which change occurred. Unfortunately for us, that relegates most of what we can recover, count, and analyze to the category of contextual rather than causal information, suggests that archaeological research more often provides us with tools to monitor the consequences of change than to understand its causes, and implies that in many cases we give objects and other things that we excavate far more importance as motivating forces than they deserve in the processes we hope to understand.

Conclusions

What can we conclude from this examination of political change in medieval Iceland? First, the Icelandic documentary material implies that actor-centered perspectives on social change *are* ultimately likely to be the most appropriate tools for understanding *why*, *how*, and *when* major social transformations took place, and for interpreting ways in which people adapted to and used those conditions of change to create the social landscapes in which they operated. However, currently we can only rarely resolve chronologies or material patterning to the extremely fine-grained resolution necessary for monitoring actors archaeologically at temporal scales similar to those in which critical actions took place—periods of years or decades at the longest. Consequently, most actor-based theories are probably unverifiable and unfalsifiable using current archaeological data. As a result, one has to question whether such approaches emphasize current theorists' roles as actors more than they reflect the interests of the actors being theorized about.[3]

Conversely, the perspectives gained from observing long-term or system-level patterning in the archaeological record appear to highlight processes that happened too subtly, too slowly, over periods of time too long, and across areas too extensive to have been perceived as important by most actors in past societies. Subtle changes through time in the scale and organization of households, variations in the frequencies with which exotic goods passed through the system, shifts in the proportions of cattle or sheep herded, or fluctuations in the condition of regional resource bases appear to have occurred at temporal scales too much longer than individual lives to have been observed by participants in the system or to have been motivations for political action by real actors. While these archaeologically defined processes and patterns are important, the Icelandic data suggest that actions leading to feud chains, alliance cascades, and transformative processes of political change found their origins and motivations in conflicts and events that would have happened and did happen regardless of these external factors. This suggests that much of what we currently measure as archaeological data may record the *contextual* fabric of life during periods of change, without being directly related to the *causes* of change. It may be, however, that this changing context helps

to explain why similar actions undertaken at different points in time led to quite different results: cycling of simple chiefdoms during some periods, the appearance and collapse of complex chiefdoms in others, and complete transformations of the system at still other times.

The social, spatial, and temporal scales at which we build our models directly influence the ways we expect the past to have been, color the answers we get back from our studies, and lead us to accept some explanations for why change happens rather than seeking alternatives. Models such as those that posit conflict as a prime mover in the evolution of complex societies generally presume longer than sub-generational temporal scales for processes to play out and describe abstract social groups, rather than individuals (at least non-elite individuals), as the agents through which change occurs (Carneiro 1970, 1981). Chieftains represented as social types rather than individual people become strategists engaged in trans-generational campaigns to capture resources, with the assumption that their authority was felt in bounded polities into which non-elites were slotted as passive pawns. The Icelandic data, on the other hand, suggest that the social scale at which political actions took place was very personal and fast-paced. Regional crises could turn on the obligations that existed between a chieftain and any one of his followers. And, most critically, the Icelandic situation implies that non-elites' interests and activities were as essential to processes of political change as were the elites' (cf. Pauketat 2000). Successful modeling of political change may therefore require multi-centric approaches for understanding the past, rather than a choice of "top-down" or "bottom-up" models.

Re-envisioning the concept of the chiefdom from one that necessarily equates chieftains with control over territories to one that sees them occupying positions of negotiated and potentially decentralized authority over their supporters may throw into question many established models, but fits well with ethnographic and ethnohistoric accounts of life in chiefdoms and small states. Reorienting our conception of chiefdoms to allow for decentralized and negotiated political processes, rather than assuming centralized decision-making in bounded polities, provides a social basis for understanding why chieftains were endured, asking what useful services they provided, examining how they were able to manipulate the system, and considering how the dynamics of those interactions may have shaped trajectories of social change.

I am not arguing that all chiefdoms were organized like those in Iceland, yet the emergence of state-like formations here, within the context of a network of interacting and competing chieftaincies, is essentially similar to social frameworks inferred behind other cases of state formation around the world (Collis 1994; Flannery 1999; Renfrew and Cherry 1986; Wright 1984) and meshes well with ethnohistorically described cases of political cycling in chiefdoms worldwide (e.g. Anderson 1994; Kristiansen 1991; Johnson 1999; Persson 1983). These considerations alone suggest that Iceland's detailed documentary sources and emerging archaeological record are worthy of investigation by archaeologists and can be used for testing and developing explanatory theories that incorporate actors' motivations and rapid, on-the-ground dynamic processes into the longer-term perspectives pro-

---

[3] However, see Wright et al. (1989) for an encouraging example of high-resolution archaeological analysis, Schele (1990) and others for advances made in understanding dynastic changes in the Maya world, and Kohler and Gumerman (2000) for a range of promising approaches employing multiscalar modeling.

vided by the archaeological record itself. In fact, several anthropologists and archaeologists have already explored the potential value of using Iceland's records as a model for understanding the "Germanic mode of production" in European prehistory (Gilman 1995), comparing the economic structure of European and Polynesian chiefdoms (Earle 1997:123-124; 2000:47), and examining the dynamics of stratified societies without state-like integrative mechanisms (Byock 1982, 1988, 2001; Durrenberger 1992; Smith and Parsons 1989).

The Icelandic case also suggests that the numerical superiority of non-elite actors must always be considered a potent force when modeling the dynamics of complex societies, especially in contexts where the weaponry everyone held was basically the same. Where no evidence exists to indicate a coercive monopoly of force by the elite—or when the point of interest is *how* an elite obtains a coercive monopoly on force—it must be considered that the acceptance of the elite by the non-elite could rarely, if ever, be taken for granted. Their mutual obligations and needs were quite possibly critical elements of any complex system's true dynamics. As archaeologists, this means that we must put far more time into understanding past societies at the scales of the household and community, attempting to understand the divergent interests of actors occupying different positions within social, political, and economic institutions (Brumfiel 1992; Brumfiel and Fox 1994), and refining our chronological control to scales adequate for monitoring the interaction of actors with one another and with their surroundings.

Acknowledgments

Fieldwork in Iceland, on which many of the thoughts expressed here are based, has been done in coordination with the Department of Archaeology of the National Museum of Iceland, with funding generously provided by the National Geographic Society, the American-Scandinavian Foundation, Norðurál, Eimskip, Sparisjöður Myrasýslu, the Buffalo Museum of Science, Brown University, and the University of Michigan. A large number of individuals and Icelandic community organizations, too many to name here, have provided material, financial, emotional, and intellectual support over the years. Special thanks are due to Sér Geir Waage of Reykholt, Guðmundur Ólafsson, Sigurður Bergsteinsson, all of my crew members, my doctoral committee members, the patient editors of this volume, Michèle Hayeur Smith, who cares for and encourages me, and Jessica and Émilie, who keep me smiling. Any errors remaining in this presentation, despite their well-meant comments and warnings, remain the sole responsibility of the author.

Biographical Sketch

Kevin P. Smith has conducted archaeological excavations and surveys in Iceland since 1985, working primarily with the National Museum of Iceland. He received his B.A. in Anthropology from Haverford College (Haverford, PA) and his M.A. in Anthropology from the University of Michigan (Ann Arbor, MI). He is currently ABD in the Department of Anthropology at the University of Michigan and Deputy Director/Chief Curator for the Haffenreffer Museum of Anthropology at Brown University (Providence and Bristol, Rhode Island, USA).

References Cited

Anderson, David G. 1994 *The Savannah River Chiefdoms: Political Change in the Late Prehistoric Southeast* University of Alabama Press (Tuscaloosa, AL).

Amorosi, Thomas 1991 'Icelandic archaeofauna: a preliminary review' *Acta Archaeologica* 61:272-284.

Amorosi, Thomas 1992 'Climate impact and human response in northeast Iceland: archaeological investigations at Svalbarð, 1986-1988' in C.D. Morris and D.J. Rackham (eds) *Norse and Later Settlement and Subsistence in the North Atlantic* University of Glasgow (Glasgow):103-138.

Arnold, C.J. 1997 *An Archaeology of the Early Anglo-Saxon Kingdoms* 2nd ed. Routledge (London).

Bagge, Sverre 1991 *Society and Politics in Snorri Sturluson's Heimskringla* University of California Press (Berkeley, CA).

Bourdieu, Pierre 1977 *Outline of a Theory of Practice* (translated by R. Nice) Cambridge University Press (Cambridge).

Brain, Jeffrey P. 1989 *Winterville: Late Prehistoric Culture Contact in the Lower Mississippi Valley* Mississippi Department of Archives and History, Archaeological Report No. 23 (Jackson, MS).

Brumfiel, Elizabeth M. 1992 'Distinguished lecture in archaeology. Breaking and entering the ecosystem: gender, class, and faction steal the show' *American Anthropologist* 94(3):551-567.

Brumfiel, Elizabeth M. and J.W. Fox (eds) 1994 *Factional Competition and Political Development in the New World* Cambridge University Press (Cambridge).

Byock, Jesse L. 1982 *Feud in the Icelandic Saga* University of California Press (Berkeley).

Byock, Jesse L. 1988 *Medieval Iceland: Society, Sagas, and Power* Hisarlik Press (Enfield Lock, UK).

Byock, Jesse L. 2001 *Viking Age Iceland* Penguin Books (Harmondsworth, UK).

Carneiro, Robert L. 1970 'A theory of the origin of the state' *Science* 169:733-738.

Carneiro, Robert L. 1977 'Political expansion as an expression of the principle of competitive exclusion' in R. Cohen and E. Service (eds) *Origins of the State: The Anthropology of Political Evolution* Institute for the Study of Human Issues (Philadelphia):205-223.

Carneiro, Robert L. 1981 'The chiefdom: precursor to the state' in G.D. Jones and R.R. Kautz (eds) *The Transition to Statehood in the New World* Cambridge University Press (Cambridge):37-79.

Clover, Carol J. and John Lindow 1985 *Old Norse-Icelandic Literature: A Critical Guide (Islandica XLV)* Cornell University Press (Ithaca).

Collis, John 1995 'States without centers? The Middle La Tène period in temperate Europe' in B. Arnold and D.B. Gibson (eds) *Celtic Chiefdom, Celtic State* Cambridge University Press (Cambridge):75-80.

Dobres, Marcia-Anne and John Robb 2000 *Agency in Archaeology* Routledge (London).

Dugmore, Andrew J. and Paul C. Buckland 1991 'Tephrochronology and Late Holocene soil erosion in South Iceland' in J.K. Maizels and C. Casteldine (eds) *Environmental Change in Iceland, Past and Present* Kluwer Academic Press (Dordrecht, Netherlands):147-160.

Durrenberger, E. Paul 1992 *The Dynamics of Medieval Iceland: Political Economy & Literature* University of Iowa Press (Iowa City, IA).

Earle, Timothy 1977 'A reappraisal of redistribution: complex Hawaiian chiefdoms' in T. Earle and J. Ericson (eds) *Exchange Systems in Prehistory* Academic Press (New York):213-232.

Earle, Timothy 1978 *Economic and Social Organization of a Complex Chiefdom, the Halelea District, Kaua'i, Hawaii* University of Michigan Museum of Anthropology, Anthropological Papers 63 (Ann Arbor, MI).

Earle, Timothy 1997 *How Chiefs Come to Power: The Political Economy in Prehistory* Stanford University Press (Stanford, CA).

Earle, Timothy 2000 'Archaeology, property, and prehistory' *Annual Review of Anthropology* 29:39-60.

Ehrenreich, Robert M., Carol L. Crumley, and Janet E. Levy (eds) 1995 *Heterarchy and the Analysis of Complex Societies* Archaeological Papers of the American Anthropological Association No. 6 (Alexandria, VA).

Flannery, Kent V. 1999 'Process and agency in early state formation' *Cambridge Archaeological Journal* 9(1):3-21.

Flannery, Kent V. and Joyce Marcus 1983 'The origins of the state in Oaxaca: editors' introduction' in K.V. Flannery and J. Marcus (eds) *The Cloud People: Divergent Evolution of the Zapotec and Mixtec Civilizations* Academic Press (New York):79-83.

Gelsinger, Bruce E. 1981 *Icelandic Enterprise: Commerce and Economy in the Middle Ages* University of South Carolina Press (Columbia, SC).

Gestsson, Gisli and Jóhann Briem 1954 'Byggðarleifar í Þjórsárdal' *Árbók hins Íslenzka Fornleifafélags 1954*:5-22.

Giddens, A. 1979 *Central Problems in Social Theory: Action, Structure, and Contradiction in Social Analysis* University of California Press (Berkeley, CA).

Gilman, Antonio 1995 'Prehistoric European chiefdoms: rethinking "Germanic" societies' in T.D. Price and G. Feinman (eds) *Foundations of Social Inequality* Plenum Press (New York):235-251.

Helms, Mary 1979 *Ancient Panama: Chiefs in Search of Power* University of Texas Press (Austin, TX).

Hermanns-Auðardóttir, Margrét 1986 'Fornleifarannsóknir að Gásum og víðar í Eyjafirði árið 1986' *Sulur* 27:3-39.

Hermanns-Auðardóttir, Margrét 1999 'Arkeologiska undersökningar av handels-platsen vid Gásir' in A. Christophersen and A. Dybdahl (eds) *Gásir – En Internasjonal Handelsplass i Nord-Atlanteren* Tapir Forlag (Trondheim, Norway):9-36.

Hodder, Ian and Clive Orton 1976 *Spatial Analysis in Archaeology* Cambridge University Press (Cambridge).

Ingvarsson, Lúðvík 1987 *Goðorð og Goðorðsmenn* (Egilsstaðir, Iceland).

Jóhannesson, Jón 1974 *A History of the Old Icelandic Commonwealth* (*Íslendinga saga*, translated by Haraldur Bessason) University of Manitoba Icelandic Series Vol. II, University of Manitoba Press (Winnipeg, Manitoba).

Johnson, Eric S. 1999 'Community and confederation: a political geography of Contact Period southern New England' in M.A. Levine, K.E. Sassaman, and M.S. Nassaney (eds) *The Archaeological Northeast* Bergin & Garvey (Westport, CT):155-170.

Joyce, Arthur A. 2000 'The founding of Monte Albán: sacred propositions and social practices' in M-A. Dobres and J. Robb (eds) *Agency in Archaeology* Routledge (London):71-91.

Joyce, Rosemary and Julia A. Hendon 2000 'Heterarchy, history, and material reality: "communities" in Late Classic Honduras' in M.A. Canuto and J. Yaeger (eds) *The Archaeology of Communities: A New World Perspective* Routledge (London):143-160.

Kemp, Barry J. 1989 *Ancient Egypt: Anatomy of a Civilization* Routledge (London).

Knight, Vernon J., Jr. 1997 'Some developmental parallels between Cahokia and Moundville' in T.R. Pauketat and T.E. Emerson (eds) *Cahokia: Domination and Ideology in the Mississippian World* University of Nebraska Press (Lincoln, NE):229-247.

Knight, Vernon J., Jr. and Vincas P. Steponaitis 1998 'A new history of Moundville' in V.J. Knight and V.P. Steponaitis (eds) *Archaeology of the Moundville Chiefdom* Smithsonian Institution Press (Washington, DC):1-25.

Kohler, Timothy A. and George J. Gumerman 2000 *Dynamics in Human and Primate Societies: Agent-Based Modeling of Social and Spatial Processes* Oxford University Press (New York).

Kowaleski, Stephen A. 1990 'The evolution of complexity in the Valley of Oaxaca' *Annual Review of Anthropology* 19:39-58.

Kristiansen, Kristian 1991 'Chiefdoms, states, and systems of social evolution' in T. Earle (ed) *Chiefdoms: Power, Economy, and Ideology* Cambridge University Press (Cambridge):16-43.

Kristjánsson, Jónas 1997 *Eddas and Sagas: Iceland's Medieval Literature* (translated by P. Foote) Hið Íslenska Bókmenntafélag (Reykjavík).

Lárusson, Björn 1967 *The Old Icelandic Land Registers* C.W.K. Gleerup (Lund).

Lehner, Mark 2000 'The fractal house of Pharaoh: Ancient Egypt as a complex adaptive system, a trial formulation' in T.A. Kohler and G.J. Gumerman (eds) *Dynamics in Human and Primate Societies: Agent-Based Modeling of Social and Spatial Processes* Oxford University Press (New York):275-354.

Marcus, Joyce 1998 'The peaks and valleys of ancient states: an extension of the dynamic model' in G.M. Feinman and J. Marcus (eds) *Archaic States* School of American Research Press (Santa Fe):59-94.

McGovern, Thomas H. 1990 'The archaeology of the Norse North Atlantic' *Annual Review of Anthropology* 19:331-351.

McGovern, Thomas H., Sophia Perdikaris, and Clayton Tinsley 2001 'The economy of landnám: the evidence of zooarchaeology' in A. Wawn and Þ. Sigurðardóttir (eds) *Approaches to Vínland* Sigurður Nordal Institute Studies 4 (Reykjavík):154-165.

McGrew, Julia (trans.) 1970 *Sturlunga Saga, Volume 1: The Saga of Hvamm-Sturla and The Saga of the Icelanders* Twayne Publishers and The American-Scandinavian Foundation (New York).

McGrew, Julia and R. George Thomas (trans.) 1974 *Sturlunga Saga, Volume 2: Shorter Sagas of the Icelanders* Twayne Publishers and The American-Scandinavian Foundation (New York).

Mehrer, Mark 2000 'Heterarchy and hierarchy: the community plan as institution in Cahokia's polity' in M.A. Canuto and J. Yaeger (eds) *The Archaeology of Communities: A New World Perspective* Routledge (London):44-57.

Miller, William I. 1990 *Blood-taking and Peacemaking: Feud, Law, and Society in Saga Iceland* University of Chicago Press (Chicago).

Oberg, Kalervo 1955 'Types of social structure among the lowland tribes of South and Central America' *American Anthropologist* 57: 472-487.

Ogilvie, Astrid E.G. 1991 'Climatic changes in Iceland A.D. c. 865 to 1598' *Acta Archaeologica* 61:223-251.

Ólafsson, Guðmundur 1996 *Friðlýstar Fornleifar í Borgarfjarðarsýslu (Rit hins Íslenska Fornleifafélags og Þjóðminjasafns Íslands 2)* Hið Íslenska Fornleifafélag og Þjóðminjasafn Íslands (Reykjavík).

Pauketat, Timothy R. 1994 *The Ascent of Chiefs: Cahokia and Mississippian Politics in Native North America* University of Alabama Press (Tuscaloosa, AL).

Pauketat, Timothy R. 2000 'The tragedy of the commoners' in M-A. Dobres and J. Robb (eds) *Agency in Archaeology* Routledge (London):113-129.

Peebles, Christopher S. and Susan M. Kus 1977 'Some archaeological correlates of ranked societies' *American Antiquity* 42:421-448.

Persson, Johnny 1983 'Cyclical change and circular exchange: a re-examination of the Kula ring' *Oceania* 54(1):32-77.

Rafnsson, Sveinbjörn 1990 *Byggðaleifar í Hrafnkelsdal og á Brúardölum (Rit Hins Íslenska Fornleifafélags 1)* Hið Íslenska Fornleifafélag (Reykjavík).

Renfrew, Colin 1974 'Space, time, and polity' in M. Rowlands and J. Friedman (eds) *The Evolution of Social Systems* Duckworth (London):89-114.

Renfrew, Colin 1975 'Trade as action at a distance' in J.A. Sabloff and C.C. Lamberg-Karlovsky (eds) *Ancient Civilization and Trade* University of New Mexico Press (Albuquerque):3-59.

Renfrew, Colin and John Cherry 1986 *Peer Polity Interaction and Socio-Political Change* Cambridge University Press (Cambridge).

Renfrew, Colin and E.V. Level 1979 'Exploring dominance: predicting polities from centres' in C. Renfrew and K.L. Cooke (eds) *Transformations: Mathematical Approaches to Culture Change* Academic Press (New York):145-168.

Schele, Linda M. 1990 *Forest of Kings: The Untold Story of the Ancient Maya* Morrow (New York).

Scull, Christopher 1999 'Social archaeology and Anglo-Saxon kingdom origins' in T. Dickinson and D. Griffiths (eds) *The Making of Kingdoms* Anglo-Saxon Studies in Archaeology and History 10, Oxford University Committee for Archaeology (Oxford):17-24.

Service, Elman R. 1971 *Primitive Social Organization: An Evolutionary Perspective* 2nd ed. Random House (New York).

Sigurðsson, Jón Viðar 1989 *Frá Goðorðum til Ríkja: Þróun Goðavalds á 12. og 13. Öld (Sagnfræðirannsóknir 10, Sagnfræðistofnun Háskóla Íslands)* Bókaútgáfa Menningarsjóðs (Reykjavík).

Sigurðsson, Jón Viðar 1999 *Chieftains and Power in the Icelandic Commonwealth* (translated by Jean Lundskær-Nielsen) Odense University Press (Odense).

Smith, Kevin P. 1995 'Landnám: the settlement of Iceland in archaeological and historical perspective' *World Archaeology* 26:319-347.

Smith, Kevin P. nd *The Economic Structure of Medieval Icelandic Chiefdoms: Political Economy in the Sturlung Period, AD 1150-1264* Doctoral dissertation, in prep., Department of Anthropology, University of Michigan, Ann Arbor.

Smith, Kevin P. and Jeffrey R. Parsons 1989 'Regional archaeological research in Iceland: potentials and possibilities' in E.P. Durrenberger and G. Pálsson (eds) *The Anthropology of Iceland* University of Iowa Press (Iowa City, IA):179-202.

Spencer, Charles S. 1990 'On the tempo and mode of state formation: neo-evolutionism reconsidered' *Journal of Anthropological Archaeology* 9(1):1-30.

Stein-Wilkeshuis, Martina 1982 'The right to social welfare in early medieval Iceland' *Journal of Medieval History* 8:343-352.

Steponaitis, Vincas P. 1998 'Population trends at Moundville' in V.J. Knight, Jr. and V.P. Steponaitis (eds) *Archaeology of the Moundville Chiefdom* Smithsonian Institution Press (Washington, DC):26-44.

Sveinbjarnardóttir, Guðrún 1992 *Farm Abandonment in Medieval and Post-Medieval Iceland: An Interdisciplinary Study* Oxbow Monograph 17, Oxbow Books (Oxford).

Thorsson, Örnólfur (ed) 1988 *Sturlunga Saga* Svart á Hvítu (Reykjavík).

Thurston, Tina 1996 'Landscapes of power and landscapes of conflict: geographical approaches to culture change in Iron Age Denmark' in D.A. Meyer, P.C. Dawson, and D.T. Hanna (eds) *Debating Complexity, Proceedings of the 26th Annual Chacmool Conference* The Archaeological Association of the University of Calgary (Calgary, Alberta):428-442.

Vésteinsson, Orri 1998 'Patterns of settlement in Iceland: a study in pre-history' *Saga-Book of the Viking Society* 25:1-29.

Wright, Henry T. 1984 'Prestate political formations' in W. Sanders, H. Wright, and R.M. Adams (eds) *On the Evolution of Complex Societies: Essays in Honor of Harry Hoijer* Undena Publications (Malibu, CA):41-77.

Wright, Henry T., Richard Redding, and Susan Pollock 1989 'Monitoring interannual variability: an example from the period of early state development in southwestern Iran' in P. Halstead and J. O'Shea (eds) *Bad Year Economics: Cultural Responses to Risk and Uncertainty* Cambridge University Press (Cambridge):106-113.

Zutter, Cynthia M. 1992 'Icelandic plant and land-use patterns: archaeobotanical analysis of the Svalbarð midden (6706-60), northeastern Iceland' in C. D. Morris and D. J. Rackham (eds) *Norse and Later Settlement and Subsistence in the North Atlantic* University of Glasgow (Glasgow):139-148.

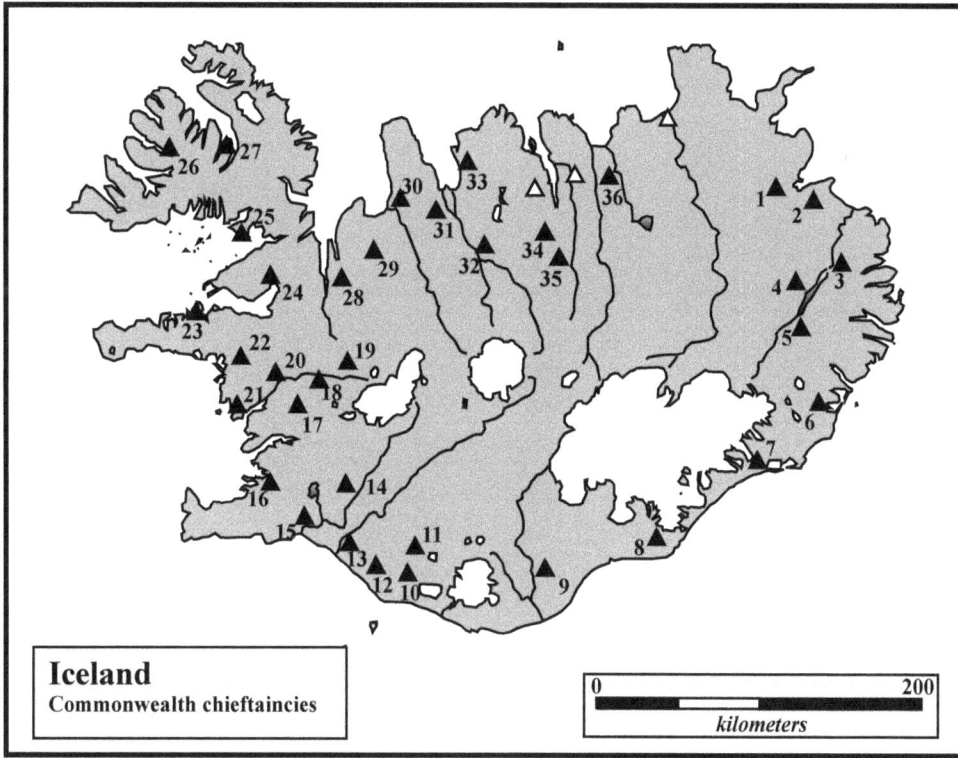

Figure 1: According to medieval Icelandic sources, thirty-six chieftaincies (goðorð) were recognized by law in AD 930; three more were added in 965. The actual number of chieftaincies may have varied through time but these offices endured in name, at least, throughout the Commonwealth period (AD 930-1264) even if some were later absorbed into larger polities. Dark triangles locate the areas where the 36 "full and ancient" goðorð had their seats; white triangles identify the three chieftaincies added after 965. Numbers carry through to Figures 2 and 3.

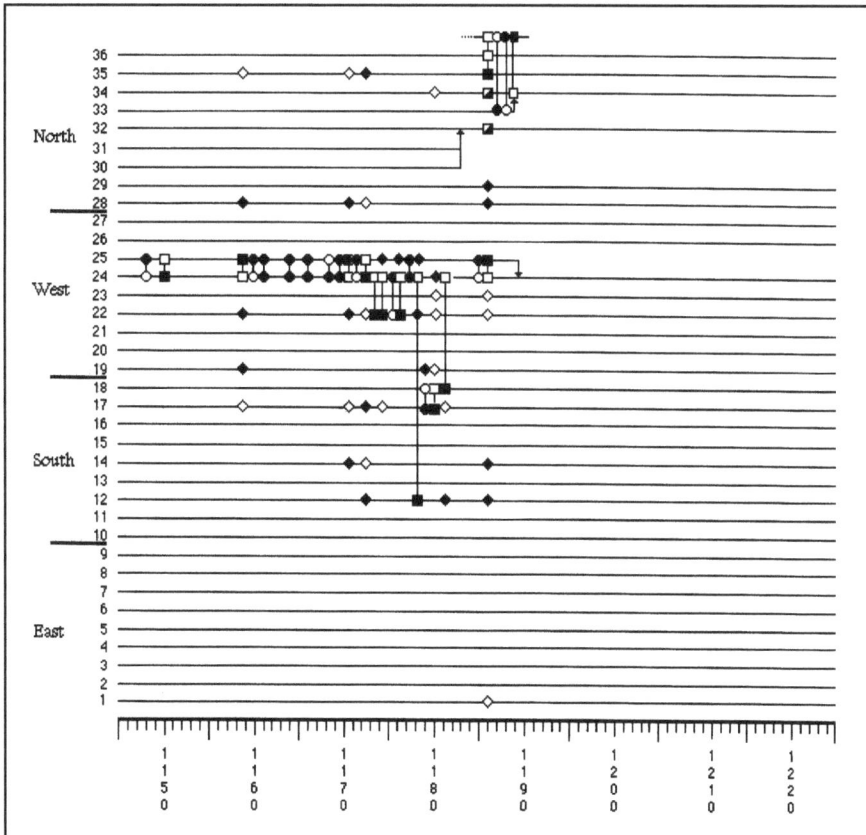

Figure 2: Graphic representation of the feud chains and alliance cascades in The Saga of Hvamm-Sturla (McGrew 1970). This dispute between two adjacent western Icelandic chieftaincies began in AD 1147 and ended circa 1190 with the absorption of one chieftaincy by another, the entanglement of chiefly houses in three Quarters of Iceland, and the initiation of another feud chain in the North Quarter. Numbers on the y-axis refer to the chieftaincies mapped in Figure 1; symbols are as described in the text (half black/half white squares identify mediators called to arbitrate settlements).

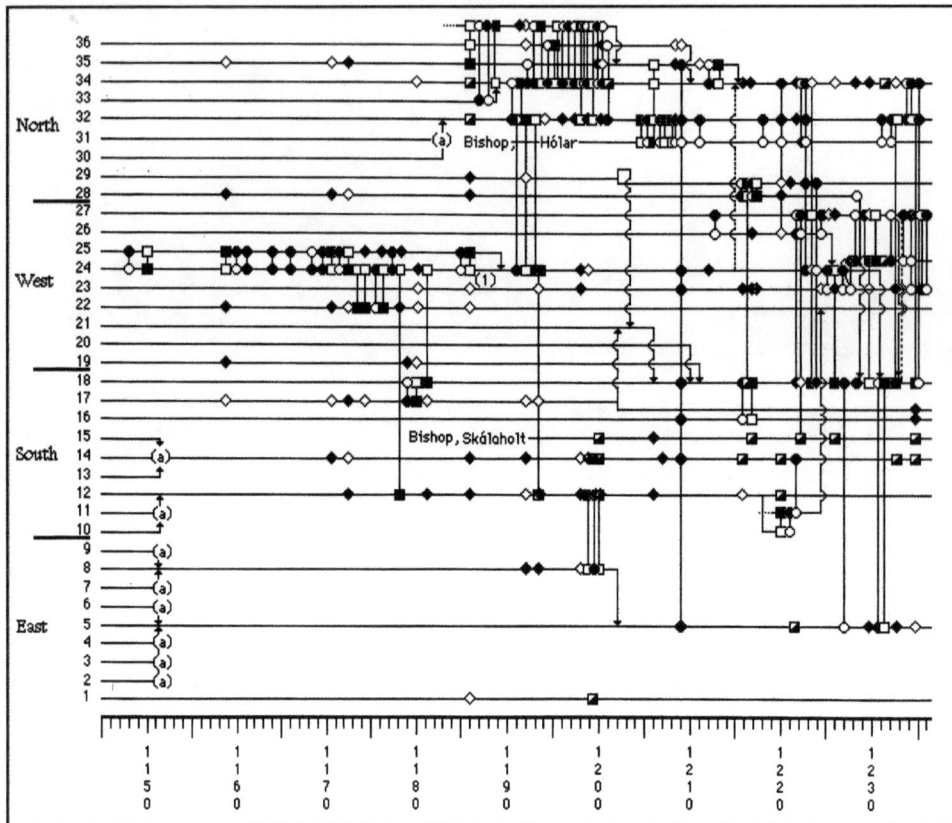

Figure 3: Graphic representation of intersecting and concurrent feud chains and alliance cascades across Iceland, circa AD 1147-1235, according to Íslendinga Saga (McGrew 1970). Note the ever-decreasing number of independent chiefly lines and the increasing tempo and spatial extent of hostilities as time progresses. Numbers on the y-axis refer to the chieftaincies mapped in Figure 1; symbols are as described in the text (half black/half white squares identify mediators called to arbitrate settlements).

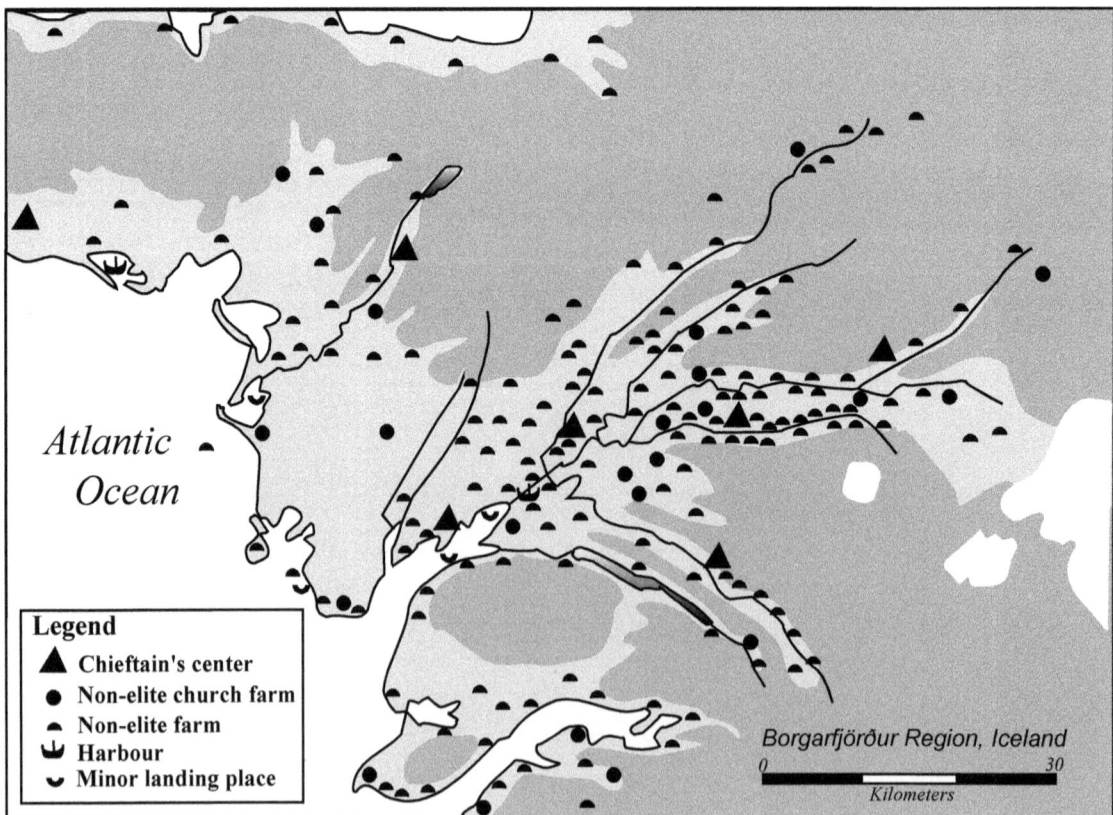

Figure 4: The Borgarfjörður region of western Iceland, circa AD 1180, according to medieval texts and archaeological research. While the number and location of chieftains' centers, non-élite church farms, harbours, and landing places are probably accurate, non-élite farms are certainly under-represented. Dark gray shading identifies land over 200 meters AMSL; white areas are glaciers.

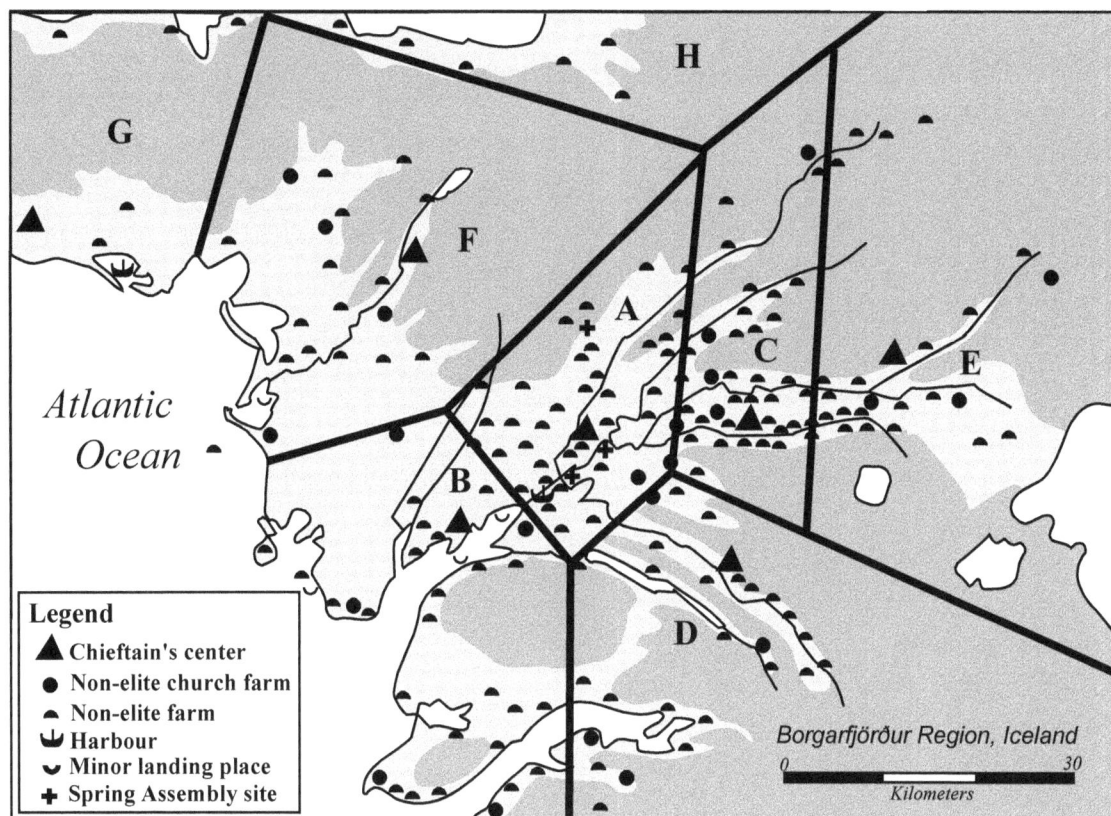

Figure 5: The Borgarfjörður region of western Iceland, circa AD 1180, with Thiessen polygons drawn around seven chieftains' centers located within the district and one (H) in the adjacent Breiðafjörður district. Dark gray shading identifies land over 200 meters AMSL; white areas are glaciers.

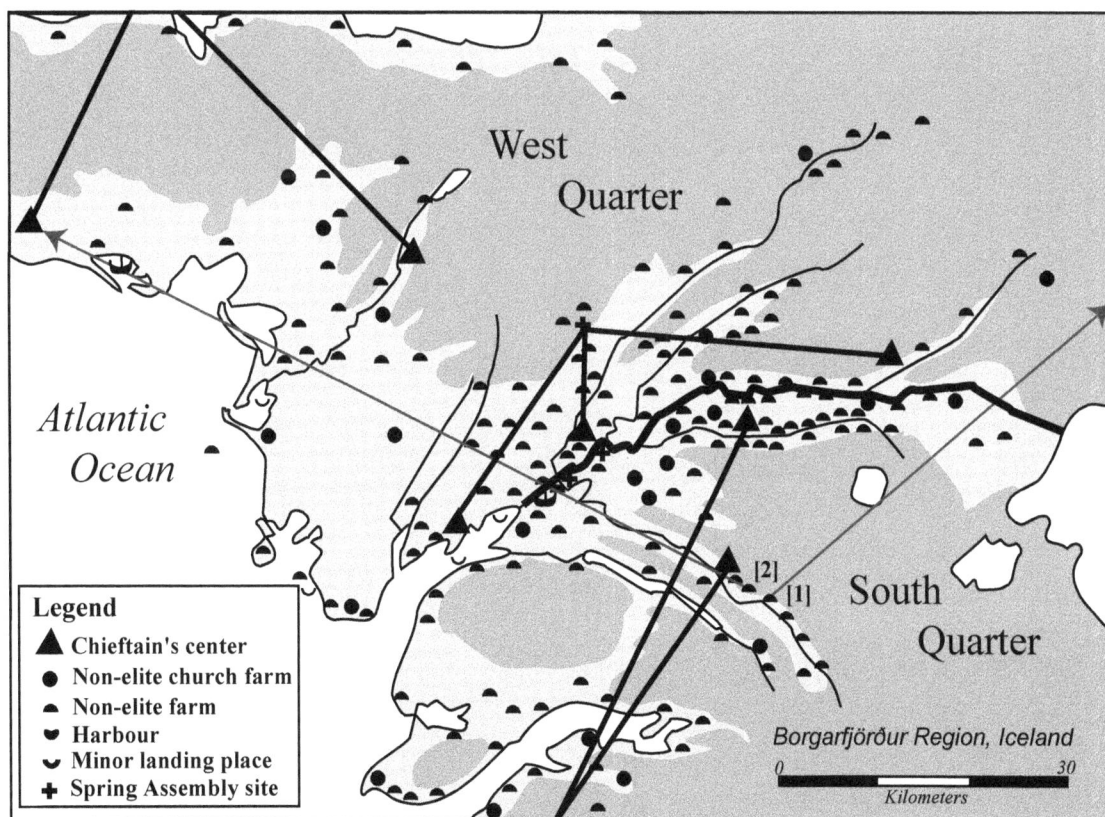

Figure 6: The Borgarfjörður region of western Iceland, circa AD 1180, showing political boundaries and alliances known from historical sources and discussed in the text. The bold line following the line of the river Hvítá through the center of the map is the boundary between the South and West Quarters. Dark lines link chieftains' centers to the Assembly Sites where they and their followers met each spring. [1] and [2] identify the farms of Þorð the Red and Hámund Gilsson, respectively, with gray lines linking them to their chieftains.

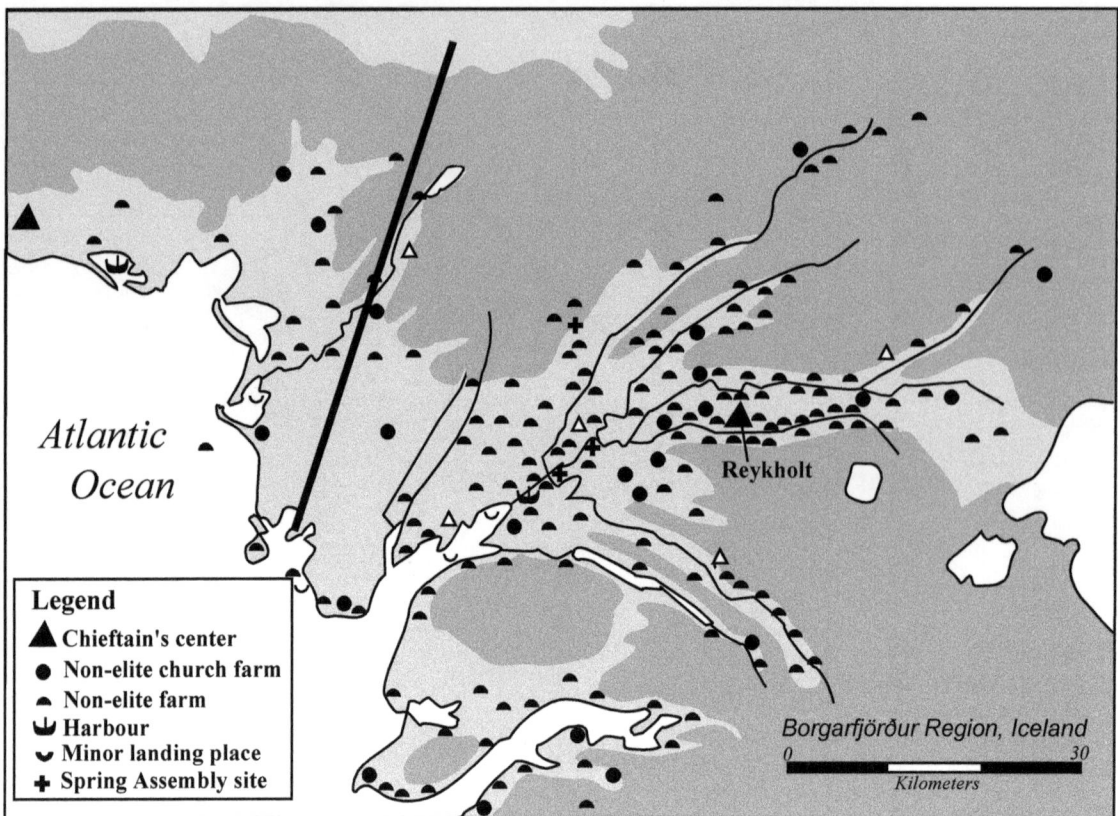

Figure 7: The Borgarfjörður region, circa AD 1240, with a Thiessen polygon boundary drawn between the paramount centers of Reykholt and Staður. White triangles identify formerly independent chieftains' centers incorporated into Reykholt's polity.

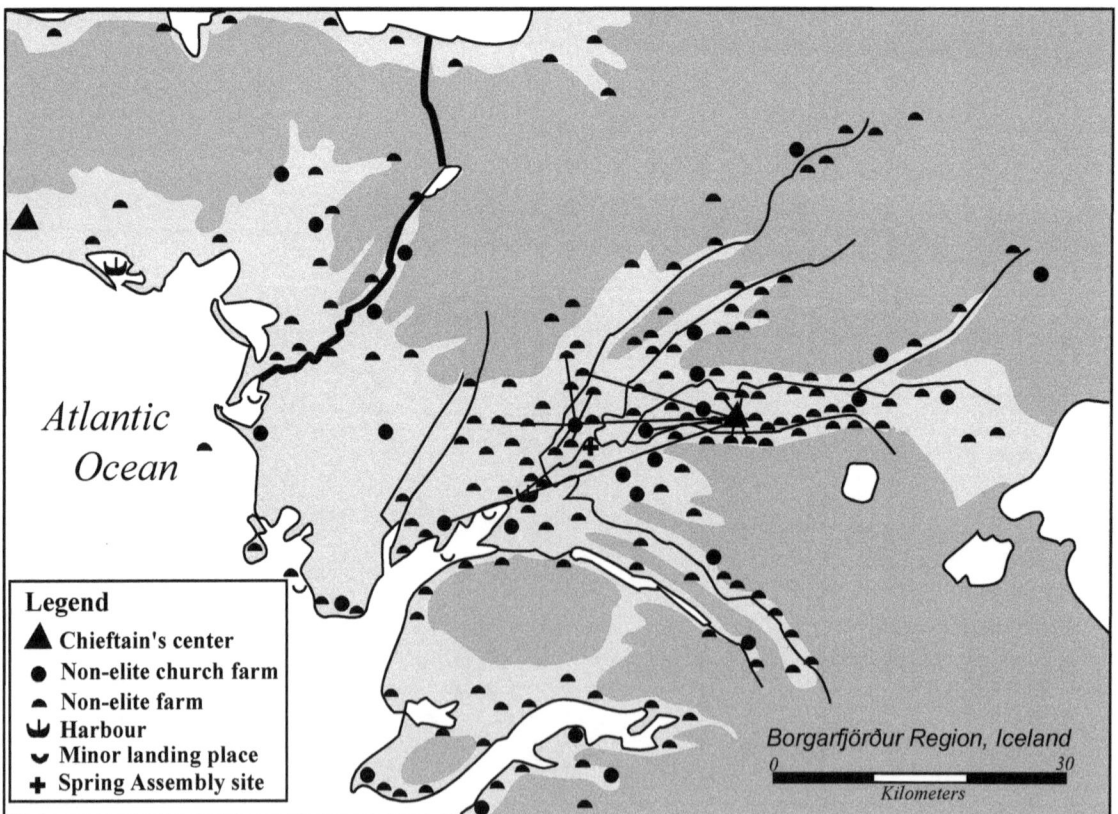

Figure 8: The Borgarfjörður region, circa AD 1240, according to historical sources. The dark line separating the chieftaincies of Reykholt and Staður is approximate and follows hreppur boundaries. Formerly independent chieftains' centers within Reykholt's domain have been reduced to local non-elite church farms. A single Spring Assembly site remains and the Quarter boundary, although maintained in theory it no longer existed in practice. Thin lines connect Reykholt to farms that it owned within the district.

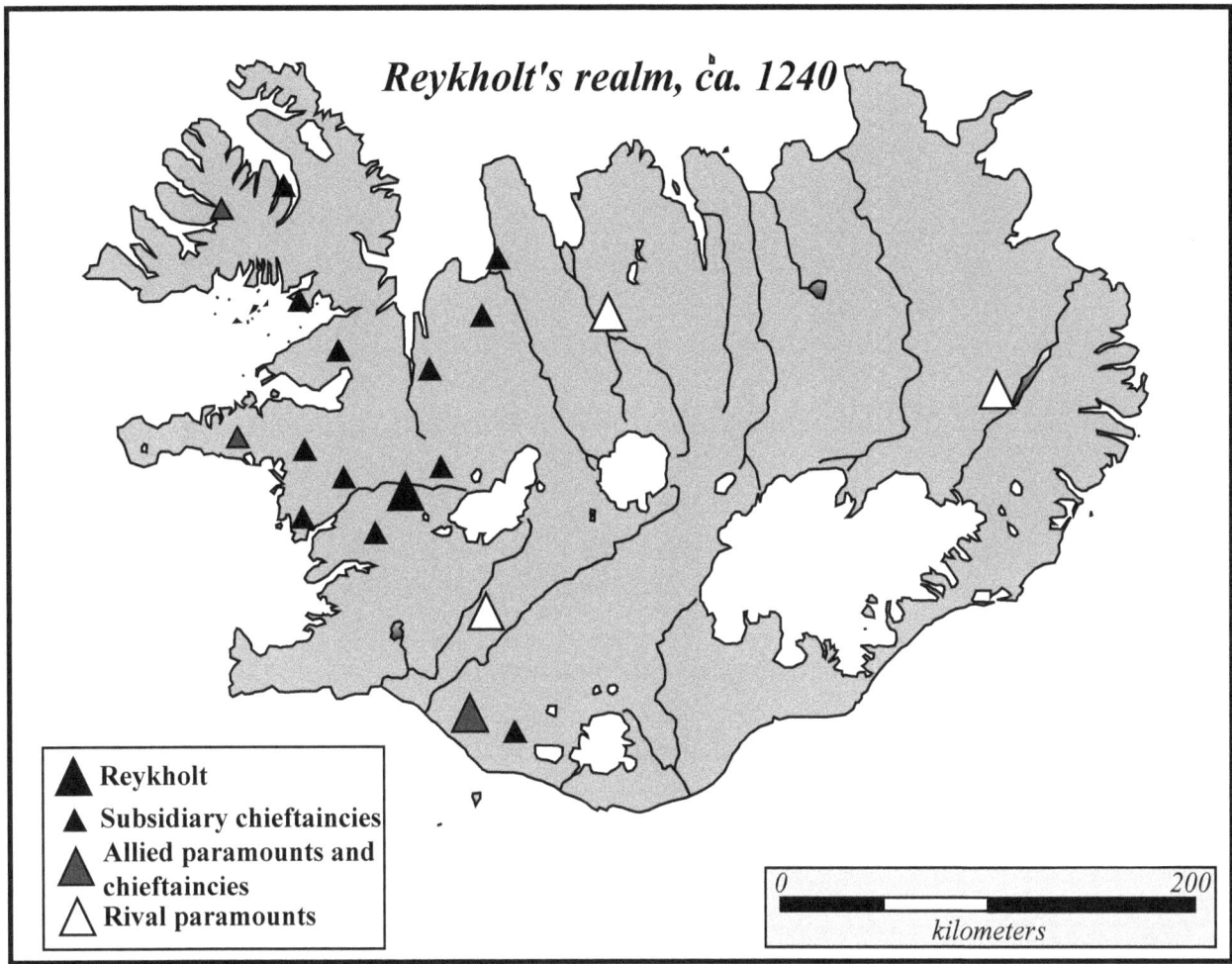

Figure 9: The paramount chieftain (*hofðingi*) Snorri Sturulson controlled most of western and northwestern Iceland from his principal residence at Reykholt. He consolidated the Borgarfjörður district (see Figures 6-8) between 1203 and 1210, then extended his power through most of western and northwestern Iceland by the time of his death in 1241. Strategic alliances through kinship and marriage brought other paramounts and smaller chieftaincies in southern and western Iceland into his sphere of influence. Subsidiary chieftaincies controlled by his rivals are unmarked.

Discussion

Peter S. Wells

The papers in this volume address the issue of scale in the context of a variety of theoretical issues and of data sets. All of the specific contexts treated here concern European archaeology, and the time range extends from the Mesolithic period to the 13ᵗʰ century AD. The topics discussed pertain not only to Europe, but to the field of archaeology as a whole, and indeed to research concerns in other social sciences as well. This collection of essays should be of interest to a wide and multidisciplinary readership.

As Mathieu and Scott explain in their introductory chapter, while all archaeologists conduct their research and writing at specific scales of investigation and analysis, these scales are rarely made explicit, and the implications of selecting one or another scale as the basis for fieldwork, synthesis, and interpretation are rarely discussed. The papers presented in this volume should inspire archaeologists to think more systematically about this subject and to apply the ideas developed here to their research designs, fieldwork strategies, reports, syntheses, and interpretations.

My remarks will address several themes that stand out among the eight thematic papers. Most important is the point that data and the patterns of which they are part can vary greatly, depending upon the questions that the investigator asks; the formulation of every question includes a decision regarding scale, whether or not the researcher explains the process of making that decision. As several authors make clear, the archaeological evidence does not speak for itself. There is no single, objective interpretation of the data to be discovered by the investigator. Instead, collecting, analyzing, and interpreting the material evidence require the creation of a research design, which must take account of the question of scale. The investigator creates the reality of the data by formulating a question and selecting an appropriate scale through which to research it.

As several of the papers demonstrate, the issue is not just a matter of shades of meaning to be derived from the evidence, but of fundamentally different interpretations of change in the past. Regarding the adoption of agriculture and all of the complex cultural changes involved, Bogucki shows that the scale of research—whether it focuses on parts of a settlement, on whole settlements, on regions, or on entire continents—determines to a large extent how we interpret the archaeological evidence recovered. The entire process of the Neolithic transformation looks different, depending upon the scale of analysis applied. Ostman demonstrates that if we focus our research attention on urban centers in the late Roman period, then the evidence suggests a time of disintegration and of economic and social decline. If, on the other hand, we examine the whole landscapes of which urban centers were parts, then the evidence can be understood to indicate instead a period of economic and social vitality. In So-

derberg's presentation, a close study of the archaeological and faunal materials from the monastic site of Clonmacnoise provides a detailed view of the specific circumstances of growth and provisioning at that site. But if we investigate the changes evident at Clonmacnoise in the context of contemporary changes in the rest of Ireland, of the British Isles, and of northwestern Europe as a whole, then the changes at that site take on new meanings.

Several of the papers address subjects that are fundamental issues in archaeology and in other social sciences, underscoring the importance of this topic around which Mathieu and Scott organized their SAA session and this volume. The points that Bogucki makes pertain to problems of investigating the origins and spread of agriculture in other regions of the world in addition to the central European landscape upon which he focuses. Ostman's paper on the changing patterns at Volterra and in its hinterlands provides an approach that could be profitably applied to any urban center in the Roman Empire, and indeed to any central place in an ancient civilization in the process of apparent decline. It would be instructive to see how the model would play out at, say, Mohenjo-Daro in the Indus Valley or Copan in Honduras. Soderberg's study has implications far beyond the site of Clonmacnoise in the center of Ireland. It addresses directly the long-asked and still much-debated question, why and under what circumstances did commercial towns emerge in early medieval northern Europe?

Themes of relatively new but rapidly growing interest in archaeology are well represented among these papers—the issues of recognizing and distinguishing individual and community agency and identity. As several authors note, archaeologists most often examine economy, social structure, and identity on the scale of the community, not of the individual. Only recently, individual agency has come to the fore as a topic for archaeological research. Among the papers in this volume, Darvill, Fisher, and Smith address this theme, and all suggest useful approaches to dealing with the distinctions between communities and individuals. Darvill uses the concept of individual agency as a way to understand action over space during the time commonly known as the Mesolithic and Neolithic. Fisher employs associations within Anglo-Saxon burials to examine patterns of brooch ornamentation on an individual scale, and contrasts this scale with that of the community as a whole, represented by the entire cemetery. In Smith's case, individual agency and action can be investigated through the textual sources available in medieval Iceland to complement the material evidence of archaeology. As I read Smith's paper, I wondered whether ongoing research in Iceland would present investigators with a challenge to weigh the relative merits of the textual and the archaeological evidence for understanding change in that context. As Smith indicates, in a sense these two sources can be considered as two different scales. Texts can provide information on the level of the individual, while archaeological data pertain more readily to the level of the community or of the society as a whole. But as more data are collected, and as attempts inevitably are made to bring the textual and archaeological data together to address specific questions, what will be the outcome of those efforts?

While the majority of the papers emphasize the role of scale in processes of analysis and interpretation, several demonstrate the importance of scale in the formulation of research design and in the process of collecting data. Hamilton's is the most explicit in this regard, identifying four distinct scales of analysis that can be applied to technological investigations in archaeology. Gibson links the issue of scale in archaeological research to larger theoretical issues, demonstrating how scale relates to topics that have been much debated in archaeology over the past several decades.

Already in Mathieu and Scott's introductory chapter, it becomes clear that scale is an important issue for archaeologists to think about. Like most large ideas, the need for consideration of scale seems obvious now, as a result of these papers. I think that most practicing archaeologists, after

reading this volume, will be convinced that scale is an issue that they need to address in their work. More attention to this subject has the potential to inform theory (as Gibson shows), to aid in research design (as Darvill and Hamilton illustrate), and to contribute to more clearly articulated interpretations of archaeological information (as Bogucki, Fisher, Ostman, Smith, and Soderberg demonstrate in their treatments of specific archaeological data sets). The principal contribution of this volume will be in showing archaeologists how important it is for them to consider the matter of scale in all stages of planning, conducting, analyzing, and interpreting in the course of their archaeological investigations.

Biographical Sketch

Peter S. Wells is Professor of Anthropology at the University of Minnesota. His recent publications include *The Barbarians Speak: How the Conquered Peoples Shaped Roman Europe* (Princeton 1999), *Beyond Celts, Germans and Scythians: Archaeology and Identity in Iron Age Europe* (Duckworth 2001), and *The Battle that Stopped Rome: Emperor Augustus, Arminius, and the Slaughter of the Legions in the Teutoburg Forest* (W.W. Norton 2003).

Discussion

Dean R. Snow

Introduction

A clever reader of this volume might elect to read this discussion first, hoping to acquire a quick overview and a guide to those chapters that are of greatest relevance to the reader's research interests. I will try to provide them, but with the caveat that what follows is only my own view, not necessarily a beacon for the future of archaeology.

James Mathieu and Rachel Scott have stated clearly their own perspective on the volume in their brief preface, and they elaborate upon it in their introduction. Their premise is that the scale at which we pursue our research has an effect on our interpretations. It is useful for me to outline here why I judge this to be true.

The editors note that Spaulding, under whom I was lucky to study, pointed out that we work in three dimensions: spatial, temporal, and formal (Spaulding 1960). Our analytical scale varies along these dimensions, and it makes a difference if we set the temporal scale at years, decades, centuries, or millennia. There can also be orders of magnitude between spatially small or spatially large analyses, there being a world of difference between a single storage pit and a continent. We have come to control the temporal dimension better and better with improvements in dendrochronology, radiocarbon, and other dating techniques. We can control the spatial dimension even better with GPS and GIS tools, although I judge that we should be embarrassed by how frequently we publish inaccurate low-resolution maps and neglect to provide even simple coordinates for site locations.

Interest in large-scale problems has grown in recent years because of, or despite, various technical limitations. Analysis at a relatively large temporal scale actually helps the researcher overcome error that is inherent in radiocarbon dating and most other dating techniques. For example, my own regional analysis of the origins and spread of Iroquoian sites in the northeastern part of North America covers the founding and abandonment of several hundred Iroquoian villages over the course of 1250 years. While it is true that I cannot be sure of the exact dates for a particular village that my animated GIS says was (for example) founded in AD 1400 and abandoned in AD 1475, it is nevertheless the case that one can easily perceive overall demographic trends when this approximation is aggregated with hundreds of others for a period of 1.25 millennia. By defining the problem at large temporal scale, I reduced standard error to a tolerable level, a tenth of what it would be if the temporal context was only 1.25 centuries.

Increasing the spatial scale also reduces error, but here the advantage is less impressive because if archaeologists are compulsive about anything, it is about precision in the spatial dimension. Most of us could put nearly everything back where we found it, often to within a centimeter or two. Curiously, our compulsion for spatial accuracy breaks down when we move beyond the boundaries of our excavations. Crude published maps often do not permit readers to locate sites to their proper counties, and we rarely publish precise spatial coordinates, even when site security is not an issue. I hope that this will change soon, for site security can be preserved by simply dropping a digit or two from the coordinates and researchers will still have more accurate locations to plot in their search for regional patterns.

Unfortunately, we are left with yet another serious problem when we move to larger scales. We have generated a very large number of archaeological databases, and these are increasingly digital ones. Large grants and contracts have funded the compilation of many digital databases in recent years, yet these remain largely incommensurate and for the most part are used by only those researchers who compiled them. The reason for this is that we have never truly agreed upon standard vocabularies and ontologies. A researcher interested in topics such as the spread of equestrian equipment across Eurasia or the spread of maize across the Americas must invest unconscionable amounts of time searching for bits of information in unpublished reports, obscure archives, rare publications, and gray literature, all the while compensating for variations in excavation techniques, measurement systems, and language. This situation will persist and large-scale analyses will be hampered until the profession adopts a cyber-infrastructure that can search efficiently for the desired data and at the same time compensate for variations that currently render databases incommensurate. I predict that this problem will be solved in the relatively near future, but for the time being it is a serious impediment to large-scale analyses.

There are interesting and useful problems to be solved when one changes one of these dimensions while holding the other constant, or changes the scales of each in opposite directions. Thirty years ago I undertook a project on the Saratoga Battlefield in upstate New York. The project was supported by the National Park Service, which at the time was getting ready for the bicentennial of the American Revolution. I found the project interesting because the spatial scale of the battlefield was large, about the size of the great urban center of Teotihuacan in Mexico. At the same time the temporal scale was very brief, a couple weeks in the fall of 1777 (Snow 1977a). Later I undertook excavation of an Archaic period site in the same region, a spatially small excavation with a very long temporal range covering a few millennia (Snow 1977b). The two cases are examples of the range of scalar variation that archaeologists typically indulge.

But notice that I have not included the formal dimension as a parameter that we vary as freely as we do the temporal and spatial dimensions. The formal dimension differs importantly from the other two. The unit of selection in both biological and cultural evolution is the individual human being, although the two evolutionary processes differ significantly (Snow 2002). The objects that archaeologists study tend to be scaled accordingly. Projectile points, pots, and the like typically do not scale up by orders of magnitude. Households do scale up modestly in some situations, and settlements can vary from a handful of people to millions of them, but the unit of selection remains the individual and our units of analysis tend to remain at or near that scale as well. This is revealed even in archaeological contexts, where the actions of individuals can only rarely be detected directly but where the processes that interest us still tend to be modeled at that level. The recent increase in agent-based analysis is evidence of it (Axtell et al. 2002; Dean et al. 2000).

Thus the reason that processes are different at larger temporal and/or spatial scales is that individuals and the things they create and deposit in the archaeological record do not scale up equivalently. For our purposes we can postulate that the formal dimension remains fundamentally static, while the other two dimensions vary considerably. A simple analogy from physics illustrates the underlying principle. At relatively small spatial scale gas molecules escaping into a vacuum will distribute themselves randomly and evenly through the available space. However, at much larger scales of time and space, gas molecules will clump because of mutual gravitational forces, forming solar systems and galaxies. The gas molecules do not scale up with time and space, but remain the same absolute size. Mutual gravitational forces that are unimportant at small scale increase in importance as scale increases, leading to the scale-dependent differences in the behavior of gas molecules.

If the universe doubled in size every minute, that is if form, time, and space all scaled up commensurately, the effect would be unnoticeable, because change is merely equivalent to cutting the standard unit of reference (meter, mile, or whatever) in half. In other words, for scalar change to make a difference, and thus be interesting to archaeologists, one of the dimensions must remain static, or at least change at a rate that is significantly out of proportion to those of the other scalar dimensions. And in those observations lies the importance of this volume.

Cases in Point

James Mathieu's mapping of all the royal buildings in England, Wales, and Scotland for the period AD 1066-1650 is interesting in part because some of them are royal castles that are connected by a network of main roads. Thus the royal castles are like modern cities connected by links in a road network. The larger array of royal buildings was linked to the royal castles by means of a secondary set of local networks, each being a set of local links between royal buildings and a single royal castle. One maps such networks in a two-dimensional plane because the Z-axis is largely irrelevant to the exercise. If one plots a rank-size distribution of nodes in Mathieu's two maps, with size measured by the number of links connecting each node to other nodes, one discovers that the royal castles have more links than do the royal buildings, but there is no single node having a very large number of links. This is because the number of links per node is constrained by the two-dimensional character of the example. The number of Interstate Highway links connecting U.S. cites is similarly constrained. However, the number of links per airport node in the U.S. is not similarly constrained, leading to a few cases like the airports at Atlanta and Chicago, which have many links, and many cases like the small airport near where I live, each of which have only a few links. The Internet imposes even fewer constraints, such that Google was able to explode as a super node having billions of links while most Internet nodes have only a few links each.

Mathieu was able to track the number of coexisting nodes across the 1066-1650 period at a resolution of one year, which in turn allowed him to identify peaks and valleys in their frequency over time. These, in turn, gave him a few key dates at which to examine spatial distributions and draw inferences about the reasons for their contrasting patterns. Something similar was done by Robert Laxton for just one county in England (Laxton 1994). He did a rank-size analysis of settlements in Nottingham as part of his analysis, using settlement population size rather than the number of links to other settlements as his size measure. There were, of course, a few large communities and many small ones, such that a log-normal (semilogarithmic) graph of their rank-size distribution produced a straight line, albeit with the tiny curve at the lower end.

It is important to note that neither Mathieu's nor Laxton's data produce a normal curve, not even a highly skewed normal curve, when size and frequency are plotted. That is because both are power distributions, not normal ones. We are so accustomed to plotting normal distributions that we sometimes fail to recognize power distributions when we encounter them. For a fuller discussion see Barabási's (2002) work. Another important observation made by Laxton is that his data are self-similar, in the sense that a random sample of the full dataset will produce the same power curve. It is very likely that Mathieu's data are also self-similar, something that encourages one to conclude that studies like his would produce valid results if replicated at smaller or larger scale. Just as importantly, if smaller-scale analyses of these data do not produce like results, then one has a new research problem that awaits solution.

Peter Bogucki provides just such a case for the period during which agriculture was spreading across northern Europe. While there appears to be continuity over time in many specific locales in the region, a larger-scale analysis of regional patterns suggests discontinuity over the same period. The temporal scale has been held constant in this case, revealing that variability that is not detectable at one special scale is detectable at another. The difficulty is not in our analytical abilities, but in the practical constraints encountered by any archaeologist seeking to examine the problem at large scale. Bogucki cites 26 sources written in 4 languages. Were it not for the practical difficulty inherent in working at large scale, Bogucki might not have been the first to observe that there is little or no connection between the Black Sea flood and the spread of agriculture into Europe.

Perhaps we would all be better off if we were forced, as Timothy Darvill was, to take a broader spatial view. The general lack of deeply stratified settlements or shell middens documenting the Mesolithic-Neolithic transition in the British Isles prompted him to take a broader view. In the end it will almost certainly be a more productive approach. Pinning inferences about a regional phenomenon on the excavation of a single key site can be and sometimes has been misleading. One tree does not make a forest.

Yet failure to see the forest for the trees can sometimes be the product of disciplinary canons, as D. Blair Gibson points out. The ecological approach taken by many archaeologists, perhaps most notably my colleague William Sanders, has been roundly criticized by researchers who regard political economy as a more productive approach. Gibson cites in particular those critics who debunk the role of population pressure in cultural evolution. The problem, I judge, is that human adaptation is neither consistently Malthusian nor consistently Boserupian, but rather cycles between the two depending upon both exogenous factors such as climate change and endogenous ones such as technical, social, and political innovations. All systems seek equilibrium, but dynamic circumstances change the direction a particular system must move in order to approach an equilibrium state. Changing conditions, either endogenous or exogenous ones, can radically alter, even reverse, that direction. Moreover, both kinds of changing conditions might be expressed at one scale but not another. Droughts can be short- or long-term, local or regional, prompting very different effects accordingly. New technology, for example irrigation, can offer a short-term solution while nurturing the seeds of its own destruction in the long term by causing a gradual buildup of salts in the soil. Gibson concludes that "ultimately, one must conclude that the interpretations of the political economy school rest on untested and unreliable assumptions." I judge that he is correct in this observation, as he is when he speculates that the rejection of evolutionary ecology by some researchers is based on their incorrect belief that to accept it is to accept oppression and human inequality as the natural order of things. A clarifying observation is that spatial scale by itself does not necessarily tell us much, for similar sociopolitical organizations can exist at different spatial scales and at different population sizes. Thus it is important to assess sociopolitical scale separately, using temporal and spatial scales to set the context within which exogenous constraints allow systems to cycle. No one claims that this will be easy.

If it were easy we would have no need for theory. We need theory because without it we have no means to fill in the blank areas on the archaeological palimpsest. However, I omit from my definition of theory any framework for interpretation that does not allow for the generation of testable hypotheses. That does not mean that it must be esoteric; the best theory is both testable and simple. A good example can be found in Gibson's discussion of the debate between the evolutionary ecological and political economic schools. If some archaeologists reject evolutionary ecology because it "is tantamount in their eyes to accepting oppression and human inequality", it is necessarily an example of the rejection of good theory for extraneous reasons. It would be better for us to set our human sensibilities aside and deal objectively with the ways in which sociopolitical systems really work.

The tendency for normal distributions to morph into power distributions is perhaps the best example, a phenomenon already touched upon above. Left alone and in the absence of constraints, economic systems will generate small numbers of very wealthy individuals and large numbers of poor ones. This tendency is both inherent and strong. One can generate a curve showing the relationship of wealth per individual with income on the X-axis and the number of individuals on the Y-axis. The first thing one should notice about such a curve is that it is not a normal distribution, not even a highly skewed normal distribution. Rather it is a power distribution that is best displayed on a rank-size graph with the ranks of individuals on the X-axis and number of dollars on the Y-axis (**Figure 1**). Converting this to a log-normal (semilogarithmic) graph produces a straight line, as mentioned above. There is only one richest person and a nearly countless number of poor ones. No one could predict that Bill Gates would today occupy the top position on a rank-size distribution, but twenty years ago anyone should have been able to predict that *someone* surely would.

The log-normal power curve generated by wealth distribution is remarkably similar to many other distributions, for example, the population density fall-off from the center to the periphery of urban settlements (Young 2002:152-154). Many such distributions are observable in the archaeological record, as Mathieu's data show. Other examples may be more visible in documentary records that clarify otherwise obscure archaeological records, as Kevin Smith describes.

Elizabeth Hamilton defines the hierarchical units of production that she finds appropriate for Iron Age Europe as the individual, the production unit, the culture, and the interaction area. These are dynamic human units of production that make sense in terms of the patterns she has discerned in the archaeological record. One might seek corresponding spatial units to define as containers for them. Biogeographers use a standard set of terms to describe units of space, and I have found them useful. The most inclusive terms are realm or kingdom, depending upon whether one is discussing plants or animals. The lower order terms are the same, covering units of space between the levels of site and region, and they work reasonably well. The hierarchy, from smallest to largest, is as follows: site, district, province, and region. These are not commensurate with Hamilton's terms, for they omit the individual and provide more distinctions at the macro end of the scale. Similarly we often use socio-economic-political terms like band, household, community, tribe, society, culture, nation, and so forth, sometimes expanding to larger political terms such as chiefdom, state, and empire as needed. My point is that while we have different classes of terms that are often incommensurate, they all fall into a small number of classes and they all begin at the level of the individual (albeit implicitly in some cases) and parallel each other reasonably well up to macro levels. Should Hamilton choose to refer to an interaction area as either a province or a region, and should she describe the political entity of that unit as a kingdom, no one will have much difficulty grasping her meaning. Yet I find myself wishing that there were more consistency in our terminology. We waste time defining terms *de novo* with each publication, and part of me laments that we are still fussing over them in the 21st century.

Genevieve Fisher has to cope with the same problem in her discussion of scalar variation in medieval dress. Anyone who has ever observed generations of teenagers, or has been one, can appreciate the implications of the themes and variations of dress that she describes. She does so with commendable restraint. At the base of various scales and the phenomena deployed along them resides the individual or the artifact(s) produced by the individual. Rae Ostman adds another dimension to scalar variation above that level, reminding us of our persistent, if not always explicit, notions of progress. Darwin, of course, insisted that adaptive change did not necessarily imply progress, an insistence made necessary by the dominant religious convictions of his time. But if there is no progress in biological evolution (or by implication in cultural evolution either) must not the idea of entropy also be false? The problem is resolved if we separate the idea of progress from the idea of complexity. Gould fails to do so in his lengthy effort to show that evolution is not progressive (Gould 1996).

The full argument is too lengthy to detail here, but in biological evolution there is a demonstrable tendency for organisms to become more complex over time rather than less complex. The effect is more pronounced in cultural evolution. Culture is in constant flux because it is always a work in progress, an evolving system that constantly adapts to changing conditions. The process is exaggerated by innovation, a uniquely human capacity that often increases the opportunity for numerical growth and increased complexity. The system is seeking equilibrium, but innovation raises the bar. If runaway innovation keeps raising the bar, as would seem to be the case today, the system evolves swiftly but seemingly never reaches equilibrium. This is the adaptive circumstance described by Boserup, and it contrasts with the more constrained adaptive conditions described by Malthus (Boserup 1965). Malthusian misery can return quickly if exogenous (or sometimes even endogenous) circumstances lower the bar. This is what Ostman is talking about when she says that referring to a specific case of change as "decline" or "collapse" misrepresents the process. Culture can evolve by becoming less complex when circumstances make such a change adaptive, and the actors involved in the process may well regard the change as progressive.

John Soderberg's chapter describes two kinds of academic debate that are often conflated in practice. There is on the one hand debate over archaeological reality, disagreements about what is being observed and low-level inferences about its meaning. On the other hand there is also a debate about the nature of explanation itself, an epistemological debate, which when conflated with the previous one is almost certain to produce argument without end. Add to that the apparent lack of a standard definition of the term "urbanism" and the lack of a generally accepted procedure for identifying it in the archaeological record, and it is little wonder that much work lies ahead. Despite these difficulties, Soderberg concludes that the production of agricultural surplus is insufficient to explain the emergence of urbanism in his case study. To get beyond necessary but insufficient factors, he invokes elite competition and the exchange of prestige goods. This in turn allows a full and convincing understanding of what went on in at least one part of first millennium CE Europe.

More tangible is Kevin Smith's description of what appears to be our only well-documented case of the rise of complex chiefdoms from simpler polities. Medieval Iceland provides the case in point, where documents allow an agent-based analysis. Smith provides useful distinctions between "chiefdom," "chieftaincy," and "chieftain" that ought to become part of our standard ontology. As is usually the case with well-documented cases, proximal causation dominates the discussion, and this involves competition between elites. It is reasonable to ask what then was in it for non-elites, who like everyone else had come to Iceland to get away from just this process. In this case, the opportunity of migratory expansion had allowed population growth and avoidance of participation in the emerging centralized kingdom of Norway.

Snorri Sturluson's centralized chiefdom later emerged in a matter of only six decades. It was adaptive because most Icelanders were better off, and they were better off because the new polity reduced the cascading cycles of retribution that had attended earlier competition between petty elites. It was a phase change at the regional level that was accompanied by little change at the local scale. Thus it is not surprising that Smith concludes that we must be mindful of both proximal and ultimate causation. The documents reveal (unsurprisingly) that writers perceived only proximal causes in the process, which played out at an archaeologically invisible scale. Things are archaeologically more visible at larger scale, where processual models are appropriate. The gap between an agent-based model operating at an archaeologically invisible scale and more visible larger-scale phenomena could be bridged by the kind of analysis I described earlier for Long House Valley (Axtell et al. 2002; Dean et al. 2000). To that end Smith's case study provides us with a unique and invaluable source of applicable theory.

Conclusions

Models that function at very large scale are of use to archaeologists only if they can be operationalized. Scale of analysis is important. It is also full of traps for the unwary archaeologist. It is often the case that the most productive scale for archaeological analysis is at neither the fine scale at which we normally gather our data nor at the very large scale of grand synthesis. Yet these are the two extreme scales at which we frequently operate. Archaeological excavation draws us into ever more particularistic exercises of observation and recording. Mindful of the destructive nature of our fieldwork, we drive ourselves and our students to capture every detail. I can imagine one of us committing a whole field season to a single house, or a single room in a single house, or even to a single hearth in that room, all for the sake of thoroughness. At the other end of things, public archaeological lectures are full of airy generalizations born of broad experience but not well-rooted in empirical reality.

Look at it this way, if one wishes to understand how traffic jams build up around urban centers, one does not do it by modeling all the cumulative behaviors of all the drivers in all the cars involved. This would be empiricism run wild and it would lead to uninformative results. However, neither can one capture understanding of the situation by studying only the broadest large-scale patterns, for one would thereby ignore the underlying mechanisms necessary to explain the dynamics of traffic jams.

Another example of this point can be found in the relationship of theoretical physics to rocket science. NASA engineers ignore relativity theory when launching rockets, because Newtonian mechanics work well enough and have the advantage of actually producing practical solutions to ballistic problems. My point is that archaeologists too often gather data at scales too small to allow them to address problems of general interest. For interesting problems to be properly addressed the data must be aggregated and the results shared.

Units of Analysis

John Locke was utterly convinced of the primacy of mind, and before Darwin, so was just about everyone else with the intelligence to think about it seriously. It seemed then inescapably obvious that organization and design had to have been created by an intelligent mind. All watches required watchmakers. Order in the universe required the presumption of some pre-existing intelligence. In the context of biology this view led to what Daniel Dennett has called a "deliciously crisp and systematic vision of the hierarchy of living things" (Dennett 1995:37). Plato's view that everything, whether living or not, had an ideal core essence allowed Locke and others to explain variation within kinds of things, and this worked reasonably well much of the time.

But Locke's system of thought did not account for why some key attributes always occurred together while others did not. In the real world snakes never had feathers and horses never had wings. These and a myriad other empirical observations could only be explained after Darwin made it clear that there were no core essences. Instead, he showed us, kinds are populations of individuals that vary, and evolution guarantees that there will be trajectories of change through time that do not allow for the mixing and matching of features from many different sources. After Darwin, Linnaeus's dendritic organization of the tree of life suddenly made sense. Sure eyes evolved several times because they are so very useful, but the separately evolved forms of eyes are not identical. And many other specific forms, like feathers, probably evolved only once. Snakes will never acquire feathers through evolution, even though their scales could conceivably evolve into something analogous to feathers, or some geneticist might someday create a modern Quetzalcoatl.

Archaeologists could observe that cultural evolution operated by a set of rules quite different from those of biological evolution. Ancient Mexicans had no problem creating imaginary feathered snakes and ancient Greeks were just as adept at inventing myths of flying horses. Clearly in the realm of cultural evolution attributes can be assembled from several sources, and the dendritic tree created by the processes of biological evolution is not a particularly good analogue. Nevertheless, our archaeological ancestors were so impressed by the dendritic model that it became established as part of archaeological exposition, and came to reside as an implicit model in archaeological analysis. Darwin himself had observed that "the formation of different languages and of distinct species, and the proofs that both have been developed through a gradual process, are curiously the same" (Darwin

1871:59). Languages and societies often map on to one another rather nicely, so it was not difficult to sweep exceptions to the side and let Darwin's insights about biology overtake rational thought about cultural evolution.

At the same time, archaeologists decided to retain an essentialist view of the prehistoric cultures they studied rather than adopt a Darwinian view of them as populations exhibiting a certain amount of internal variability. Thus I judge that our archaeological ancestors erred at least twice in a big way. They inappropriately borrowed the dendritic model from biological evolution and just as inappropriately retained a pre-Darwin essentialist definition of prehistoric cultures, their basic units of analysis.

We see the evidence of these conceptual problems in many of the current debates documented in *Antiquity* and *The European Archaeologist*. The question of whether the Celts ever existed in Great Britain or on the continent depends in part on one's appetite for semantic quibbling, but also in part on one's view of "Celt" as an essential (in the Platonic sense) unit of analysis. A term like "La Tène" seems to me to have no utility as a unit of analysis if one rejects Platonic essentialism, which I do. And amidst the archaeological chaos, the dendritic diagrams created by linguists studying languages they classify as "Celtic" may or may not be meaningful for archaeological analysis. And so forth; this is just one example.

So what can be done? Models that function at very large scale are of use to archaeologists only if they are realistic in terms of cultural evolution and if they can be operationalized. Such models cannot be realistic in terms of cultural evolution if the units of analysis are the essentialist categories that we have often used in exposition, as chapters in this volume illustrate. Yet historical and archaeological atlases are full of them. Neither can we expect to make much progress if we concentrate myopically on artifacts, artifact types, and features.

On the other hand, treating sets of sites as populations allows us to investigate models that operate at an appropriate scale, as some of the chapters here also demonstrate. The implications go far beyond the parochial interests of regional specialists; they are informative and useful for archaeologists everywhere. The emergence of geographic information systems (GIS) as a powerful new tool facilitates more research at this scale. Computerized databases can be linked to GIS in ways that successfully connect regional specifics to global models. However, the linkages are necessarily direct ones, and the intermediate units (phases and the like) that archaeologists have become accustomed to using in recent decades can actually prevent researchers from making them.

Archaeologists everywhere must also pay more attention to models of human behavior at large scale that are available to us from ethnology and linguistics. If we are to have any hope of solving problems like the spread of Indo-European languages across Europe we will have to marry realistic models of language propagation to archaeological site population models. I judge that commonplace terminology has frustrated attempts to forge these linkages. So has an implicit acceptance of a dendritic model of the development of languages (and, by implication, cultures) over time. Such a model ignores the role of language switching, which I judge has to have been a major process in the success of Indo-European languages.

Biographical Sketch

Dean R. Snow received his B.A. in Anthropology from the University of Minnesota (1962) and his Ph.D. in anthropology from the University of Oregon (1966). His doctoral research was conducted in Mexico. He has had additional field experience in Minnesota, Wisconsin, Alaska, New England, New York, and Ireland. His research interests include large scale phenomena, including paleodemography, trade and exchange, linguistic prehistory, and the spread of cultigens and technological innovations. He is best known for his work on Iroquois (especially Mohawk) archaeology.

References Cited

Axtell, R.L., J.M. Epstein, J.S. Dean, G.J. Gumerman, A.C. Swedlund, J. Harburger, S. Chakravarty, R. Hammond, J. Parker, and M. Parker 2002 'Population growth and collapse in a multiagent model of the Kayenta Anasazi in Long House Valley' *Proceedings of the National Academy of Sciences* 99:7187-7316.

Barabási, A.-L. 2002 *Linked: The New Science of Networks* Perseus (Cambridge).

Boserup, E. 1965 *Conditions of Agricultural Growth: The Economics of Agrarian Change under Population Pressure* Aldine (Chicago).

Darwin, C. 1871 *The Descent of Man, and Selection in Relation to Sex* J. Murray (London).

Dean, J.S., G.J. Gumerman, R.L. Axtell, A.C. Swedlund, M.T. Parker, and S. McCarroll 2000 'Understanding Anasazi culture change through agent-based modeling' in T.A. Kohler and G.J. Gumerman (eds) *Dynamics in Human and Primate Societies: Agent-Based Modeling of Social and Spatial Processes* Oxford University Press (New York): 179-205.

Dennett, D.C. 1995 *Darwin's Dangerous Idea* Simon and Schuster (New York).

Gould, S.J. 1996 *Full House: The Spread of Excellence from Plato to Darwin* Three Rivers Press (New York).

Laxton, R. 1994 'A new look at the rank-size rule as applied to field survey data from Laconia' in I. Johnson (ed) *Methods in the Mountains: Proceedings of Congrès International des Sciences Prèhistoriques et Protohistoriques Commission IV Meeting, Mount Victoria, Australia, August 1993* Sydney University Archaeological Methods Series Vol. 2, Sydney University (Sydney).

Snow, D.R. 1977a *Archaeological Atlas of the Saratoga Battlefield* University at Albany (Albany).

Snow, D.R. 1977b 'The Archaic of the Lake George region' in W.S. Newman and B. Salwen (eds) *Amerinds and their Paleoenvironments in Northeastern North America* Annals of the New York Academy of Sciences Vol. 288, New York Academy of Sciences (New York):432-438.

Snow, D.R. 2002 'Individuals' in J.P. Hart and J.E. Terrell (eds) *Darwin and Archaeology: A Handbook of Key Concepts* Bergin and Garvey (Westport, CT):161-181.

Spaulding, A.C. 1960 'The dimensions of archaeology' in G.E. Dole and R.L. Carneiro (ed) *Essays in the Science of Culture* Cromwell (New York):437-456.

Young, D.A. 2002 'A new space-time computer simulation method for human migration' *American Anthropologist* 104(1):138-158.

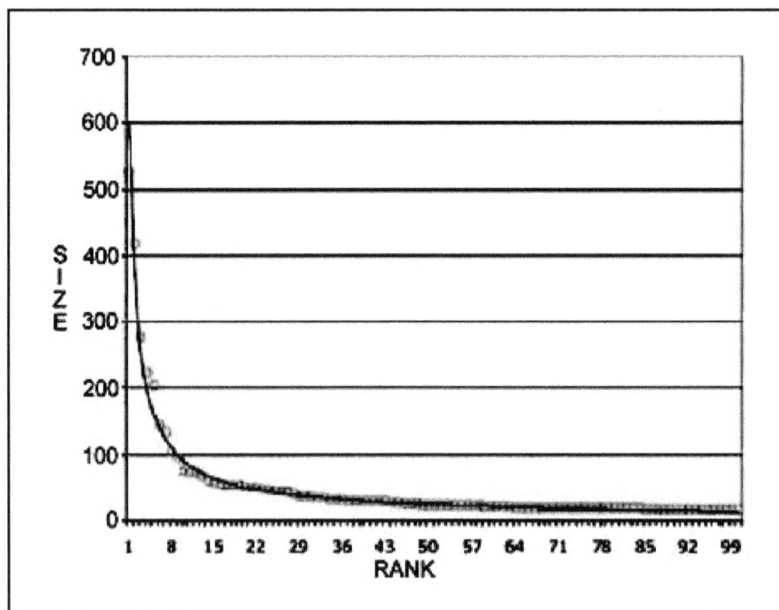

Figure 1. Power distribution curve.